Language, Technology, and Society

Language, Technology, and Society

RICHARD SPROAT

OXFORD

UNIVERSITY PRESS

OXFORD
UNIVERSITY PRESS

Great Clarendon Street, Oxford OX2 6DP

Oxford University Press is a department of the University of Oxford.
It furthers the University's objective of excellence in research, scholarship,
and education by publishing worldwide in

Oxford New York

Auckland Cape Town Dar es Salaam Hong Kong Karachi
Kuala Lumpur Madrid Melbourne Mexico City Nairobi
New Delhi Shanghai Taipei Toronto

With offices in

Argentina Austria Brazil Chile Czech Republic France Greece
Guatemala Hungary Italy Japan Poland Portugal Singapore
South Korea Switzerland Thailand Turkey Ukraine Vietnam

Oxford is a registered trade mark of Oxford University Press
in the UK and in certain other countries

Published in the United States
by Oxford University Press Inc., New York

British Library Cataloguing in Publication Data

Data available

Library of Congress Cataloguing in Publication Data
Library of Congress Control Number: 2010920353

Typeset by SPI Publisher Services, Pondicherry, India
Printed in Great Britain
on acid-free paper by
CPI Antony Rowe, Chippenham, Wiltshire

ISBN 978-0-19-954938-2

1 3 5 7 9 10 8 6 4 2

Contents

Preface

In 1986, soon after I arrived at AT&T Bell Laboratories as a postdoc, I received an offer of an assistant professor position in a linguistics department at a major university. I decided not to accept it, but to accept instead the technical staff position that Bell Labs proposed as a counter-offer. Had I accepted the academic position, it is a virtual certainty that I would not have written this book. For my eighteen-year tenure at Bell Labs and its various offshoots gave me an opportunity to explore language and speech technology in a way that would not have been possible in an academic linguistics department in those days. I became heavily involved in multilingual speech synthesis, and later on in speech recognition. I had a chance to dabble in machine translation and information extraction. My interest in speech synthesis, and in particular the problem of how to get computers to read from ordinary text, got me interested in the question of how text actually represents language, and thus how writing systems work. The present book is in many ways a synthesis of a wide variety of areas that it has been my good fortune to work on over the years.

The book also grew out of a course that I developed during my five and a half years at the University of Illinois at Urbana-Champaign, which was called 'Language, Technology and Society'. In that course, which was aimed at sophomores, I explained how language technology works—from the very first writing, to modern speech and language systems. But I also brought in a social dimension, where we discussed the social implications of some of the systems we were discussing.

This is a broad set of issues, and my level of expertise in the different areas varies a lot. I have benefitted greatly from comments and suggestions by a number of people. My greatest debt goes to Steve Farmer, a comparative historian who has worked for years on how writing, literacy, and textual traditions shape thought. Steve and I have discussed many of the topics in this book, especially those that relate to the social impact of writing and literacy. Others have read or commented on various chapters, in particular Chilin Shih the chapter on speech technology, and Brian Roark the chapter on machine translation. Cecilia Alm gave me many useful comments on the lecture notes for my course at the University of Illinois that eventually developed into this book. Since this book is intended for the educated layman, I asked my father to read a couple of the chapters, which helped me improve on the presentation.

Michael Erard suggested several points that helped me expand my discussion of the typewriter. Martin Howard answered my questions about typebar placement on the earliest Remington models, and graciously provided me with several photographs of the mechanism in action. Peter Weil, another typewriter expert, also gave me some useful discussion.

Anneke Neijt helped with some technical issues on the Dutch spelling reform. Benjamin Barrett, Wolfgang Behr, and William Boltz responded to my query on the Linguist List as to whether the character 鱈 *tara* 'codfish' was invented in Japan.

On the technical side of book production, I would like to thank Simon Ager for granting permission to use a number of tables of different scripts from his wonderful Omniglot site (http://www.omniglot.com). My daughter, Lisa Sproat, drew three of the figures used in Chapter 1. I would also like to thank my editors at Oxford, Julia Steer and John Davey, who supported this project, and were patient with my (admittedly unavoidable) shifting completion date.

Finally, the author and publishers have made every effort to contact copyright holders of figures reprinted in *Language, Technology, and Society*. This has not been possible in every case, however, and we would welcome correspondence from those individuals/companies we have been unable to trace.

August, 2009   Portland, Oregon

List of Figures and Tables

Figures

Tables

1

Preliminaries

What sets humans apart from other animals is surely a contentious issue; ideas on this vary radically depending upon one's religious or philosophical views. But surely two human characteristics stand out that few would disagree with: our ability to use language; and our ability to create and use complex tools—that is to create and use technology.

Both of these statements require qualification.

By 'language' here we mean not just any communication system, but a communication system that allows the user to create and understand essentially unlimited numbers of messages, which can be as long as the user wants them to be, and which are made up of basic units of meaning (words, or in more accurate linguistic terminology, *morphemes*), that themselves number in the tens of thousands of types. Spoken languages and signed languages all have these properties. Language characterized thus is a quintessentially human ability. Language is central to who we are and what we are capable of. Not a single human achievement, whether one is thinking of the earliest settled agricultural civilizations, or the most advanced endeavors in theoretical physics, would have been possible without language.

By 'tool' we mean any artificial device that is created to augment our abilities in one way or another. Humans are not the only tool-building species, but our technology is clearly orders of magnitude more complex than anything known from non-human animals.

This book is about language and it is about technology, and it is in particular about the technologies that have been developed over the millennia to enhance and mimic our linguistic abilities. For much of history, that technology came down essentially to one thing: writing. Thus, the first half of this book will deal with the technology of writing and its effects on society. The second half of the book will trace the history beyond writing to modern computer speech and language systems.

But before even writing could develop, language and technology had to come together. This chapter traces the confluence of those two human abilities.

1.1 Language and technology

All animals, and many other life forms, communicate, and several species are now known to use tools; but in both these areas, humans have developed skills that are significantly different from what other animals are able to do.

Consider first communication. At its simplest, communication between members of a species may consist of chemical signals. Plasmodial slime molds—a common example is *Fuligo septica*, the large yellowish "blobs" that one often finds on bark mulch in one's garden—use chemical signals to communicate among the individual free moving cells to indicate that it is time for the cells to congregate into a single acellular plasmodium. Everyone knows about the dances of bees that communicate important information about the locations of food sources, and the territorial and mating calls of birds. The more we learn about animal communication, the more it is becoming clear that many of the features that we attribute to human language, such as "words" which are used to refer to things in the world, and "syntax" (the ability to combine these terms together), are not uniquely human. For example, Siberian jays use different calls to signal predators depending upon what the predator is doing,[1] showing that for these birds, the calls refer to different things.

Quite sophisticated uses of communication can be found. The bonnet macaques of Southern India have an elaborate set of calls that are used to convey various kinds of information, such as the presence of predators. These monkeys even use their communication system in ways that are quite reminiscent of humans: for example they may use it to deceive other members of the troop. Anindya Sinha has documented the use of fake predator calls by lower ranking monkeys to distract higher ranking monkeys who are attacking them, affording the deceiver a chance to escape.[2]

But human language is different, in that the messages that human languages can encode are far more complex than anything found in any other known communication system. There has been an often ferocious debate among linguists, psychologists, and other cognitive scientists as to what, precisely, is the measure of complexity that is most distinctively human. In a paper in *Science* that was published in 2002, Marc Hauser, Noam Chomsky, and W. Tecumseh Fitch[3] argued that the defining feature is *recursion*. One type of recursion is involved in sentences of the form *X thinks that S*—for example *John thinks that Mary is pretty.* An analysis of the structure of this sentence would say that the *embedded* clause *(that) Mary is pretty* is an object of the verb *think*, since it is a statement about what John is thinking. We can repeat this embedding, and in fact repeat it as long as we want: *John thinks that Mary believes that Bill said that Michael opined that Jill is cute.* Here we have clauses, that contain other clauses, that contain other clauses with a recurring structure, hence the term recursion. Dan Everett (2005), on the other hand, has argued that there are some languages—most notably the Amazonian language Pirahã—that lack recursion (as well as a great many other features that are often deemed to be "universal"), and if Everett is right, then presumably recursion cannot be the defining feature of human language.

Two things that are certainly characteristic of human language are:

- Large numbers of words: the vocabulary size in any human language runs (at least) into the tens of thousands of items.
- A rich set of ways of combining the basic elements to form more complex units (phrases, sentences), which have no predetermined bound on their length; no language has a rule that says that utterances may be no longer than, say, twenty words.

In contrast, no animal communication system has more than a few basic vocabulary items, and the "syntax"—ways of putting together—basic terms in animal communication systems are decidedly simpler than those of human language. While linguists, psychologists, and philosophers will continue to debate what is distinctive about human language, it is in fact hard to show that the difference consists in *anything other than the two items listed above.* In any event, as a practical matter, even if these are not the defining characteristics of human language they do have the distinct advantage of being true.

Now consider tools. There are far fewer tool-using species than there are species that communicate, but the number is nonetheless non-negligible. The woodpecker finch (*Cactospiza pallida*—one of Darwin's finches of the Galapagos Islands) uses cactus spines to retrieve insects from holes in trees. Many hunting birds use gravity and rock surfaces as a kind of passive tool to break hard shells of prey. There are even reports of crows in Japan that have learned how to take advantage of traffic to crush walnut shells: the birds have learned to drop nuts at pedestrian crosswalks, wait for cars to run over them and crack them, and then wait for the walk sign to come on to safely retrieve the cracked nuts. Impressive though that is, more interesting and more restricted are species that actually manufacture tools. The most famous of these are our closest relative, the chimpanzee. Tool manufacture in chimps was first reported by Jane Goodall, who observed them stripping the leaves of twigs to manufacture a probing stick that they could use to collect termites from otherwise inaccessible holes. A recent report[4] shows that some colonies of chimps have learned to manufacture brushes from twigs for collecting termites. But of course, here again, humans have far surpassed any other animals in their abilities to invent, produce, and use tools, and our tools have enabled us to transform our environment, in ways that are now becoming all too apparent to us.

1.2 First signs

It was inevitable that these two core aspects of humankind, language and technology, would eventually come together, but one other thing was needed in order for that to happen, and that was the ability to create depictions or symbols that represented objects in the world and other natural phenomena. Language itself is, of course, a representational system: the English word *dog* is used as a way of referring to dogs, and thus can be said to represent dogs. For tens of thousands of years, humans have also been depicting objects in the real world: the earliest examples of graphic art are the cave paintings from the Chauvet Cave, dating back possibly as much as 32,000 years. It is not obvious that these, or other similar early art, was used for anything other than a simple depiction of every day events: animals familiar to the people who painted the pictures, and the hunters who chased after the animals. Presumably the paintings were just a form of artistic expression with no deeper symbology, much as a landscape painting is today.

But at some point, around 10,000 years ago, in Mesopotamia, a true representation system, one that was purely functional in nature, was developed, apparently for the purpose of accounting for goods. The system consisted of stone or, more commonly, clay tokens that represented units of commodities such as grain, sheep, or oil. Some examples are shown in Figure 1.1.

The first person to propose the "token theory" was Leo Oppenheim in a paper in 1959, but the theory has become most associated with Denise Schmandt-Besserat of the University of Texas, who showed that tokens were used as early as 8000 BC and developed the theory that they were the precursors of writing.[5]

Oppenheim, in his 1959 paper, discussed the "clay envelope" shown in Figure 1.2, which dates from the second millennium BC from Nuzi (present-day northern Iraq). The outer surface contains a description of the contents:

- 21 ewes that lamb;
- 6 female lambs;
- 8 full-grown male sheep;
- 4 male lambs;
- 6 she-goats that kid;
- 1 he-goat;
- 3 female kids.

FIGURE 1.1 Mesopotamian tokens. From left to right, first row: type of garment, unit of metal, unit of oil, sheep. Second row: unit of honey, *unknown*, type of garment

Source: Image © 2009 Lisa L. Sproat, used with permission.

The envelope contained forty-nine tokens corresponding to the animals listed.

This established the denotation of the tokens, but what of the connection to writing? The received wisdom on the origin of writing, and a view that is still widely assumed, was the 'pictographic theory' due to an eighteenth-century English bishop, William Warburton. The idea was that writing developed out

FIGURE 1.2 A "clay envelope" from Nuzi

Source: After Schmandt-Besserat (1996: 10, fig. 2); image © 2009 Lisa L. Sproat, used with permission.

of pictographs, the kind made by stone-age cultures the world over, and which gradually took on fixed denotational significance as people realized they could use these symbols to record ideas. A picture of a sheep gradually evolved into a pictograph for a sheep. Until Schmandt-Besserat's work, the theory remained essentially unchallenged. For example, pictography figured prominently in Ignace Gelb's landmark *Study of Writing* (1963) as an important precursor to writing.

Certainly pictographs can evolve into written symbols: the modern Chinese character for 'sheep' 羊 was originally a pictograph of a sheep. But the problem with the pictographic theory, at least as it applied to Mesopotamian writing, is that while some symbols were clearly pictographic in origin, many others were quite abstract. The 1929–30 excavations at Uruk unearthed early Sumerian tablets dating to the fourth millennium BC. In these early instances of 'proto-writing', the 'pictograph' for 'sheep' was a circle with a square in it, not a particularly faithful rendition of a sheep. But while the early glyph for 'sheep' ⊕ does not resemble a sheep, it does bear a striking resemblance to the *token* that was used for 'sheep'; see again Figure 1.1. Arguably the symbol for sheep was a pictograph of the token for sheep, but clearly not of the sheep itself.

Evidence from Mureybet (Syria) shows that tokens were associated with agriculture: the first occurrence of tokens at that site corresponds to a 'quantum jump' in the quantity of cereal pollen.[6]

The token system presented a problem of convenience: if you had a lot of commodities for which you wanted to keep records, you would end up with a lot of tokens. Obviously there is the potential to lose tokens, so ways were invented to keep the tokens together. One way was to pierce the tokens so that they could be strung together as old Chinese coins were. Another method was to seal the tokens in a *bulla*, a clay 'envelope'. But this latter method presented a further problem: once the envelope was sealed, the only way to know what was inside was to break the envelope. So the method was developed of stamping an impression of the tokens inside the envelope on the outside of the envelope before it was sealed. An example of one of these envelopes is shown in Figure 1.3. Of course once this technique was developed, the natural next step was to realize that one could stamp the symbols themselves on a solid clay tablet instead of an envelope, and thus do away with the tokens. This insight seems to have occurred in the late fourth millennium BC.

The result of this innovation was a way of representing concepts like 'twenty sheep', by stamping the tablet with twenty impressions of the sheep token. But this was not writing. There is no reason to analyze the 'documents' as representing some canonical spoken form. Presumably an impression of twenty sheep tokens might elicit the reading *twenty sheep* in whatever language

FIGURE 1.3 A envelope with its contents and the corresponding markings of the contents on the outside

Source: After Schmandt-Besserat (1996: 52, fig. 15); image © 2009 Lisa L. Sproat, used with permission.

the users spoke, but other ways of conveying the same information linguistically would not be wrong. Consider a modern analog: it is perhaps canonical to read *$2,000* as *two thousand dollars*, but it is not wrong to read it instead as *two grand* or *two k dollars*.

To make the transition to language the system had to grow in complexity so that it could cover a much wider range of meanings than just accounting texts, and it had to become conventionalized in the mapping between language and the visual forms. The exact evolution of this process is still not fully understood, but Schmandt-Besserat points to two other steps in the evolution of this process. One was the development of conventional ways to represent numbers. It is awkward to have to stamp twenty sheep symbols every time one wants to indicate twenty sheep, not to mention a hundred or six hundred sheep. The number symbols (see Figure 1.4) evolved from symbols representing amounts of grain, an interesting leap of imagination itself, since it required the abstraction of the concept of *quantity*—a larger number of individual sheep is analogous to a larger volume of grain.

The second step was the need to represent one other crucial piece of information in economic transactions, namely the *names* of the parties involved. Some way had to be found to write the names of the buyers and

FIGURE 1.4 Glyphs for numbers, originally symbols for quantities of grain

sellers of the goods, and this presented an interesting and important problem. In any language, some personal names are clearly based upon concrete depictable nouns: consider *Rose, Robin, Smith*. Others, however are harder to depict: *Charity, Felicity, Noble*. Still others (in English and many other modern languages, the majority) are not even interpretable semantically: *Robert, John, Philips*. In order to write most names, a system had to be developed to represent them in terms of their sounds, that is to write them *phonetically*.

Two methods were known to have been operative in the development of early writing systems, the *rebus* principle and the *acrophonic* principle. The *rebus* principle is familiar to most people in the form of visual punning, as in a drawing of an eye, a can, waves, and a (female) sheep, to represent the English sentence *I can see you*; the method simply depends upon picking easily depictable terms that are identical or similar in sound to the target term, and using the depictions purely for their sound values, not for their meaning. The acrophonic principle is somewhat more abstract, but otherwise is similar to the rebus principle: rather than the sound of the whole word, just the sound of the beginning of the word is relevant. Thus a picture of a cucumber could be used to represent the word *cue*, because *cue* is pronounced the same as the first syllable of *cucumber*. Or it might even be used to represent just the first consonant /k/.

Once the earlier Mesopotamians started being able to write names phonetically, it was inevitable that they would learn to write other words using the same technique. We should stress here, that we have as yet only the skeleton of a story. As Schmandt-Besserat herself stresses, there are only a few tens of known examples of envelopes and tablets stamped with tokens, representing the development of a system over several thousand years. We have no direct evidence of exactly how the leap of understanding transpired that allowed people to move from representing things like '20 sheep' to being able to write anything. But in Mesopotamia we have far more evidence of how writing developed from pre-writing than in any of the other ancient cultures—Egypt, China, or Central America—where writing is believed to have evolved independently. Whatever the exact trajectory, this slow coming together of language and technology culminated in the world's earliest full writing system, that of Sumerian, around 2800 BC. Of no development could it be more aptly said that the rest is history.

2

Writing as a Language Technology

We start by stating what I will assume is the obvious: writing systems are systems of symbols. Furthermore—and this is also presumably obvious—as a symbol system, the individual symbols, whether they be letters in English, Chinese characters, or Egyptian hieroglyphs, represent something. That, after all, is what symbols do. The next question is *what* they represent, and this turns out to be much more subtle. In some cases the answer seems obvious. For a language like Spanish where there is a very regular correspondence between the letters on the page and the way the words are pronounced (Spanish is 'written as it is pronounced'), then it is pretty clear that the individual symbols represent sounds. But what about in English, where the correspondence between letter and sound is much less regular? Or Chinese, where for centuries many people have believed that the individual symbols represent ideas? Or Egyptian hieroglyphs?

We shall argue in this chapter that all writing systems represent elements of *language*—not ideas or something else; and we shall argue in the next chapter that more specifically all writing systems mostly represent sound (rather than some other kind of linguistic object). But before we get to these points there are some issues that we need to understand about symbol systems in general so as to be able to better understand what it means to say that writing is a symbol system that represents language. To anticipate the conclusions of this chapter, we will first show that symbol systems are necessarily *conventional*, and second we will argue that all non-linguistic symbol systems are necessarily limited in what they can express. Writing is the one kind of symbol system that is virtually unlimited, but that is precisely because it is tied to language, and language is the only medium of communication that humans know which allows them to convey effectively any idea.

Over the course of the millennia, humans have invented a myriad of symbols to represent all kinds of concepts. Some symbols are simple in that they are typically used alone, and not in any conventional combination with other symbols. Consider the traditional three balls representing a pawnbroker, or the swirling spiral of a barber's shop. In other cases, as in the case of mathematical symbology, the symbols can be part of a complex system that has its own rules about how symbols are combined and what the combinations mean.

In order for something to be a symbol, there has to be a convention for what it means and how it is used. When these conventions are absent, the would-be symbol has no definite interpretation; when they are violated, the result can be confusion. A case in point: few symbols are as universally recognized as the red octagon of a stop sign. Note that it is the red octagon that is crucial: in the United States, the word *stop* also appears, but you can remove that, or replace it with another word (e.g. *alto* in Mexico) and the interpretation will not change. Change the color to blue, or the octagon to a circle, and you will no longer have a stop sign. The conventional denotation of the red octagon is clear: you must stop here. And so when that convention is violated, the result is confusing. In January 2008 I was traveling near Chennai (Madras) and noticed that the red octagon was being used to indicate a bus stop. True, the words *bus stop* actually appeared inside the octagon: yet the usage still violated my conventions of what the symbol means, since in my interpretation, any driver who sees that sign should stop—evidently not the intended interpretation in this case.

Conventionality is critical and attempts to create symbols that are "universal" in that they do not depend upon prior convention are generally doomed to fail. Unfortunately there are practical consequences of this state of affairs, and none is more poignant than the case of the Waste Isolation Pilot Plant (WIPP) in Carlsbad, New Mexico, the final resting place of several tens of thousands of tons of transuranic waste; we describe the symbological problem posed by the WIPP in the Appendix to this chapter.

Yet despite the practical experience of people who have tried and failed to come up with symbologies that transcend culture and convention, there has been no shortage of others willing to try. The idea is remarkably seductive. Perhaps the most extreme example of an attempt to design a convention-free symbology are the *Golden Records*, which were sent into space on the two Voyager spacecraft, both of which are now outside the solar system (Figure 2.1). The record is intended as Earth's message to alien intelligent beings. The record contains (analog) images of Earth along with audio clips of greetings in many human languages (from Akkadian, to Wu), music from a variety of cultures, as well as some written texts. The markings on the surface of the record are explained as follows:

Each record is encased in a protective aluminum jacket, together with a cartridge and a needle. Instructions, in symbolic language, explain the origin of the spacecraft and indicate how the record is to be played.[1]

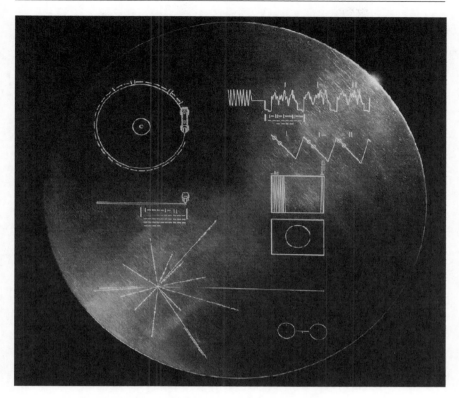

FIGURE 2.1 The *Golden Record* from the Voyager missions
Source: Used with permission: see http://www.jpl.nasa.gov/images/policy/index.cfm.

Before you read on, you should now take a closer look at the markings on the record and try to figure out what the 'symbolic language' instructions mean.

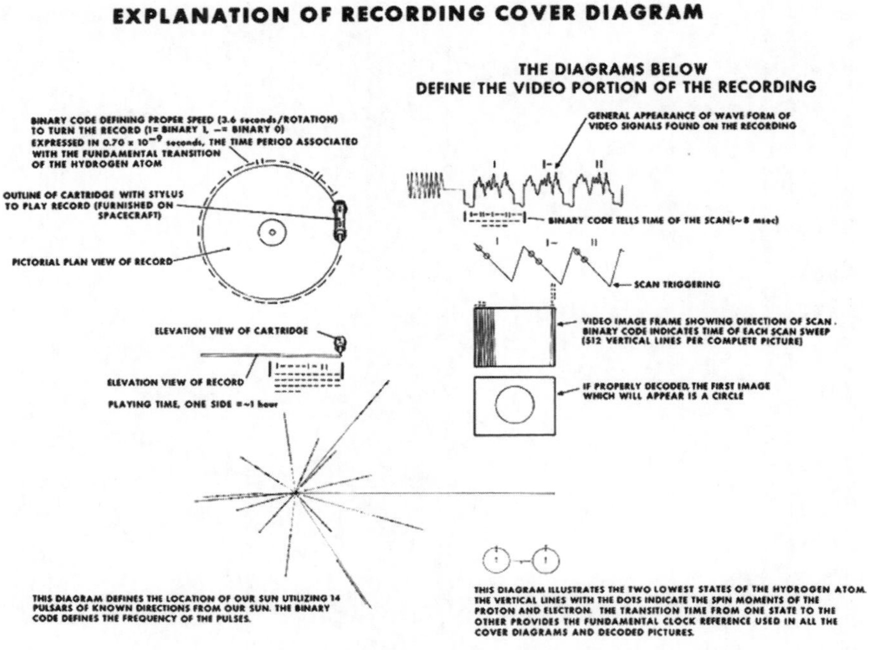

EXPLANATION OF RECORDING COVER DIAGRAM

**THE DIAGRAMS BELOW
DEFINE THE VIDEO PORTION OF THE RECORDING**

FIGURE 2.2 The explanation of the symbols from the *Golden Record*
Source: Used with permission: see http://www.jpl.nasa.gov/images/policy/index.cfm

Now that you have no doubt figured out what the symbols mean, you can check that you got it right by comparing your solution with Figure 2.2, which gives the official explanation from the Jet Propulsion Laboratory website devoted to the Voyager missions.

Of course you probably did not figure it out, because you likely did not have enough background information to know what some of the symbols would mean. Now this is significant, when you consider the purpose of this artefact. You are equipped with a human brain, the same kind of brain that designed the Record. We have some reason to believe that human brains all share some properties and tend to think along similar lines. But what about whatever alien creatures may eventually find this record? What assumptions can we make about how their brains work? Now consider that if you, with your human brain, could not figure out what this 'symbolic language' meant, how could we ever suppose that an alien with a presumably quite different set of cognitive abilities would be able to figure it out?

Assuming the team that designed the *Record* (which was headed by the late Carl Sagan) seriously intended it as a mode of communication, then this is yet another demonstration of the seductiveness of the notion of a universal language. Since we will never know if the *Record* falls into alien hands and is correctly interpreted, we can but speculate: but your own experience at trying to understand this message should leave you with serious doubts.

To be fair, we can hardly be said to have proved that unfamiliar symbols can *never* be interpreted. It is certainly conceivable that some of the symbols proposed for the WIPP (see Appendix 2.A) might still make sense to our descendants 10,000 years hence. For all we know, the Voyager missions may have been intercepted by aliens who are even now playing the *Golden Record*, and planning a trip to Earth, having figured all this out from the instructions. But none of this seems likely.

Conventional symbol systems are, of course, an entirely different matter. We deal with them on a daily basis: road signs, financial symbols, mathematical symbols, musical symbols—all of these are familiar to most of us, and some of them are familiar to all of us. Clearly such symbols are effective at communicating information, so the next question one would ask is what kind of information they communicate and how constrained or unconstrained that information is. Convention in symbology involves an agreement about what the individual symbols mean, and in non-trivial symbologies, it includes agreements on how to combine symbols and what those combinations mean. In mathematics we know that $\int$ represents "integral", x can denote a variable, a superscripted number often means "raise to the power of that number", and d is conventionally used to represent the differential. There is a conventional way of combining these, so that we write $\int f(x)\,dx$ for some function f of variable x, and thus $\int x^2\,dx$ is the integral of the quadratic function x^2. Thus any non-trivial symbol system has both a *syntax* (how the symbols are combined) and a *semantics* (what the symbols mean and what the combinations mean).

What is limited for most symbol systems is the kind of information they can encode—their *scope*. Traffic symbols such as the stop sign are limited to denoting ideas related to traffic. Mathematical symbology is substantially more intricate than this, but even so the scope is fairly limited compared to the full range of ideas that humans can conceive and, crucially, can convey using language. To see this, it is sufficient to observe that no matter how complicated a mathematical expression may be, it is possible to put that expression into words such that someone who is sufficiently skilled in mathematics can correctly reconstruct the intended expression: this may be a painful exercise, but it is nonetheless always possible in principle to do it. Now consider the inverse case of an arbitrary set of ideas expressed in language—the *Gettysburg Address* for example: there is simply no way this can be expressed using mathematical symbology. The same thought experiment can be done for any symbol system that one can think of, and it will quickly become apparent that all of these other systems are limited in a way that language is not.

But is it possible to develop a graphical symbol system that is universal in that it is as expressive as language, and yet is not tied to language in the way that writing is? Certainly this idea has been a dream dating back hundreds of years. The idea that language is a barrier to communication between people of different cultures is one that is deeply entrenched in our cultural psyche: it is expressed in the Biblical story of Babel, as well as in the efforts to develop artificial universal languages such as Esperanto. It was an idea that became particularly popular during the Age of Enlightenment, encouraged at least in part by the first contacts of the West with Chinese culture, and the (mistaken) belief that Chinese characters were somehow disconnected from language and conveyed ideas directly; Leibniz for a while dabbled with this notion. It was spoofed by Jonathan Swift in *Gulliver's Travels*—a sure indicator that it was a popular idea at the time:

The other project was, a scheme for entirely abolishing all words whatsoever; and this was urged as a great advantage in point of health, as well as brevity. For it is plain, that every word we speak is, in some degree, a diminution of our lungs by corrosion, and, consequently, contributes to the shortening of our lives. An expedient was therefore offered, 'that since words are only names for things, it would be more convenient for all men to carry about them such things as were necessary to express a particular business they are to discourse on.' And this invention would certainly have taken place, to the great ease as well as health of the subject, if the women, in conjunction with the vulgar and illiterate, had not threatened to raise a rebellion unless they might be allowed the liberty to speak with their tongues, after the manner of their fore-fathers; such constant irreconcilable enemies to science are the common people.

However, many of the most learned and wise adhere to the new scheme of expressing themselves by things; which has only this inconvenience attending it, that if a man's business be very great, and of various kinds, he must be obliged, in proportion, to carry a greater bundle of things upon his back, unless he can afford one or two strong servants to attend him. I have often beheld two of those sages almost sinking under the weight of their packs, like pedlars among us, who, when they met in the street, would lay down their loads, open their sacks, and hold conversation for an hour together; then put up their implements, help each other to resume their burdens, and take their leave.

But for short conversations, a man may carry implements in his pockets, and under his arms, enough to supply him; and in his house, he cannot be at a loss. Therefore the room where company meet who practise this art, is full of all things, ready at hand, requisite to furnish matter for this kind of artificial converse.

Another great advantage proposed by this invention was, that it would serve as a universal language, to be understood in all civilised nations, whose goods and utensils are generally of the same kind, or nearly resembling, so that their uses might easily be comprehended. And thus ambassadors would be qualified to treat with foreign princes, or ministers of state, to whose tongues they were utter strangers.

(*Gulliver's Travels*, Part III: "A Voyage to Laputa, Balnibarbi, Luggnagg, Glubbdub-drib, and Japan", Chapter V).

Let us state the case boldly and bluntly: there has never been a 'universal' system of communication that can be used to communicate everything that humans can communicate in language, which does not somehow parasitize off language the way writing does. This is not for want of people trying. Perhaps the most noteworthy attempt—noteworthy in both the perseverance of its author and the moderate degree of success that his system enjoyed—is *Blissymbolics*.

Charles Kasiel Bliss (Karl Kasiel Blitz, 1897–1985) was an Austrian chemical engineer. He was Jewish, and in 1938, after the Anschluss, the Nazis sent him to the concentration camp of Dachau, and then Buchenwald. His wife—a German Catholic—managed to win his release, but he was forced to move immediately to England, leaving his wife behind. He had hoped to get her to England, but the outbreak of the Second World War foiled these plans. She was able to get out of Austria via Romania, then Greece, and when Mussolini invaded Greece in 1940, they decided that the only way for her to be safe and for them to meet up again was to go independently to Bliss's cousin in Shanghai. They met up again on Christmas Eve, 1940.[2]

In Shanghai he was exposed to Chinese and to Chinese writing, which he believed (falsely) to be a purely meaning-based writing system. Indeed, he believed, as had many before him, that the Chinese writing system was independent of language, and was thus a universal system of communication. Unfortunately, he recognized that Chinese writing is rather difficult to learn, and so he set out to create something simpler but equally universal in its character. He worked on his system for a number of years and in 1949—by which time he had moved to Australia—he published the first edition of *International Semantography*, and set up his own publishing outfit, Semanto-graphy Press in Sydney, to do this. He continued to develop and promote the system further over the course of his life.[3]

It should be stated at the outset that Bliss was concerned first and foremost that the symbology he developed be *international*, and *easy to use*. Inter-national, because he felt very strongly that his symbol system should not be tied to any one culture and should work across cultures. Easy to use, since he felt that one of the reasons for the high illiteracy rates in many countries was the difficulties of the traditional orthography. He viewed his semasiographic approach as a way to achieve these goals, since the symbols were not supposed

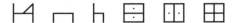

FIGURE 2.3 Pictographic Blissymbolics symbols: 'bed', 'table', 'chair', 'chest of drawers', 'wardrobe', 'window'

FIGURE 2.4 Iconic Blissymbolics symbols: 'man', 'woman', 'above', 'mind', 'feeling'

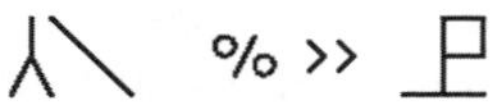

FIGURE 2.5 Compositional Blissymbolics words: 'writer' (man + pen), 'taxes' (percentage for State)

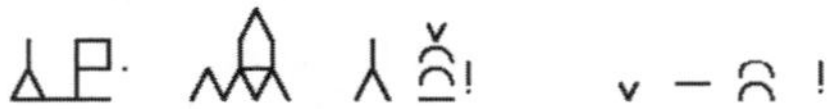

FIGURE 2.6 Compositional Blissymbolics words, from left to right: (1) 'foreigner' (man + outside + State); (2) '(insect) vermin' (insect undermining house); (3) 'bad man'. The four symbols separated off to the right represent the components of 'bad': 'evaluated', 'negative', 'conscience', intensifier

FIGURE 2.7 Compositional Blissymbolics words: 'apology' (saying, feeling, down, reasoning, negative, exclamation); 'into'; 'understanding' (into knowledge)

to be tied to the details of any one language, in particular the way it was pronounced. But he was perfectly comfortable with adopting symbols that were already international, including the symbols of mathematics and those of chemistry, a point we return to later on.

The basic symbols of Blissymbolics are either pictographic or iconic, as exemplified in Figures 2.3 and 2.4.[4] Obviously, though, this can get one only so far, and so the bulk of concepts are expressed by compounds of these more basic symbols. Some examples of these are given in Figures 2.5–2.7. Thus the word for (presumably male) 'writer' is the icon for 'man' followed by the icon for 'pen'. The notion of 'tax' is conveyed by the universal symbol '%' followed by the

FIGURE 2.8 Use of indices in Blissymbolics: 'waterfowl', 'duck' (waterfowl + 1), 'goose' (waterfowl + 2)

FIGURE 2.9 Use of indices in Blissymbolics: 'horse', 'mule', 'ass'

icons for 'for' and 'State'. A (again, presumably male) foreigner is a 'man outside the State'; '(insect) vermin' are insects that undermine houses; and a 'bad man' is a complex construction involving 'man', an evaluation symbol "$\vee$", the 'con-science' symbol (dome), a negative symbol ('−') and an intensifier (here the universal symbol '!').[5] An 'apology' could be glossed as something like 'saying that your feeling is down (bad) and there is a negative reason for it.'

Even for concepts that can be depicted, there are only so many things that one can distinguish if one wants a script that can be written easily. The general symbol for 'waterfowl' is given on the left of Figure 2.8: it represents the symbol for bird above the symbol for water. So far so good. What about, for example, different kinds of waterfowl: ducks, geese, marsh hens, swans, herons, ibises, flamingoes,...? Bliss proposes to use numerical indices for these. Thus a 'goose' is 'waterfowl + 1'; a duck is 'waterfowl + 2'. Similarly, in Figure 2.9 we see the representation for three horse-like animals.

Similar to the use of indices, Bliss proposes using letters to represent different countries. In many cases, it is straightforward to distinguish coun-tries by their flag, but in many other cases, this runs afoul of the fact that many flags are only distinguished from other flags by color: witness the many European tricolors. To get around this problem, Bliss uses the initial letter of the country name alongside an icon of its flag (Figure 2.10). Here we are already able to see a small crack in the system: clearly many names of countries are language-dependent. Germany is *Deutschland* in German and *Allemagne* in French; which letter do we pick: 'G', 'A', or 'D'? Obviously picking any one requires that one know at least this minimal amount about the language of origin of the name, if one is to be able to guess what the symbol denotes (assuming one does not already know).

FIGURE 2.10 Use of letters in Blissymbolics: 'Belgium', 'Italy', 'Mexico'

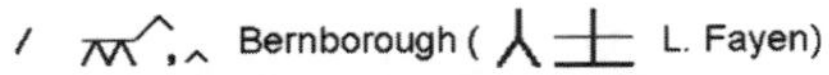

/   𝗺̂,ᴧ   Bernborough (人 ⊥ L. Fayen)

FIGURE 2.11 Blissymbolics for 'the stallion Bernborough (owner L. Fayen)'

Further material from particular languages can be borrowed. The most obvious example is names. The fragment of a sentence in Figure 2.11 illustrates this. The words 'the', 'stallion' ('horse' + 'male'), and 'owner' are written in Blissymbols. The names 'Bernborough' and 'L. Fayen' are written in English. One could argue that Bliss had no choice: how else are you going to write names that, on the face of it, have no obvious semantic interpretation and just seem like arbitrary strings of sounds? But note that all naturally occurring writing systems have a way of dealing with this via the mechanism of *transliteration*. Thus despite Bliss's belief about Chinese writing, as we shall see in the next chapter, most of the system is based on phonetics and there are conventional ways of representing foreign names in Chinese by using characters that represent sounds that are similar to the name's pronunciation in the original source language. Thus 'Fayen' would likely be written with characters that would be pronounced in (Mandarin) Chinese as *fa-yan*. 'Bernborough' would likely be written with characters that would be pronounced as *bo-en-bo-luo*. Since Blissymbolics explicitly avoids reference to sound, there is no straightforward way to represent names other than in their original form.

Once we get beyond individual Blissymbolics concepts, we get into the realm of *syntax*, or the combining of words into sentences. There are three issues here. One is the modification of words when they are combined in order to convey certain kinds of meaning in the sentence context; linguists call this kind of modification *inflection*. The second is the particular words needed. The third is the order in which the words occur.

Consider the sentence 'I fear you' in Figure 2.12. There are three basic concepts corresponding to 'I' ('person 1'), 'you' ('person 2'), and a complex expression denoting 'fear'. This sentence is *active*, meaning that the subject is the one who does the action, or in this case feels the emotion. The comparable passive sentence 'you are feared by me' is given in Figure 2.13, where here it is the subject who is the feared entity, not the one doing the fearing. The active versus passive distinction is indicated by the symbols < (active—pointing at the word on the left) and > (passive, pointing at the word on the right). This is an instance of

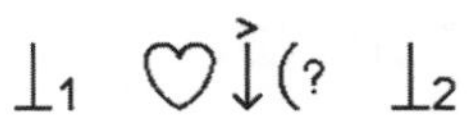

$$\bot_1 \quad \heartsuit \dot{\mathsf{l}}_{(?} \quad \bot_2$$

FIGURE 2.12 Active verb in Blissymbolics: 'I fear you'

⌄
⌊₂ ♡↓(? ⌊₁

FIGURE 2.13 Passive verb in Blissymbolics: 'You are feared by me'

⌐▤ ⊕ ♡↓(? ›ₗ ⌐▥

FIGURE 2.14 Use of passive verb 'fear' as 'danger': 'Czechoslovakia is a danger to (Nazi) Germany'

FIGURE 2.15 Blissymbolics for 'danger'

inflection, and the example presents an issue, since many languages lack the active/passive distinction that English happens to have, and would express this alternation in some other way. Indeed, Bliss himself (1965: 162), notes that the two sentences mean the same thing, and one might then wonder why, in a purely semantographic system, one would not be able to do away with the distinction entirely. Bliss goes on to argue for the use of the passive of 'fear' to represent the concept of 'danger' as in his example in Figure 2.14, since a danger is something that is (mentally) feared. But there are other ways to express this idea, and indeed, later versions of Blissymbolics represent 'danger' with the more iconic symbol in Figure 2.15.

In Blissymbolics, verbs may be marked for tense so that you can mark the difference between 'see', 'saw', and 'will see'. Many languages do this. But many do not. Chinese, for example, has no marking of tense on verbs.

The word order of the examples in Figures 2.12–2.14 is also reminiscent of English insofar as the subject is before the verb and the object after. While this is a common word order, it is important to realize that many languages differ in this regard. So whereas in English we would say 'John saw a dog', in Korean you would say *John-eun gaereul bwasseoyo* (literally, 'John dog saw') with the verb at the end. In Welsh you would say 'Mi welodd Siôn gi' (literally 'saw John dog') with the verb at the beginning. Blissymbolics follows English usage in the ordering of its words.

Similar language-particularities involve examples like Figure 2.11, which includes a symbol for the definite article 'the' (many languages—Russian,

$$\underset{3}{\overset{\square}{L}} \quad \hat{\Phi} \quad \overset{\vee}{-\frown} \qquad \underset{3}{\overset{\square}{L}} \quad \hat{\Phi} \quad \overset{\vee}{\lambda,-\frown}$$

FIGURE 2.16 Blissymbolics for 'he is stupid'; 'he is an idiot'

Chinese, Korean—lack a definite article); and various ways of expressing the so-called *copular* (literally 'joining') verb 'be' in sentences like those in Figure 2.16. Chinese does not use a form of 'be' in 'he is stupid', but says 'he stupid'. And in present-tense sentences, Russian does not use a copular in either case.

It is worth stressing that when Bliss claimed his system was 'readable in all languages', he never meant that one could read word-for-word:

> Now that boast 'readable in all languages' never intended to mean [sic] that a sentence in semantography can be read *word after word* in any language. It is to be understood that the reader would (1) glance over the symbols composing the whole sentence, would then (2) get its meaning and then (3) translate it in the proper word order in his native language.   (1965: 174, emphasis original.)

But interpreting sentences that may involve some amount of language-particular information is surely something that requires practice. Chinese speakers would learn to ignore tense marks, and definite articles. Korean and Japanese speakers would reorder the words—something highly reminiscent of the situation in Old Japanese where texts were actually written in Chinese characters *in Chinese word order*, with indices that expressed how to order the words in the output.[6] So much for the universality of Chinese writing. Clearly all of this *can* be learned, but it is also clear that no matter how one configures it, there is no hope of designing the system so that it will be equally accessible to speakers of any language.

There are three questions that must be asked of Blissymbolics:

1. How language-independent is it?
2. Can you make the fine-grained distinctions that natural languages, and writing systems based on those languages, can make?
3. How much easier is it to learn than the standard writing system for one's own language or indeed any language?

We have already addressed the question of language-independence. Certainly in Bliss's writings there are a number of features of English (and presumably his native German) that appear. One can argue that one could have based it on some different language: Chinese, or perhaps the native Australian language Warlbiri. But no matter: inevitably some language-dependence will seep through into the system. In some cases, one cannot avoid reference to sound, if only in the representation of proper names.

With respect to the second question, it is clear that even in its most elaborated form, Blissymbolics is inferior to natural spoken language (and the accompanying sound-based writing systems) in the number of distinctions it can make. The example 'bad man' in Figure 2.7 is explicitly intended as representing a whole range of English words that are related to this concept: *scoundrel, miscreant, blackguard, villain, hooligan,* and so forth. But are these words really synonyms? Bliss argues that they are close enough, and that one can get by without all these distinctions. This may be true in principle, but no one has shown that one can engage in the full richness afforded by conversations or written correspondence in natural language with only a subset of the vocabulary representing some 'key' concepts. Bliss cites as a precedent C. K. Ogden's 'Basic English'—a proposal to reduce the number of English words to a bare minimum of about 850—a concept that was promoted for a while as an international language. Clearly this might suffice for some cases: buying vegetables in a market, one can usually get by with gestures and some basic number terms, and perhaps words or phrases like 'fresh', 'how much', 'too expensive', and so forth. But to get beyond these simple kinds of interactions, a much larger number of words would be needed, even for everyday conversation, not to mention technical discourse. Pidgin languages—languages that are constructed by people who want to communicate (e.g. for purposes of trade) and who do not share a common language—have this property of being very limited.[7]

How much easier is Blissymbolics to learn than full systems of communication? Beyond limited applications with a subset of the full richness of the system (see below), I am not aware that the question has been addressed. But the design of the system suggests that there would be difficulties. Language-particular infiltrations such as word order and the marking of certain kinds of non-universal information (e.g. definite articles) could certainly be learned. Chinese speakers must do the same when they learn English and learn that marking definiteness with 'the' is required in some cases. From that point of view Blissymbolics is much more lenient than English: in English if you say 'I saw horse', it is simply wrong; the Blissymbolics equivalent would presumably not be.

But what about devices such as indices? Bliss is right that it is possible to learn a small set of indices so that one could remember that 'goose' is 'number one waterfowl' and 'duck' is 'number two waterfowl'. The issue is how many such sets there are to keep straight, since clearly the more there are, the more burden this places on the learner to memorize what are clearly just arbitrary facts. Some of these proposals become baroque. For colors, Bliss proposes that there be a single color symbol and numbers to indicate which color is intended. Clearly this must break down beyond the basic colors of the rainbow. How do I indicate 'chartreuse', or 'mauve', or 'sienna'? Bliss offers

$$\underline{\odot}_1 \quad \underline{\odot}_2 \quad \underline{\odot}_3 \quad \underline{\odot}(87)$$

FIGURE 2.17 Some colors in Blissymbolics: 'red', 'orange', 'yellow', 'Persian blue'

two suggestions: one is that the index be to a position in a standard color chart; see Figure 2.17. The other that one be able to give the colors in terms of wavelength. Obviously the latter would be problematic for mixed colors, and these days one would presumably use some kind of standard digital representation of colors, such as Red–Green–Blue (RGB). But no matter. I think I know chartreuse when I see it. I would find it very difficult to name the RGB values for it, much less the particular entry in a color chart.

For chemicals Bliss suggests simply using the standard chemical formulae. This is hardly surprising given his chemical engineering background. But this would be rather hard to implement in practice. Readers presumably will have no trouble with H_2O for "water"; but how many know 'ethanol' as $C_2 H_6O$, much less 'caffeine' as $C_8H_{10}N_4O_2$, or 'capsaicin' as $C_{18}H_{27}NO_3$? For chemists this might not be a problem. But there are at least hundreds of terms for chemicals that are used in everyday language where most speakers know pretty much what the substance is, but where they could not name the chemical formula. The alternative of using the common-language name for the chemical obviously immediately brings up the question: which language?

Bliss had conceived of his system as a universal system of communication, one that would be easy to learn (unlike the Chinese writing system, his misconception of which was his model), and that could be used by people from all cultures and languages. But language is complex, and the requirement that words be decomposed into meaning "atoms" makes it hard to capture all the subtle distinctions that language can convey. Inevitably the system will be impoverished with respect to ordinary writing. Furthermore, the more distinctions one is able to capture in the system, the more difficult the system becomes to learn, since, as we have seen, the graphical devices for capturing the distinctions are often arbitrary. So the benefits of having a "transparent" meaning-based script are eroded.

Despite plaudits from Bertrand Russell and other major intellectual figures, Blissymbolics did not make much headway as a practical system. Hardly anyone has ever heard of it, and even scholars of writing systems are largely ignorant of it.[8]

One area where Blissymbolics has had an impact is in the teaching of children with severe cognitive impairment and communication disorders. The Toronto-based organization Blissymbolics Communication International (http://www.blissymbolics.org) is devoted to promulgating Blissymbolics and has had some success in applying it to situations where children with impairments have severe difficulties with ordinary language, but are evidently able to learn to use Blissymbolics to communicate effectively within a somewhat limited range of topics.[9] This in itself is not unique: other symbol systems are used for people with severe cognitive impairments, and there is no evidence that Blissymbolics is particularly beneficial compared to other systems. Indeed, *Augmentative and Alternative Communication* practitioners these days tend to prefer systems such as Picture Communication Symbols (PCS), where the symbols are much more pictorial than Blissymbols, since their patients find them easier to learn.

The notion of a universal 'semantic' language is, as we have noted, an extremely seductive one. But as with other kinds of seduction, once the initial attractiveness of the idea wears off and one is tasked with developing an entire system, it becomes clear that the task is probably impossible. The easy cases—a heart for 'love', a smiley face for happiness, some combination of a humanoid figure and heart for 'lover, paramour'—often blind us to the fact that there is really a very limited set of things that you can express in language which, are so easily broken down into atoms. And there are never enough of these atoms to make all the distinctions that spoken—and written—language can make. As speakers of English we are all aware of the words 'annoyance' and 'consternation'. They are clearly distinct words, and have different usage patterns and imply different things when you use them. How would you represent these two words if you had to do it purely on the basis of some collection of semantic primitives? Or take 'achievement' versus 'accomplishment', 'goal' versus 'objective', 'summit' versus 'peak', and, unless you are an artist with a very fine knack for subtle detail, 'spaghetti' versus 'vermicelli'. One may look at a system like Blissymbolics and note that it is possible to distinguish perhaps several thousand words. This may seem like a lot, but compared to the active vocabulary of averagely educated people, which numbers in the tens of thousands of words, it is still quite small.

Writing—real writing that literate societies use to communicate the full range of what can be communicated in spoken language—works because it is tied to language. We have labored this point, because it is important to understand why it is the case. The second claim of this chapter, that writing is a language *technology*, is a much simpler claim to justify, and we can do that in just a couple of paragraphs of text. At first glance it does seem a bit odd to think of writing as a technology. After all, things like pen and paper, or chalk and chalkboard, are canonical instances of 'low tech' devices. Yet, often, what seems like a primitive device to those of us familiar with it will immediately seem less primitive when we observe the reactions to it of someone who has never seen the device before. To them it is a wondrous artefact, something whose principles they will likely not initially understand, that seems to be capable of performing a task that they cannot explain. To them it will seem like magic, and we can fall back on the well-known quotation from the late Arthur C. Clarke that "any sufficiently advanced technology is indistinguishable from magic".

The point is rather poignantly made by the following example recounted by Thomas Williams, a Wesleyan missionary in Fiji in the 1840s:

In the erection of this chapel, a circumstance occurred which will give a striking idea of the feelings of an untaught people, when observing, for the first time, the effects of written communication. As I had come to work one morning without my [carpenter's] square, I took up a chip and with a piece of charcoal wrote upon it a request that Mrs. Williams should send me that article. I called a chief, who was superintending his portion of the work, and said to him, "Friend, take this: go to our house, and give it to Mrs. Williams."... [He] asked "What must I say?" I replied "You have nothing to say; the chip will say all I wish." With a look of astonishment and contempt, he held up the piece of wood and said, "How can this speak? Has this a mouth? "... On arriving at the house, he gave the chip to Mrs. Williams, who read it, threw it away, and went to the tool chest; whither the chief, resolving to see the result of this mysterious proceeding, followed her closely. On receiving the square from her, he said, "Stay daughter, how do you know that this is what Mr. Williams wants? " "Why," she replied, "did you not bring me a chip just now? " "Yes," said the astonished warrior, "but I did not hear it say anything." "If you did not, I did" was the reply, "for it made known to me what he wanted, and all you have to do is to return with it as quickly as possible." With this the chief leaped out of the house; and [caught] up the mysterious piece of wood.... On giving me the square, he wished to know how it was possible thus to converse with persons at a distance. I gave him all the explanation in my power; but it was a circumstance involved in so much mystery, that he actually tied a string to the chip, hung it around his neck and wore it for some time. During several following days, we frequently saw him surrounded by a crowd who were listening with intense interest while he narrated the wonders which this chip had performed.[10]

Only a technology could have such a magical effect.

Appendix

Appendix 2.A The Waste Isolation Pilot Plant

The Waste Isolation Pilot Plant (WIPP) is designed as the final resting place for "transuranic" waste, consisting mostly of items rendered radioactive during the production of nuclear weapons; the sister site at Yucca Mountain in Nevada is designed for "high-level" waste from spent nuclear fuel from the civilian sector.[11] According to the WIPP website (http://www.wipp. energy.gov), the United States has produced 55,000 tons of this waste, and continues to produce about 2,000 tons annually. Transuranic waste is highly toxic (though less so than the "high-level" waste at Yucca Mountain). More importantly it will remain toxic for approximately 10,000 years. Waste at WIPP is stored half a mile underground in structures embedded in a 250-million-year-old salt formation. It has been in operation since 1999.

Finding an appropriate site and designing containers and structures that can isolate such material and render it 'safe' is clearly a major task, but there is another and potentially more serious problem. To see this, it is worth bearing in mind that 10,000 years is more than twice as long as all of recorded history. Though one might not like to contemplate it, it is quite easy to imagine that civilization could collapse within the next thousand years, and that the survivors of this collapse could live relatively primitive existences for a few millennia. Then the cultural level might start to increase again until, say eight thousand years in the future, another civilization roughly comparable to our own in terms of technical ability comes into being. They will be a lot like us: biological evolution is sufficiently slow that we can be fairly certain that humans will not change very much biologically in the next 10,000 years. So, we can be sure that they will be both smart and curious. Suppose then that they come across what's left of the WIPP. They have no idea what it is, and like archaeologists of today who come across the remnants of a Sumerian city from five thousand years ago, they would very likely try to dig it up. Obviously this would be bad news, but how do we prevent it from happening?

If you were thinking of warning signs—for example the standard nuclear trefoil symbol (Figure 2.18), along with some phrases like *Danger!*, *¡Peligro!* in various languages—then consider this: what is the likelihood that eight thousand years from now people will read or speak any of the languages that we speak today, or understand any of the conventional symbols that we use? If you did not know what the nuclear trefoil meant, how would you hope to figure it out?

The designers of WIPP were sufficiently concerned by this problem that they asked Sandia National Laboratories to convene two panels of experts to study the problem and come up with a recommendation. The report[12] makes fascinating reading since both panels comprised experts from several fields, who brought a wide range of points of view to bear on the problem, and proposed a variety of solutions. The first panel (Team A) included the linguist Fritz Newmeyer and the linguistic anthropologist Ward Goodenough, and, not surprisingly, they were well aware of the difficulties of designing any symbology that would retain its meaning over so long a period.

Fritz Newmeyer was particularly pessimistic about designing a clear message:

If the WIPP is ever operational, the site may pose a greater hazard than is officially acknowledged. Yet the problems involved in marking the site to deter inadvertent intrusion for the next 10,000 years are enormous. Even if knowledge exists that would allow translation of the message on the markers, there might be little motivation to solicit such knowledge. Pictorial messages, however, are unreliable and may even convey the opposite of what is intended.   (Trauth et al. 1993: F–142)

One of the tasks assigned to the panels was to assess the probability, whatever messages were selected, that those messages would be correctly interpreted. A variety of different purposes for the future intruders were posed, among them drilling for water and archaeological investigations. Different time periods up to 10,000 years in the future were to be considered, as well as considerations of the possible future technological state of the people at the site—higher, the same, or lower than our current technological state. Table 2.1 gives Team A's

FIGURE 2.18 What does this symbol mean if you didn't already know?

TABLE 2.1 Probability of correct interpretation of message—drilling for water as mode of intrusion

Expert	200 Years technology level			500 Years technology level			1,000 Years technology level			5,000 Years technology level			10,000 Years technology level		
	H[a]	M	L	H	M	L	H	M	L	H	M	L	H	M	L
Ast	.99	.98	.98	.98	.95	.60	.95	.85	.20	.90	.10	.05	.90	.05	.01
Brill	.99	.99	.95	.95	.95	.90	.95	.95	.70	.95	.95	.60	.95	.95	.50
Goodenough	.99	.99	.99	.96	.95	.70	.90	.90	.50	.65	.60	.15	.50	.40	.02
Kaplan	.99	.98	.95	.98	.90	.70	.95	.85	.60	.80	.70	.40	.75	.50	.01
Newmeyer	.99	.99	.90	.90	.85	.80	.80	.70	.50	.70	.60	.40	.50	.30	.20
Sullivan	.95	.95	.80	.90	.90	.60	.85	.85	.40	.70	.70	.10	.40	.40	.01

	500 Years			2000 Years			10,000 Years		
Team B	.90	.90	.80	.90	.85	.70	.99	.80	.30

Notes: The table shows Team A's analysis of the probability of the correct interpretation of a message by an intruder given that the purpose of the intruder was to drill for water. Probability estimates from each of the panel members are given in the rows. The columns represent different times in the future, under different scenarios of technology that was higher, the same or lower than ours. The most pessimistic predictions are, not surprisingly, for the most remote times for the lowest technological levels.

[a] H, M, and L represent the assumptions that technology level is respectively more advanced than today (H), similar to today's level (M), or less advanced than today (L).

assessments for the intrusion purpose of drilling for water. Not surprisingly, the predictions are reasonably optimistic for the near future, but drop off substantially for the distant future, especially if we assume that the people living at that time are less technologically advanced than we are.

Needless to say, the panel recognized the pointlessness of using the nuclear trefoil, and pointed out that even if it *were* understood so far into the future, apparent circumstances (no measurable radioactivity on the surface) might lead future would-be intruders to discount the message:

A difficult question is whether or not to include the familiar radiation hazard trefoil as a part of our design. It is indeed an internationally recognized symbol with a 40-year history, but its long-term intelligibility when applied to all cultures over a period of 10,000 years is dubious at best. Furthermore, one of its standard uses means "do not go into this space unless properly protected" whereas we are not trying to keep people away from the surface above the WIPP repository. So even if the symbol were understood in the future, once no radioactivity was measured on the surface, we might lose our credibility in the eyes of future investigators.   (Trauth et al. 1993: F–112–113)

Team A was thus fairly dubious about the use of abstract symbols, even seemingly universal symbols of disgust or frightening faces. As they point out: "museums and private collections abound with such guardian figures removed from burial sites. These earlier warning messages did not work because the intruder knew that the burial goods were valuable" (Trauth et al. 1993: F–34). Instead they put their faith in linguistic messages and provided a set of texts in multiple modern languages including (presumably for reasons more having to do with political correctness than practical need) the Native American language Navajo. Also provided on the surfaces on which these messages were to be inscribed was space to translate the texts into the modern languages of future millennia (Figure 2.19). They claim 'there will always be scholars capable of reading the major languages of the twentieth century' (Trauth et al. 1993: F–36), though they preface this statement with the rather crucial caveat 'barring some drastic cultural discontinuity'. They should perhaps also have included the caveat that periodically updating the translation requires someone to be the caretaker, a concern also raised by Newmeyer in his comments.

Obviously if we can assume that people will still be able to read, say, twentieth-century English several thousand years from now, then the best we could do would be to write the warnings in English. Non-linguistic symbols surely will fail, without the cultural context to help interpret them. But it seems to me in any case that one needs to be highly doubtful of the assumption that eight thousand years from now there will be scholars who

These standing stones mark an area used to bury radioactive wastes. The area is … by … Kilometers (or … miles or about … times the height of an average full grown male person) and the buried waste is … kilometers down. This place was chosen to put this dangerous material far away from people. The rock and water in this area may not look, feel, or smell, unusual but may be poisoned by radioactive wastes. When radioactive matter decays, it gives off invisible energy that can destroy or damage people, animals, and plants.

Do not drill here. Do not dig here. Do not do anything that will change the rocks or water in the area.

Do not destroy this marker. This marking system has been designed to last 10,000 years. If the marker is difficult to read, add new markers in longer-lasting materials in languages that you speak. For more information go to the building further inside. The site was known as the WIPP (Waste Isolation Pilot Plant) site when it was closed in ….

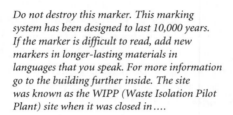

FIGURE 2.19 One of the proposed marker texts from Team A

Note: The text explains what the WIPP is, and in addition to English was proposed to be translated into Arabic, Spanish, French, Russian, Chinese, and Navajo. A blank space was to be left to allow future peoples to translate into their language. The text was to be flanked by two iconic faces, one (by Edvard Munch) representing fear and the other representing sickness.

can read present-day languages. Just consider the large number of languages from only three or four thousand years ago which were forgotten and had to be deciphered in modern times (see Chapter 4): Sumerian, Akkadian, Old Persian, Elamite, Ugaritic, Egyptian, Mycenaean Greek. In most of these cases, the loss was not due to any 'drastic cultural discontinuity', but merely because they fell out of use and were forgotten.

There is a simple moral to this story, which returns us to the main point: symbols, whether they be linguistic symbols, mathematical symbols, stop signs, or nuclear trefoils, are conventional. Simply put, you have to know what they mean, and if you don't know, and if you do not share the cultural background of the people who created them, it is unlikely in general that you are going to figure them out.[13]

3

How Writing Represents Language

This chapter introduces the various ways in which writing systems represent the information they do, with a particular focus on how they represent sound. I will say at the outset that this is not a comprehensive introduction to the history of writing systems, nor does it dwell on what is perhaps the most salient feature of writing in many cultures, namely the esthetic aspects of scripts. There are other works that cover these aspects in more detail, most notably Andrew Robinson's *Story of Writing*,[1] and Amelia Gnanadesikan's *Writing Revolution*.[2] Similarly, I will have little to say here about the mechanics of writing—pens, brushes, styluses. We will cover this a bit at the end of this chapter. Again, one can find more extensive treatment of these issues in other places, such as Robinson (2006b). Here, we focus on how writing works as a technology for encoding language.

The two most obvious questions to ask of any technology are: (1) what does it do, and (2) how does it work? We have already defined writing as a technology for representing language, so the answer to the first question is that writing provides a mechanism for recording ideas that are expressed in language. How, then, does it do this?

Before we answer that question in the bulk of this chapter, it is worth stepping back a moment to remind ourselves that any linguistic expression, whether a single word or a long complex sentence, can be broken down into smaller units, each of which can be viewed as a more or less simple building block of the language. Let's try to understand this point by way of example.

Suppose I say the sentence *My dog likes avocados*. To emphasize the fact that I am talking here about speech or language and *not* writing, I will re-render this sentence, based on my own pronunciation, in the International Phonetic Alphabet, which is the standard symbol set used in linguistics for indicating pronunciation:

maɪ dɔg laɪks ævəkadoz

This transcription, which is fairly coarse—it omits many details, which a careful phonetician might wish to represent—gives one level of representation at which I can describe this utterance, but there are several others.

The *phonemes* or *segments* that make up the utterance are combined into syllables. Roughly speaking, a syllable is a sequence of zero or more consonants, a vowel, or vowel-like sound, followed by zero or more consonants. A more precise definition would take us too far afield (and in any case linguists have found it hard to provide an exact definition), but actually syllables are a fairly intuitive concept, much more so than phonemes. Indeed, experimenters have shown that that illiterate speakers show 'awareness' of syllables, whereas it has been argued that people only become aware of phonemes if they have been exposed to writing, and in particular alphabetic writing.[3] So readers who have had no background in linguistics will already know that *my, dog,* and *likes* each have one syllable, whereas *avocados* has four syllables.

So here is the sentence again, with parentheses indicating the groupings into syllables:

(maɪ) (dɔg) (laɪks) (æ)(və)(ka)(doz)

There are higher-level groupings that linguists consider: syllables are often grouped into *feet*; if you are familiar with poetic scansion, then this is the same basic concept as feet in poetry. In our case, a foot is a stressed syllable grouped together with a series of following unstressed syllables. This is only interesting in the case of *avocados* in our example, where in my pronunciation there is a main stress on *ca*, and a secondary stress on the initial *a*, so that the foot structure would look as follows:

[(æ)(və)][(ka)(doz)]

So far we have been talking about *phonological* structure, that is structure that involves sound. But there is clearly more. There are words, four of them to be precise, so that is another level of structure. But we can do better than that: two of the words—*likes* and *avocados*—are clearly complex in that they have two identifiable bits. *Likes* consists of the verb *like* plus an ending *-s* that indicates that the subject of the verb is a third person singular noun phrase. *Avocados* consists of the noun *avocado* and an ending, also *-s*, that marks it as plural. Each of these subword pieces is what linguists would term a *morpheme*.[4] Roughly speaking, the morpheme is the minimal unit of meaning in a word in that (again roughly speaking) one can often identify a particular meaning or function with a given morphological component of a word. Thus in *avocados* there is a bit that denotes the avocado, and there is a bit that denotes plurality. Using a " + " to mark a morpheme boundary, we have another level of representation for our sentence in terms of morphemes:

maɪ dɔg laɪk + s ævəkado + z

Words in a sentence are related to one another and one common way to express this relationship is to group them into *phrases*. (Those of you who did sentence diagramming in school will have done something akin to this.) In our sentence *my* is related to *dog* in that it restricts the sense of dog to one of that set of dogs that belong to me. The sentence asserts something about my dog: that she likes avocados. So the verb phrase *likes avocados* expresses this predicate. The noun phrase *my dog* and the verb phrase *likes avocados* combine to form the whole sentence.

We can also think of things at the level of semantics. This is a lot more vague than what we have discussed so far, but linguists often think of individual words as having semantic features that relate them to other words. Indeed, thesauri are organized around this principle, and one such electronic thesaurus, WordNet, produced by psychologist George Miller's group at Princeton, has been extensively used in natural language processing to model semantic relations between words. Thus dogs share a semantic relation to wolves and jackals, a more distant relation to cats, and so forth. Avocados are thought of as vegetables by many people. And so forth.

In the foregoing discussion, we have enumerated a number of levels of linguistic representation: phonemes, syllables, feet, morphemes, words, phrases, and semantic features. Now, as the British linguist Geoffrey Sampson observed in his 1985 book on writing systems,[5] in principle writing systems could choose to represent any of these levels. But in practice the choice is quite a bit more limited, and much of this has to do with simple combinatorics.

Most linguists (as well as commercial firms that sell courses in phonics) will tell you that there are about forty-five phonemes in English, depending upon the dialect and upon particular choices about what to consider a phoneme. How many syllables are there? This is much more difficult to answer, but one way to give a sense of the number is to look in a dictionary and count the number of distinct syllables that one finds. To give a basic idea, I took the CMU Lexicon,[6] a dictionary containing 127,000 English words and names with their (American) pronunciations, that is widely used in speech and language technology. The CMU lexicon does not mark syllable boundaries, which means that in order to deal with a polysyllabic word, it would be necessary to first parse the pronunciation into syllables. This is easy enough to do, but requires some decisions about in which syllable to place a consonant that straddles two syllables. So to obviate those decisions, I simply considered monosyllabic words, and I counted how many distinct syllables were found for these words in the dictionary. I counted ten thousand syllable types. If we had included polysyllabic words, we would have observed many more types. But ten thousand is already enough to make you realize that for a language with syllable structures as complex as English, it is impractical to have a separate symbol for each syllable. In fact, syllabaries—writing systems based on syllables rather than phonemes—are common, but they rarely have more than a hundred or so symbols and they are used either for languages that have a *much* simpler syllable structure than English (one example is Japanese), or else they represent the actual syllables of the language quite imperfectly (as we will see in the case of Linear B for Mycenaean Greek later on). In general, while the units of syllabaries do represent syllables, it is actually pretty rare that you will find a language where there is a distinct single symbol for each and every one of the syllables. To my knowledge this point was first made explicitly by the linguist William Poser in a presentation at the Linguistic Society of America in the early 1990s, but it really basically comes down to common sense: writing systems have to be designed and learned, and it is simply too hard to design and learn a system with thousands of arbitrary symbols.

Given the large population of syllable types in many languages, it seems pointless to proceed further up the phonological hierarchy, because the numbers of distinct symbols one would need simply grows out of hand. There are, for example, no writing systems that are based on feet.

What about the other levels—morphemes, words, phrases, or semantic features? We can eliminate phrases from consideration for the same reason we can eliminate syllables: there are far too many of them. Even words are suspect, since the number of distinct English words is in reality open-ended, but even if you insist that it is finite, it at least numbers in the hundreds of thousands: as we noted, the (relatively small) CMU lexicon has 127,000 words. Morphemes are a safer bet (though that set is large too), so could one design a writing system that has separate symbols for morphemes but, crucially, does not make any reference to the *sounds* of those morphemes. Such a system would be termed *logographic*.[7] Sampson in his 1985 book thought he had found such an instance in Chinese. The Chinese scholar John DeFrancis has for many years argued vehemently against this view, pointing out that Chinese writing in fact represents sound rather extensively and that well over 95 per cent of the roughly 48,000 characters that have been created throughout the history of Chinese include a component that indicates the pronunciation (though the indication may be quite imperfect). We will return to this point later on, but for now suffice it to say that there are *no* unequivocal cases of writing systems that encode the full set of morphemes of the language, and do it in a way that ignores the sound. For a subset of the morphemes this is possible: certainly part of Chinese writing can be characterized in this way, but not the whole system.

So writing systems can encode segments and limited numbers of syllables, and maybe a small number of morphemes. What about meaning elements? Of course this was something that Bliss was trying to achieve, as we saw in the previous chapter. Having said that, many writing systems throughout history, and *all* of the original writing systems—Sumerian, Egyptian, Chinese, and Mayan[8]—include elements that denote meaning. Typically these are in the form of *determinatives* that indicate something about the meaning of the word or morpheme that they are used to write. One element in Sumerian ✳, for example, indicates that the (following) word is the name of a deity. However, such semantic systems are always quite limited in scope, consisting of at most a few hundred elements.

In the remainder of this chapter we will examine how the technology of writing works by considering how the various representable elements— phonemes, (some) syllables, (some) morphemes, and (some) semantic features—are combined into working writing systems. We start with Chinese.

3.1 Chinese writing

Few writing systems have been more misunderstood than Chinese. Although the system is basically phonological as we shall see, for centuries people have believed that Chinese writing encodes ideas directly. As we saw, this was Charles Bliss's belief, and this was the inspiration for the development of his own ideographic system. Leibniz believed it for a time, thinking that Chinese might serve as a model for a universal language, seeing that it circumvented language and encoded thought directly. The misconception has been as widespread among Chinese as among Westerners: a Chinese convert to Christianity, who wrote under the name 'Ko, Jéf', stated in 1776 that Chinese characters 'are composed of symbols and images, and that these symbols and images, not having any sound, can be read in all languages, and form a sort of intellectual painting, a metaphysical and ideal algebra, which conveys thoughts by analogy, by relation, by convention, and so forth.'[9]

The idea has yet to disappear, and it seems particularly rife in some communities. I have reviewed countless technical papers by Chinese speech technology engineers who invariably start their papers by pointing out that Chinese (in contrast to English) is an 'ideographic language'. And the Unicode Consortium has adopted the terminology 'ideograph' to denote Chinese characters. Because of these misconceptions, Chinese is a very good place to start any discussion of how writing systems really work, since if one can argue that Chinese is largely phonographic—encodes sound—then other writing systems are even more obviously so.

The basic point that I want to make is a point that was made by the University of Hawaii Chinese scholar John DeFrancis in a couple of books (*The Chinese Language, Fact and Fantasy* and *Visible Speech*) as well as in several scholarly articles.[10] DeFrancis is by no means the first (or last) to have made these points, but his presentation is in many ways the most compelling. In any discussion of Chinese characters it is useful to review briefly the so-called *six writings* (Chinese *liù shū*),[11] the traditional classification system that breaks characters into six categories. These are:

象形	*xiàngxíng*	simple pictograms
指事	*zhǐshì*	indicators
會意	*huìyì*	meaning compound
形聲	*xíngshēng*	phonetic compounds
轉注	*zhuǎnzhù*	'redirected characters'
假借	*jiǎjiè*	'borrowings'

As the name suggests, the simple pictograms originated as pictures of objects. For example, the word *rén* 'person' is written 人, which originally was a picture of a person. 'Wood', *mù* 木 was originally a picture of a tree. The word for 'turtle', *guī*, is written 龜, and is a picture of a turtle complete with head, feet, carapace, and tail. Some examples of pictograms and their original pictographic forms are shown in Figure 3.1. Indicators are characters that do not really *depict* the intended meaning, since the meaning is something that is hard to draw directly, but rather *indicate* something about the meaning. Thus 'up' *shàng* is written 上, the indicative value of which is easiest to see when you compare it with 'down', *xià* 下.

Pictographic and indicator characters are interesting insofar as they clearly contain no direct encoding of the sound of the word. Still it is important to realize that even though they are not phonographic, neither are they in any sense *ideographic*. 人 does not represent the *idea* of person: it represents a specific morpheme of the Chinese language that in Mandarin happens to be pronounced *rén*. 上 does not represent the idea of 'upness': it represents the morpheme *shàng*. When reading Chinese text, it will not do to substitute some other expression meaning 'up' for *shàng* when you encounter 上. To do so would be a mistake in reading, just as if in reading English one were to read *fowl* when encountering the printed word *bird*.

Skipping to the last two categories of the Six Writings, we come to borrowings and redirected characters. Borrowings comprise characters that were 'borrowed' into another usage because of their pronunciation.

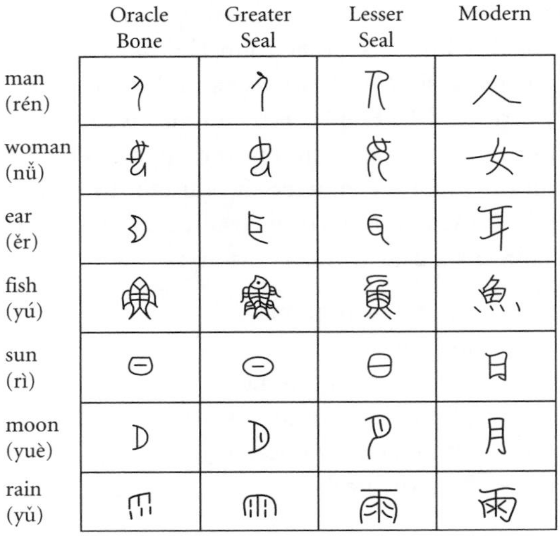

	Oracle Bone	Greater Seal	Lesser Seal	Modern
man (rén)				
woman (nǚ)				
ear (ěr)				
fish (yú)				
sun (rì)				
moon (yuè)				
rain (yǔ)				

FIGURE 3.1 Some simple Chinese pictograms and indicators and their original forms

Source: From William Wu and Hong Yi Cheng, http://www.ocf.berkeley.edu/~wwu/chinese/handout.html

The stock example of this is 來 *lái* 'come', which originally was a type of grain (indeed, was a pictograph for this) but became used to mean 'come' because of the similarity in sound. This is clearly just an application of the *rebus principle*. Redirected characters—the least clear of the traditional six categories—are characters that are supposedly 'redirected' in their meaning: thus, 信 *xìn* 'trust, believe' is composed of two pieces, on the left a reduced component form of 人 *rén* 'person' and on the right the character 言 *yán* 'tongue, speech'. The implication is that a person standing by his or her word represents the notion of trust.

The most interesting characters belong to the two middle categories, which comprise most of the compound characters (though 信, above, is also a compound character). Compound characters are composed of at least two components, each of which is itself usually a character, or a reduced 'combining' form of a character. Since Qin Shi Huang, the First Emperor, standardized the script in 219 BC, new characters have almost exclusively been formed by compounding. As long as one follows certain (mostly structural) rules about combination, one is free in principle to create new characters by combining two characters together, each of which may themselves be compounds. Thus there is theoretically no limit to the number of characters that could be formed (though modern digital representations, such as Unicode, place an effective limit) and Chinese readers often cannot distinguish between a non-existent character and a character that might well exist but that they happen not to know.

The two middle categories distinguish the ways in which the components are used. Meaning compounds combine the meanings of the two components to make a third meaning. The example that is commonly given—though DeFrancis points out that this analysis is probably wrong—is 明 *míng* 'bright', composed of two parts 日 *rì* 'sun' and 月 *yuè* 'moon'. Phonetic compounds consist of one piece that contributes something about the meaning, and another that contributes information about the pronunciation. For example, 橡 *xiàng* 'oak' is composed of (on the left) 木 *mù* 'wood, tree' and on the right 象 *xiàng* 'elephant'. The meaning 'elephant', is irrelevant here: 象 is being used *purely* for its sound, to indicate the pronunciation of the whole. In this particular case, the phonetic information is perfect because (in Mandarin) both 象 and 橡 are pronounced the same. Most of the time the match is not so good. For example, the character 鴨 *yā* 'duck' is composed of (on the right) 鳥 *niǎo* 'bird' and (on the left) the phonetic indicator 甲 *jiǎ* 'carapace'. In this case, the pronunciation match (for Mandarin) is pretty poor. Part of the reason for the poor representation of sound is that many of the characters were developed thousands of years ago, when Chinese pronunciation was quite different from any of the modern Chinese languages. The belief is that in earlier Chinese many of these phonetic components were much better indicators of the pronunciation of the characters than is the case today; indeed one of the pieces of evidence commonly used to reconstruct Old Chinese pronunciation is putative similarities based on the phonetic component of the written character. In any case, if you consider English spellings such as *knight*, *though*, or *write*, all of which represent much earlier pronunciations, you will see how poor the representation of sound in a writing system can be.

What is critical here, however, is not how well Chinese encodes sound, but the fact that it does so at all. More to the point, it has used the phonetic compound *almost exclusively* as a way of forming new characters throughout the roughly 3,500-year history of the script. For as DeFrancis notes in *Visible Speech* (1989: 99), during the period of the Shang Dynasty oracle bones (starting *ca* 1400 BC), 34 per cent of the 977 attested characters were already of the phonetic compound type. By Late Han of the second century AD, 82 per cent of the 9,353 characters then invented were of this form. And by the time that the eighteenth century Kangxi emperor of the Qing dynasty ordered the compilation of the 48,641 characters that were known to scholars of that time, fully 97 per cent were phonetic compounds.[12]

This is a powerful point. The writing system that has more than any other been misunderstood as 'writing ideas', or maybe writing morphemes (as the linguist Geoffrey Sampson has argued), but certainly not writing sound, turns out to be largely constructed on the basis of sound. As became clear in the last chapter, you cannot really avoid this in the end. It is much easier to decide that two words are similar in sound than it is to decide if they are similar in meaning. Phonetic features are much more salient. If I want to invent a way of writing a tree name, it is easy for me to take the 'tree' semantic element and stick on another piece that indicates the pronunciation of that tree name. This requires no more analysis than simply finding a phonetic indicator that sounds close enough to the word I am trying to write. If I chose to do it semantically, I would have to think about some distinctive property of this tree that I wished to highlight and then figure out a way to write that property. But what property would I emphasize?

From the point of view of the reader too, basing the system largely on phonetics makes a lot of sense. Suppose I have never seen the character 橡, but I do know the word *xiàng* 'oak'. Running across this character, I would figure it must name a kind of tree because of the 木 on the left, and the right-hand piece would tell me it is pronounced something like *xiàng*. A small mental game of charades—kind of tree, sounds like *xiàng*—would be enough to cue me to the intended meaning. Even if the phonetic cue is not so close as in this example, one could still often guess. If the cue were semantic, in contrast to phonetic, then my job of guessing would be significantly harder.

Not that such systems have not been invented. The Japanese literati, who prided themselves on how *difficult* the Japanese writing system was, added to that difficulty by inventing, over the course of time, a couple of hundred new Chinese characters that were used almost exclusively to represent native Japanese words. Japanese, like many other East Asian languages, was heavily influenced by Chinese. Not only did they adopt and adapt the Chinese writing system, but they also borrowed massively from Chinese in their vocabulary. Fully sixty per cent of the Japanese vocabulary that one would find in a standard Japanese dictionary is borrowed from Chinese or based on Chinese morphemes. Just as English has borrowed heavily from Latin (and French) but still retains a large number of native Anglo-Saxon words, so Japanese has both a Chinese vocabulary and a native vocabulary. Alongside *san* 'mountain', from Chinese, there is the native word *yama*. In this, as in many other cases, both words may be written with the same Chinese character 山. One of the difficulties of reading Japanese is figuring out in any given case how a character should be read. A wonderful example is the beautiful temple in Kyoto 清水寺 (Clear Water Temple) whose name uses native Japanese words (*kiyo mizu dera*), whereas another Kyoto Temple 大德寺 (Great Virtue Temple) is read as a sequence of Chinese-derived words (*dai toku ji*) note that both names end in character 寺, pronounced differently in each case.

Table 3.1 Japanese *kokuji* or 'national characters'

働	PERSON + MOVE	*hataraki*	'effort'
凪	WIND + STOP	*nagi*	'lull, calm'
凧	WIND + CLOTH	*tako*	'kite'
峠	MOUNTAIN + UP + DOWN	*touge*	'mountain pass'
颪	DOWN + WIND	*oroshi*	'mountain wind'
怺	HEART + FOREVER	*koraeru*	'endure'
毟	FEW + HAIR	*mushi*	'pluck'
聢	EAR + CERTAIN	*shika*	'clearly'
躾	BODY + BEAUTIFUL	*shitsuke*	'upbringing'
鴫	FIELD + BIRD	*shigi*	'snipe'
嬶	FEMALE + NOSE	*kakā*	'wife'
鱈	FISH + SNOW	*tara*	'codfish'

Notes: The second column gives the meanings of the components that make up the character. Interestingly, 鱈 'codfish', which was perhaps so written because of the snowy meat of cod, has been borrowed into Chinese, along with a few other *kokuji*. In Chinese, the 'snow' portion 雪 *xuě* is interpreted as the phonetic component, and the whole character is also pronounced *xuě*. This pronunciation has been borrowed back into Japanese, so that in addition to the native pronunciation *tara*, 鱈 also has the Sino-Japanese pronunciation *setsu* (which is also the Sino-Japanese pronunciation of 雪 'snow'). (The character also has a Sino-Korean pronunciation of *seol*.) This history illustrates an important point about characters as they are used in Chinese: the default strategy for Chinese readers dealing with an unfamiliar complex character is to attempt to interpret one of the components as a phonetic indicator.

But some native words had no Chinese-character representation, and so characters were invented. These *kokuji* (国字 'national characters') exhibited a remarkably different trend from how new characters were invented in China. For *virtually all kokuji* are semantic compounds. A sample of kokuji, some of which are found in R. P. Alexander's appendix[13] is shown in Table 3.1. It is important to realize that only a few hundred characters of this kind were invented, so the system of *kokuji* never became very large. Nevertheless it is interesting to speculate on why the Japanese did it this way.

Before we do that however, we briefly consider another adaptation of Chinese characters. Since the middle of the nineteenth century, Vietnamese has been written in an adaptation of the Latin script called *chữ quốc ngữ* (literally 'script of the national language'). But prior to that time it was written in a Chinese-based writing system called *chữ nôm* (written as 字喃), a system that dated from the tenth century. Alongside characters inherited from Chinese to write Chinese loanwords, the Vietnamese invented new characters to represent native words. A sample of such characters is shown in Figure 3.2. What is interesting about *chữ nôm*, in contradistinction to *kokuji*, is that *all* of the examples are semantic-phonetic compounds. In many cases the Vietnamese extended the system in a totally Chinese fashion, using traditional Chinese semantic components. For example the character for

FIGURE 3.2 Vietnamese *chữ nôm* characters

Note: After each character is shown the *chữ quốc ngữ* spelling, and the meaning.

Source: From Ager, Simon, "Chữ-nôm Script", in "Omniglot—writing systems and languages of the world", www.omniglot.com, accessed 3 February 2008, used with permission.

'bird' 占鳥 contains a normal 'bird' component 鳥 (on the right as in Chinese) and phonetic component 占 to represent the sound *chim*. In other cases the system was extended to use semantic components that were never used in Chinese. For example, all of the numbers use the Chinese numeral symbols plus a component indicating the pronunciation. Thus 'eight' is 八 'eight' plus 參 for the phonetic component; 'five' is 五 'five' plus 南 for the phonetic; 'three' is 三 'three' plus 巴 for the phonetic. In Chinese, numeral symbols are typically not used as semantic components of characters. But no matter: the Vietnamese system extends the Chinese system along exactly the same basic lines as Chinese itself extended its character set over the centuries.

Why then the difference between Japanese and Vietnamese? There are two possibilities that have been mooted, each of which has some measure of plausibility. The first is a linguistic explanation that plays to the differences between Vietnamese and Japanese. Neither Vietnamese nor Japanese is related to Chinese, but Vietnamese is structurally similar to Chinese in that most of its basic morphemes are single syllables. In Japanese, in contrast, the native vocabulary has a large number of polysyllabic words. Semantic-phonetic extensions to the system depend upon being able to find morphemes that are similar enough in sound to the intended morpheme that one can make a new compound that has a certain range of meanings (e.g. it is the name of a tree, an insect, a kind of vegetable, or a human emotion) and has a certain sound ("sounds sort of like *qīng*"). For this to work, a word needs to have a reasonable number of *neighbors* that are similar enough in sound. A moment's reflection will convince the reader that the shorter the words, the better chance there is of finding a good cohort of neighbors. Puns, which also depend upon close similarities of sound, are similarly constrained: it is much harder to pun in some languages than others. So one explanation for why Japanese literati took the course that they did when they invented *kokuji* was that the properties of the Japanese language made it harder to find enough morphemes that are closely similar in sound to the morphemes for which new characters were being developed. Vietnamese, in contrast, presented no such difficulties.

There is another explanation, however. As we have already mentioned, the Japanese literati were proud of their writing system, and prided themselves in particular on the difficulties that it presented to the learner. This was not merely the pride of a technologist in the intricacies of an engineering design. It also served a social function in that it raised the bar on entrance into the literacy club. Simply put, the more intricacies the system presented to the learner, the harder the learner had to work to acquire the system, and the more restricted the circle of literate people would be. Certainly a system that is divorced from sound, and which depends upon figuring out which word is intended given a set of somewhat arbitrarily chosen semantic features, is more of a challenge than one where a person, encountering a character for the first time, can guess at the intended morpheme by a combination of both semantic and phonetic evidence. If this story is correct, then there is a certain irony here, when juxtaposed with Charles Bliss's Semantography, which we discussed in the last chapter. As the reader will recall, Bliss set out to develop a system that was easy to learn precisely because it was divorced from language and depended solely upon combining meanings. But *kokuji* are very reminiscent of Blissymbolics: new elements of the system are constructed by combining semantic elements to form a more complex whole, which was then to be interpreted as a particular morpheme of the language. The result was not clearly a win, when it came to simplicity, and probably was not intended to be.[14]

Returning to the main point of this section, Chinese writing is, and always has been, largely phonetic. Extensions of the system in Vietnamese *chữ' nôm* confirm that phonetics was the major creative force in the Chinese system. Japanese purely semantic *kokuji* are the exception that proves the rule, since they likely arose either because Japanese itself makes it more difficult to apply the semantic-phonetic approach, or because the inventors intentionally used an approach that would make the system harder rather than easier to learn.

Of course, Chinese (and also Egyptian, various Mesopotamian writing systems, and Mayan) uses more semantic information in the writing system than most other systems use. Most are essentially purely phonetic and the major differences between them relate to which phonetic units they encode, a topic to which we now turn.

3.2 Syllabic writing

There is certainly something natural about syllables. Take a word like *ban-danna*, and consider how many syllables it contains. Even if you have not had any particular linguistic training, you probably will agree that the answer is three. Now if I ask you to say each syllable separately—think about this before you read on...—you would probably split it up as something like *ban-da-nna*. There may be some disagreement: maybe you'd say *ban-dan-na*. You would surely not do *ba-ndann-a*. Even if they cannot define them, people are aware of syllables. As we saw already, even illiterate speakers are aware of syllables, but phonemes are much less obvious to the untrained speaker.

So perhaps it should come as no surprise that a large number of writing systems that have been developed over time are syllabaries. If it is more natural to think in terms of syllables as a basic unit of sound, it stands to reason that people who are developing a writing system would more naturally choose to represent syllables rather than the much harder to perceive phoneme. Indeed, syllables are often believed to be such a natural unit, that the use of a syllabary is deemed to require very little deep analysis on the part of the developer of the system, or on the part of the user of the finished product. On the other hand, segmental alphabets, since they link to the much more abstract phoneme, are believed to require substantially more analysis on the part of the developer or the learner. This has led to some surprising and extreme views.

For example, in a book entitled *The Writing on the Wall—How Asian Orthography Curbs Creativity*,[15] William Hannas argued that East Asian writing systems, since they are structured around syllables, require less analysis on the part of the learner than do alphabetic systems (such as English). This in turn he relates to the oft-made claim that Asian countries lag behind the West in terms of scientific creativity: everybody is familiar with the claim that Japan has succeeded largely by imitating (though often improving upon) Western inventions. Hannas not only argues that this is the case, but believes he can pinpoint the reason: when Japanese (and Chinese, and Koreans) go to school they are taught to read in writing systems that are structured around syllables. Chinese characters of course represent syllables (as well as non-phonographic information). The Japanese also use Chinese characters—*kanji* (though in many cases *kanji* are pronounced with more than one syllable), and have their own syllabaries—*hiragana* and *katakana*, which we will say a bit more about below. Korean writing—Hangul—is actually segmental, but the segmental symbols are arranged into two-dimensional syllable blocks. (We will look at

Korean writing later on in the chapter.) And Koreans still learn many Chinese characters even if they do not use them regularly. Children who grow up in the West learning an alphabetic writing system are forced to analyze the stream of sounds in a word in terms of the very unintuitive phoneme unit. It is this early stimulation of the analytical capabilities of the brain that is critical, according to Hannas, in developing the mindset required for doing creative scientific and technological research. By focusing on the obvious syllables, children in China, Japan, and Korea are literally missing the opportunity of a lifetime to exercise the analytical powers of the brain. In part Hannas is basing his argument on a view that has been around for a while: the idea that the invention of the alphabet by the Greeks was the harbinger of the Western tradition of analytical science was touted by, among others, Marshall McLuhan in a paper in 1977.[16]

But the idea that syllabaries somehow require no analysis on the part of the user—or the designer—of the system is at best misleading. Yes, the basic units of syllabaries are (mostly) syllables, and yes, syllables are easier to 'access' than phonemes. This would seem to imply that one could simply observe how one would say a sentence, and then simply write down each syllable one for one with the corresponding *syllabogram*. It is this part that is misleading, since it is rarely the case that syllabaries represent one for one the syllables that occur in speech. There are a couple of reasons for that. First, as we saw already, the number of syllables in some languages can be rather large, and so it is simply impractical to have a syllabary with enough distinct symbols to represent all the syllables. In that case one must resort to breaking the syllables up into more manageable pieces, and to do that one has to do some analysis of the internal structure of the syllable. We will see this point in detail when we examine how Linear B and Cherokee work, so we will defer further discussion until then.

The other sense in which one can get a mismatch is because one often finds that syllables get reduced in speech in a way that may not be reflected in writing. For example, the Mandarin word for 'they' is *tāmén*, written with two characters 他們. But quite often this is pronounced as a single syllable *tam*, particularly in casual speech. Particularly in Northern Mandarin, the second syllable of the expression *bù zhīdào* 不知道 'not know' can be so elided that the whole phrase (which would normally sound something like 'boo jer dao') can end up sounding like 'boor dao'. These are natural phenomena that apply in fluent speech and have counterparts in every language: consider the common reduction in English of *going to* into *gonna*. It is natural to think of these kinds of cases as involving 'corruptions' of the 'correct' form, represented by the orthography, but in fact this has the situation exactly backwards. When children learn to speak they are not normally exposed to the form of the language that is codified in the writing system, and it is only later when they go to school that they are taught what society typically views as the 'correct' form. And when they do learn to read they are forced to go through some amount of analysis to map what they see on the page to what they are used to as the pronunciation of the word. This may result in some reconfiguring of their knowledge of the language as they begin to adopt a more standard pronunciation of some words than the ones they learned growing up. All children who learn to read and write in any culture go through this to some extent, the extent being determined in large part by how different their native dialect is from the standard language that is represented in the orthography.

Linear B serves as a good example of a syllabary where a single syllable in the spoken language may in general be represented by a sequence of more than one symbol in the written form. The syllabic elements in the Linear B script are shown in Figure 3.3. One of the things that will be immediately clear from this list is that, with just a few exceptions, every symbol represents either a vowel or a single consonant and a vowel: V or CV. The problem is that the language Linear B was used to write, an early form of Greek known as Mycenaean, spoken between about 1600 BC and 1100 BC, had more complex syllable structures than this. For example, the word for 'seed' in Mycenaean would have been something like *sper-ma*, as it was in later Classical Athenian Greek; the word for 'gold' was *kʰru-sos*. As the syllable-boundaries indicated with '-' help show, Mycenaean had syllables of the form CCV, CVC, and CCVC. More complex syllables were also possible. So how could you represent such syllables in Linear B? To make matters

FIGURE 3.3   Linear B symbols and their values

Source: From Simon Ager, 'Linear B', in 'Omniglot—writing systems and languages of the world', www.omniglot.com, accessed 3 February 2008, used with permission.

worse, Greek had distinctions in sounds for which there was no corresponding distinction in Linear B. For example, /l/ and /r/ are distinct sounds in Greek, but Linear B had no separate symbols for syllables with these sounds: the syllable |o could represent *ra* or *la*. In English we distinguish between two kinds of *stop* sounds namely *voiced* stops /b/, /d/, and (hard) /g/, and *unvoiced* stops /p/, /t/, and /k/. Greek had a three-way distinction, between voiced, unvoiced, and unvoiced aspirated stops, which were produced with an additional puff of air. Thus there was a /g/, a /k/, and what we have notated above as /k^h/. Linear B had no representation for these distinctions: *ga*, *ka*, and *k^{h}a* were all written with the same symbol.

In order to represent Greek syllables, several compromises were arrived at. First of all, syllable final consonants were generally not written. Thus the final 's' of *k^{h}ru-sos* would have been omitted: *k^{h}ru-so*. Second, sequences of initial consonants (with one systematic exception, which we will see below) were broken up into two syllables, and a vowel—usually the vowel of the syllable—was inserted into the first syllable. Thus: *k^{h}u-ru-so*. Finally, since there was no way to represent the aspirated 'k', the word was written *ku-ru-so* ⅄ ⑂ ⊓. *Phaistos*, the site made famous by the Phaistos Disk, which we will briefly examine in the next chapter, was written as *pa-i-to* ╪ ⅄ ⊤. The systematic exception to what we just said is syllables that had 's' followed by some other consonant: thus *sperma* 'seed'. In these cases, the 's' was omitted entirely: *sperma* was written as *pe-ma* ▷ ⚇.

Obviously to apply this system required some modicum of linguistic analysis: the developers of Linear B had to realize that a syllabic unit like *k^{h}ru* could be broken up into two units. They had to learn to ignore syllable-final consonants. They had to decide that the 's' in words like *sperma* was a separate unit that could be ignored. And of course they had to be sufficiently aware of basic phonetics to map all the labial sounds 'p', 'b', and 'p^h' to the single sound 'p'. None of this came for free, and all of it belies the notion that using a syllabary involves a simple mapping between obvious units of speech and their written representation.

One may wonder why Linear B was so ill-matched to Greek. The reason for this is clear enough: Linear B developed in Crete from an earlier script called Linear A. Linear A was used to write a language, often called Eteocretan or Minoan, that evidently had much simpler syllable structure than Greek. We do not know much about the language, except that it was obviously not related to Greek and indeed does not seem to be related to any other known language. The Mycenaeans evidently entered Crete some time during the fifteenth century BC, and adopted writing from the Minoans, developing their Linear A into Linear B. They ended up using the script for about four hundred years, and made very few modifications to the way the system worked. One may wonder why, in that time, they did not improve on the system. The reason presumably lies in a simple fact about writing systems, one that is often overlooked when people evaluate how rational a particular system seems to be: namely that writing systems are designed for native speakers of the language, and as long as native speakers can figure out what is being said, the writing system serves its intended purpose. The fact that Linear B documents were all of a very limited kind—all of them were accounting texts—would have helped here: although *pe-ma* might in principle have represented several different words, in the context of an accounting document about agricultural products, there really was not very much chance of misinterpretation.

If you borrow a syllabary from a language that has a simpler syllable structure than yours, inevitably you will have to do some linguistic analysis of your own language in order to figure out how to use it, and you will likely end up with a situation where individual phonological syllables are actually written with more than one syllabogram. This situation can also arise, though, when the system is specifically designed for a language, as is the case with the syllabary invented for Cherokee by Sequoyah.

Sequoyah (George Gist—or Guess, *ca* 1767–1843) worked as a silversmith in Willstown, Alabama and had a lot of contact with whites. He did not speak, much less read, English, but he was aware of the English writing system, having seen many examples and understood that this was a written representation of the English language. He also realized that literacy was one of the sources of the English speakers' power, and he set out to design a writing system for his own language. While he knew that English writing represented the English language he had no idea *how* it represented it.[17] Thus when he set out to design his own system for Cherokee he had no model other than the forms of English letters. His initial attempt was based on having a written symbol for each word, an approach that he soon realized was impossible. So he gravitated instead toward using sound, and thus went through the same stages of invention that the original inventors of writing must have gone through when they realized that one could represent sound with symbols.

Sequoyah's final system is essentially a syllabary, but has some of the same properties that we already saw for Linear B. The symbols mostly represent simple consonant–vowel syllables, but syllables in the Cherokee language can be more complicated than this, and thus syllables that are more complicated than simple CV combinations are broken up in their graphical representation. For example, the word *unohlisdi* is written as ℧ZC∘ꝺJ, whose symbols, reading from left to right represent *u-no-hli-s-di*. Note that the fourth symbol ⟨image⟩ *s* is not itself a separate syllable. Amalia Gnanadesikan (2008) speculates that Sequoyah—whose own name *S-si-quo-ya*, starts with this symbol—may have thought of *s* as being a syllable in its own right, since one can produce an *s* on its own (make an *s* sound and continue it), much like a vowel.

Not surprisingly, perhaps, given its unfamiliarity, there was a fair amount of skepticism among other Cherokees as to whether he had in fact achieved what he claimed. In order to allay the skepticism, Sequoyah taught his daughter Ah-Yo-Kah to read and write Cherokee, and this was sufficient to convince others that the system really did work. From that point on, literacy in Cherokee grew. It was made official by the Cherokee nation in 1825. Today the system is still used but, unfortunately, is less widely known. There is, however, interest in its revival, and there is a small but dedicated community of users, as well as Wikipedia pages in Cherokee.

Probably the most famous syllabary is the Japanese *kana* system—famous in that whenever writing systems are discussed and people mention syllabaries, *kana* is invariably the example chosen. There are two *kana* systems: *hiragana* and *katakana*. Japanese is a *mixed* writing system that uses three different scripts, Chinese characters (*kanji*) and the two *kana* systems. Very roughly speaking, *kanji* are used for content words such as nouns, adjectives, and verbs, whereas *hiragana* is used for writing grammatical words (case markers and other 'small' words). *Katakana* is almost exclusively used today to write foreign words and names such as *Tennessee* テ ネ シ ー *teneshii*. But the system has been in flux, in large measure because of government-mandated reductions in the number of *kanji* used, and so now many more Japanese words of either Chinese or native Japanese origin are written using *hiragana*.[18]

Japanese is a complex system, certainly the most complex writing system in use today and a contender for the title of the most complex system ever.[19] A large part of the complexity resides in the use of *kanji*, which in Modern Japanese can represent both native words and words of Chinese origin, as we discussed above: the trick in any case is to know which is the right reading, which makes reading Japanese text a challenge for the text-to-speech systems that we will examine in Chapter 7. Thus, as we saw, the common character 山 'mountain' could be the native Japanese word *yama*, or the Chinese-derived word *san*. Both mean the same thing, but one must know from the context which one to use. In general a given character may have *several* different Sino-Japanese readings, reflecting different stages at which words were borrowed from Chinese (often via Korean).

In Chinese writing, as we noted, most characters are semantic-phonetic compounds, where a portion of the character gives a hint at the pronunciation.

These still work, more or less, in Sino-Japanese words, but they are useless for words of Japanese origin. Thus 鯉 'carp' is pronounced *lǐ* in Mandarin, reflecting its composition of the fish radical 魚 and the phonetic component 里 *lǐ*. This decomposition also works for the Sino-Japanese pronunciation *ri*. But the native word, and the more common pronunciation for this character, is *koi*, for which the phonetic component of the character obviously gives one no clue.

These points, coupled with the *kokuji* that we described earlier, mean that Japanese is the writing system with the largest *logographic*—and hence smallest *phonographic*—component of any living system. But it is important to remember that the system is still not *ideographic*: 鯉 represents the word *koi*, not the *idea* of 'carp'.

When the Japanese first adopted the Chinese writing system in the fourth century AD, they quickly discovered that it was hard to write Japanese using Chinese characters. The main relevant difference between Japanese and Chinese is in word formation. Chinese is what is often termed an *isolating* language, meaning that its words undergo very few changes. In contrast, Japanese (and also Korean) are agglutinative languages, where there are many grammatical morphemes that attach to words to mark various kinds of information, such as tense on the verb, or case information on nouns. None of these markers had any obvious written form in Chinese. So the Japanese quickly hit upon the idea of using Chinese characters for their pronunciation values. By the seventh century the system was codified as 万葉仮名 *man'yōgana* '10,000 Leaf Kana'—so-named because of a famous manuscript that used the system. Over time, due to cursive writing, *man'yōgana* was simplified into *hiragana*. *Katakana* was also derived from Chinese characters, but had a different origin, being derived not by cursive simplification, but rather by explicitly extracting components of Chinese characters that were used to mark pronunciations in Buddhist texts. As a result of these different histories, *hiragana* has a much more fluid appearance than *katakana*, which is much more angular.

Table 3.2 shows the basic *kana* syllabaries, the Chinese characters from which they were derived, and the pronunciation of those characters in Modern Mandarin and in Middle Chinese (which is closer to the forms of Chinese which would have influenced Sino-Japanese than is Modern Mandarin). In nearly all cases, the *kana* pronunciation is derived from the Chinese pronunciation of the original character. The three exceptions to this are the *katakana* symbols for *e*, *mi*, and *wi*, which are derived from native pronunciations.

Kana is a syllabary, but as with Linear B, it is not a *complete* syllabary in that it is not possible to write all the syllables of Japanese with single symbols. Furthermore, the system is somewhat less arbitrary than Linear B in that

TABLE 3.2 Basic *kana* syllables

Syl.	Kata.	Char.	Mand.	Mid. Chin.	Hira.	Char.	Mand.	Mid. Chin.
a	ア	阿	ā	ʔa	あ	安	ān	ʔan
i	イ	伊	yī	ʔjij	い	以	yǐ	yiX
u	ウ	宇	yǔ	hjuX	う			
e	エ	江			え	衣	yī	ʔjɨj
o	オ	於	yú	ʔjo	お			
ka	カ	加	jiā	kæ	か			
ki	キ	幾	jī	gjɨj	き			
ku	ク	久	jiǔ	kjuwX	く			
ke	ケ	介	jiè	kɛjH	け	計	jì	kejH
ko	コ	己	jǐ	kiX	こ			
sa	サ	散	sàn	sanH	さ	左	zuǒ	tsaX
shi	シ	之	zhī	tsyi	し			
su	ス	須	xū	sju	す	寸	cùn	tshwonH
se	セ	世	shì	syejH	せ			
so	ソ	曾	zēng	tsong	そ			
ta	タ	多	duō	ta	た	太	tài	thajH
chi	チ	千	qiān	tshen	ち	知	zhī	trje
tsu	ツ	川	chuān	tsyhwen	つ			
te	テ	天	tiān	then	て			
to	ト	止	zhǐ	tsyiX	と			
na	ナ	奈	nǎi	najX	な			
ni	ニ	二	èr	nyijH	に	仁	rén	njin
nu	ヌ	奴	nú	nu	ぬ			
ne	ネ	祢	mí	nejX	ね			
no	ノ	乃	nǎi	nojX	の			
ha	ハ	八	bā	pɛt	は	波	pō	pa
hi	ヒ	比	bǐ	pjijX	ひ			
fu	フ	不	bù	pjuw	ふ			
he	ヘ	部	bù	buX	へ			
ho	ホ	保	bāo	pawX	ほ			
ma	マ	万	wàn	mjonH	ま	末	mò	mat
mi	ミ	三			み	美	měi	mijX
mu	ム	牟	móu	mjuw	む	武	wǔ	mjuX
me	メ	女	nǚ	nrjoX	め			
mo	モ	毛	máo	maw	も			
ya	ヤ	也	yě	jæX	や			
yu	ユ	由	yóu	yuw	ゆ			
yo	ヨ	興	yú	yo	よ	与	yú	yo
ra	ラ	良	liáng	ljang	ら			
ri	リ	利	lì	lijH	り			
ru	ル	流	liú	ljuw	る	留	liú	ljuw
re	レ	礼	lǐ	lejX	れ			

(cont.)

TABLE 3.2 continued

Syl.	Kata.	Char.	Mand.	Mid. Chin.	Hira.	Char.	Mand.	Mid. Chin.
ro	ロ	呂	lǚ	ljoX	ろ			
wa	ワ	和	hé	hwa	わ			
wi	ヰ	井			ゐ	為	wèi	hjwe
we	ヱ	惠	huì	hwejH	ゑ			
wo	ヲ	平	píng	bjæng	を	遠	yuǎn	hjwenH
N	ン	无	wú	mju	ん			

Notes: Shown are the *katakana* forms, the Chinese character from which each was derived, the Mandarin pronunciation, the Middle Chinese pronunciation; *hiragana* forms, and Chinese character information if different from those for *katakana*. Middle Chinese pronunciations are from William Baxter (2001). "X" and "H" mark Middle Chinese tonal categories. In three underlined cases, the pronunciation comes not from Chinese, but from the native Japanese pronunciation for the character.

many *kana* symbols are derived from others by diacritics. For example, while all of the non-nasal consonants shown in Table 3.2 are voiceless, Japanese does have voiced stops. These are generally derived from the basic symbol by use of a diacritic mark. Thus alongside *hiragana* か *ka*, there is が *ga*; alongside く *ku*, there is ぐ *gu*; alongside す *su* there is ず *zu*. In each case the voicing feature is marked by a pair of dots. Complex syllables, including syllables with long vowels, or ones that have nasalized vowels, or ones that have a /y/ between the consonant and the vowel, must be written with more than one *kana* symbol. This in the *katakana* rendition of *Tennessee*, テネシー, the final pair of symbols represents the syllable *shii*, where シ is *shi* and ー marks the vowel as being long. The *N* symbol in Table 3.2 is used to mark syllables that have a nasalized vowel: かん *kan*. The syllable *ryu*, which has the glide 'y', is written as り ゅ *ri-yu* in *hiragana*.

This is remarkable: there are fewer than 150 syllable types in Japanese, far fewer than most other languages. Mandarin, which has among the simpler syllable structures of modern Chinese languages, has over 400, excluding tonal distinctions. English has at least 10,000, as we saw. A hundred and fifty-odd basic symbols is not very many to memorize, and so one might wonder why the inventors of *kana* did not just create a separate symbol for each syllable. Certainly, if the syllable is, as some have argued, the most natural unit of speech, and given that there are so few of them in Japanese, one might wonder why it was deemed necessary to decompose syllables in writing. One commonly hears the claim that the widespread use of syllabaries is evidence for the basic status of syllables. But this little bit of propaganda ignores how most syllabaries actually work in practice.

The rare exception that proves the rule is the Yi syllabary,[20] a part of which is shown in Figure 3.4. The Yi syllabary contains 819 symbols, to cover the 819 syllable types in the language, including tonal variants. This is a highly unusual situation. But in the case of Yi, there is a reason: the Modern Yi syllabary was derived from an earlier mixed semantic-phonetic script of the

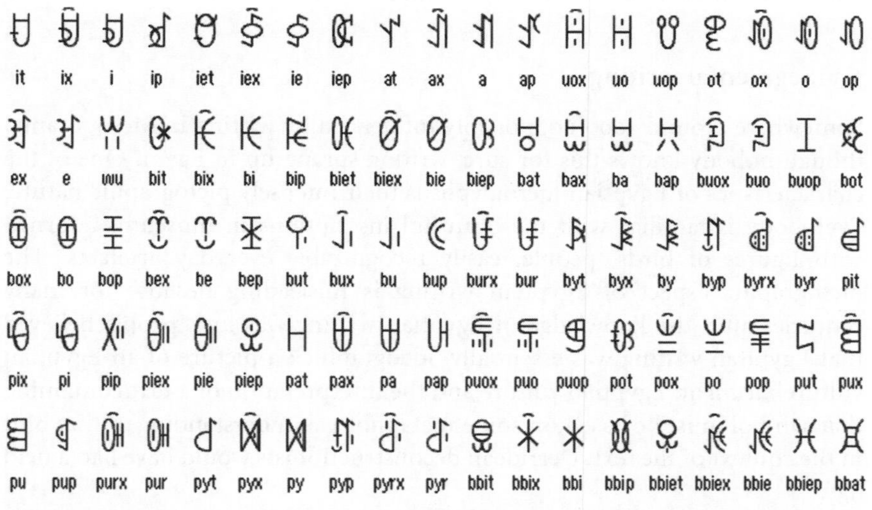

FIGURE 3.4 A portion of the Yi syllabary

Source: from Simon Ager, 'Yi Syllabary', in 'Omniglot—writing systems and languages of the world', www.omniglot.com, accessed 3 February 2008, used with permission.

Chinese type—quite distinct from Chinese, but quite clearly influenced by it—containing thousands of characters. The modern version simply selected, for each distinct syllable, one of the possibly multiple characters that had that pronunciation.[21] While this history shares some properties with the evolution of *kana* via *man'yōgana* in Japanese, the evolution of the latter was much more organic, and resulted in a system that was much more typical of what one usually finds in syllabaries. Yi is simply not the norm.

3.3 Segmental writing

Somewhere around 3000 BC, possibly influenced by writing in Mesopotamia though nobody knows this for sure, writing sprang up in Egypt. One of the characteristics of Egyptian hieroglyphs is their intensely pictographic nature. Everybody is familiar with the beautiful inscriptions in museums adorned with figures of birds, people, easily recognizable everyday artefacts. The pictographic aspect of Egyptian writing is misleading because for many centuries after the knowledge of Egyptian writing was lost, people believed that Egyptian writing was essentially 'ideographic': a picture of an Egyptian vulture *meant* an Egyptian vulture and the interpretation of a text containing that symbol must be based on some metaphorical understanding of that bird in the context of the text. Derridean deconstructionists would have had a field day.

Today we know that the symbols mostly had a more mundane meaning: nearly all of the beautiful pictures that one sees in hieroglyphic texts represent sounds. It would be as if in English instead of writing 'text' we used a picture of a tent for 't', an egg for 'e', a xylophone for 'x' and finally another tent for the second 't'. Like Sumerian or Chinese or Mayan and many other early scripts, Egyptian was a mixed script: some of the symbols did represent meanings associated with words, much as the semantic components of Chinese characters. But these were not the majority of the symbols one would find in running text.

Egyptian writing may, as we have noted, have been influenced by Mesopotamia. One argument in favor of that, apart from the obvious close proximity of the two cultures, and that Egypt became literate not too long after Sumer, was that Egyptian writing seemed to appear fully formed. Unlike Mesopotamia, where as we saw already one can trace writing back to a preliterate phase where people used tokens to represent a limited set of commodities, in Egypt there is no clear prehistory to writing.

But if the Egyptians were influenced it was only in the *idea* of writing, because there are two obvious differences between the two systems. First, and most obviously, is the outward shape. Mesopotamian writing was always somewhat abstract in its form, even in the earliest phases. Once the use of a stylus to make wedge-like incisions in clay became standard practice, the pictographical origins of the symbols became mostly unrecognizable. This was not so in Egypt, and hieroglyphs retained their highly pictographic character for three thousand years until the system eventually fell out of use in the third century AD. (Needless to say, the system was not very practical as a script for daily use, and so over time more cursive forms of the script evolved. The first was hieratic, which simplified hieroglyphic signs substantially but which was still recognizably pictographic; and demotic, which was entirely cursive: demotic is the third script on the Rosetta stone, which we will return to in the next chapter.)

The second difference was in the way the script worked. Both Sumerian and Egyptian are mixed scripts, mixed in that they have both logographic or semasiographic elements, mixed in with a large amount of phonographic representation. But whereas Sumerian phonographs represented syllables, Egyptian opted to represent only *consonants*. More specifically, they had *uniliteral* symbols that represented single consonants, *biliteral* symbols that represented pairs of consonants, and *triliteral* symbols that represented triples of consonants. Figure 3.5 gives some examples of each of these. It is important to understand something here. Consider the symbol 𓄟 for *ms*. This symbol did *not* simply represent the consonant sequence *ms* such as we have in *Amsterdam*. Rather it represented a sequence *ms*, *with a vowel possibly intervening between the* m *and the* s. Thus 𓄟 might represent *mos*, *mis*, *mus* or, indeed, even *ms*, depending upon what word one was using it to spell.

This consonantal writing, which characterized Egyptian and the later Semitic scripts that were influenced by it, was very similar to the somewhat hackneyed example from English:

f u cn rd ths u cn b trnd as a scrtry nd gt a gd jb

To make this intelligible, we cannot quite remove all the vowels, but we can remove most of them. The result is still quite readable by a competent English speaker, and this is because, knowing the language, we know how to make use of the context to supply information that is missing. This is something that is remarkably difficult for machines to do right: text-to-speech synthesizers, which we shall discuss in Chapter 7, would not be expected to perform well on the above sentence.

Of course our example above is not real English: it is a convenient short-hand that happens to work for the reason we stated. But why would one

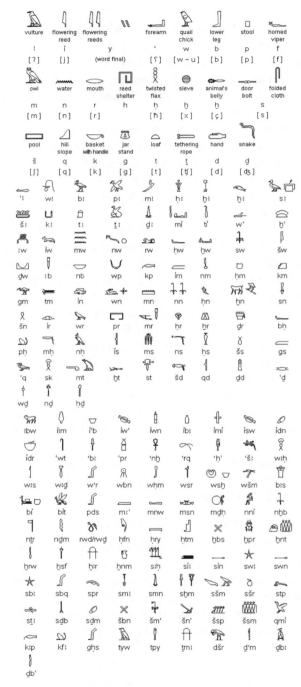

FIGURE 3.5 Egyptian uniliteral, biliteral, and triliteral symbols

Source: from Simon Ager, 'Ancient Egyptian Scripts', in 'Omniglot–writing systems and languages of the world', www.omniglot.com, accessed 3 February 2008, used with permission.

design an *entire writing system* that behaved in this way? It would seem to make little sense. Yet this is precisely what the Egyptians did.

To understand why they might have made this choice, you need to understand something about how the Egyptian language works. Egyptian belongs to the Afro-Asiatic family of languages, which includes Semitic languages like Hebrew and Arabic as distant relatives. One of the properties that characterizes these languages is a so-called *root-and-pattern* kind of word formation. In English we mostly change words into other words using some combination of *prefixes* and *suffixes*. In order to form the past tense of *study*, the suffix *-ed* is added to the word (and the spelling 'y' changed to 'i'.) The same morphological change happens to apply in the case of the *passive* voice *(was) studied* as in *The book was studied*. In Semitic languages, such as Arabic, things are a bit different. Changes such as tense or voice typically involve changes in the vowels of the stem, though there may be other changes such as prefixation or suffixation.[22] For example, the perfect aspect verb *darasa*, 'he studied', can be changed to 'it was studied', by changing the vowels to *durisa*. Addition of a prefix *ya-* and omission of the first vowel—*yadrasa*—gives us the imperfect form meaning 'he studies'. Not only are these inflectional changes handled in part by changing the vowels, but more generally one can create words in Arabic that have related meanings by changing the vowels and the general shape of the word. Thus alongside *darasa* we have *darrasa*, a related word meaning 'teach'. We also have *daarasa* meaning 'study with'. A writing system that does not represent vowels has one important advantage with languages like this. If you represent the vowels in the spelling then there are various forms that the stem will appear in: *daras, duris, dras, darras, daaras*. If vowels are not represented, however, then all of these forms will appear with one spelling: *drs*. The advantage here is that all forms of the same root *drs* will appear in the same written form, which means in turn that the graphical form will not change, and the root can immediately be recognized. Things are not quite this simple: sometimes not only vowels but other consonants intervene between the consonants of the root and these consonants would be written. And in modern Arabic (and Hebrew), some vowels—specifically those that are phonetically long—are written (using consonant symbols borrowed for this purpose.) But at least for the vowels, modern practice differs from that of Egyptian or the original Semitic scripts of the Sinai: in those earlier scripts, no vowels were written for native words. As for Semitic, so for Egyptian: the form of the verb *sḏm* 'hear' would likely have had different vowels in different aspects, yet the written form remained the same. It would be up to the reader, presumed to be a competent speaker of the language, to fill in the details.

It is possibly the linguistic form of Egyptian—its root and pattern morphology—that inspired the first writing system whose phonographic component represented segments, not syllables. Be that as it may, when Semitic speakers living in Sinai around 2000 BC developed their own writing, apparently inspired by Egyptian, they would have found that a consonantal system was well suited to their language too, and consonantal scripts spread in the Semitic-speaking world, eventually developing into the scripts for Phoenician, and thence to Hebrew, Aramaic, and Arabic.

From Semitic, the script evolved into a full alphabetic system—writing both vowels and consonants—in three separate events. The most often discussed of these is the adaptation of the Phoenician alphabet by the Greeks somewhere around the eighth century BC. While we do not know the historical circumstances of this transfer—the details were not recorded—it is fairly clear what happened, and the story has been recounted many times. If you take any pair of languages, particularly languages that are not related to each other, there will be sounds which are more or less shared between the languages, and sounds which one language has that the other does not.[23] So it was with Phoenician and Greek. Both languages shared a common core of consonants, but there were also consonants that Greek had that Phoenician did not, and vice versa (Figure 3.6). It is the latter group—the consonants found in Phoenician and not in Greek—that are of most interest for the current discussion, since it meant that Phoenician had symbols for sounds that were not needed for Greek and, more to the point, led to *misinterpretations* of what they represented. Three consonants in particular were the *'āleph* ◁, the *'ayn* ◯ and the *ḥēth* ⊟. ◁ represented a glottal stop /ʔ/, which can be described as a 'catch in the throat'. More technically, a glottal stop occurs when the vocal chords are completely closed, and then opened to allow them to vibrate for a vowel. Indeed, we have glottal stops in English in words that begin with a vowels, and one may assume that the Ancient Greeks did too. The difference was that the sound was viewed as being a *distinctive* part of the consonant inventory by the Phoenicians, whereas in Greek it was just something that happened at the beginnings of words that began with a vowel. The ◯ and ⊟ represented *pharyngeal* sounds, something that is hard to describe in English, but which involves pulling the root of the tongue as far back as it will go and thereby constricting the pharynx. ◯ is the voiced variant and ⊟ the unvoiced variant. Modern Arabic still preserves these sounds, though they are lost in Modern Hebrew (but still written).

Since the Greeks did not have these sounds, they would have been confused as to what they represented, and it would be easy for them to misinterpret them to mean something else. The name *'āleph* ◁ begins with the syllable /ʔa/,

𐤀	'āleph	ʔ	A	a
𐤁	bēth	b	B	b
𐤂	gīmel	g	Γ	g
𐤃	dāleth	d	Δ	d
𐤄	hē	h	E	e
𐤅	wāw	w	Y	u
𐤆	zayin	z	Z	z
𐤇	ḥēth	ḥ	H	ē
𐤈	ṭēth	ṭ	Θ	th
𐤉	yōdh	y	I	i
𐤊	kaph	k	K	k
𐤋	lamedh	l	Λ	l
𐤌	mēm	m	M	m
𐤍	nun	n	N	n
𐤎	sāmekh	s	Ξ	ks
𐤏	'ayin	ʕ	O	o
𐤐	pē	p	Π	p
𐤑	ṣādē	ṣ		
𐤒	qōph	q	(Ϙ)	
𐤓	rēš	r	P	r
𐤔	šin	š	Σ	s
𐤕	tāw	t	T	t

FIGURE 3.6 Phoenician letters, their names, their approximate phonetic values, the equivalents in Greek, and the approximate phonetic value of the Greek

Note: Boxed Greek letters represented vowels rather than consonants. 𐤑 had no Greek derivative. Ϙ (*qoppa*) was an archaic Greek letter, from which our 'Q' is derived.

and if you ignore the /ʔ/ you have the vowel /a/. The extension worked similarly for ◯ and ⊟, which were reinterpreted in terms of the first sounds in their names that the Greeks could make sense of (/o/ and /e/); note that a pharyngeal voiced consonant in particular makes a following /a/ sound almost like American English *aw* as in *caw*, so that the first vowel of ◯ may well have sounded something like an /o/ to Greek ears (see also Gnanadesikan 2008).

Having established the idea that some vowels could be written, it was a relatively straightforward extension to the idea that all vowels should be written. Thus *yōdh* and *wāw* became adapted, as iota and u(psilon), to represent /i/ and /u/; similarly E (epsilon) was adapted from *he*. The other written vowel of Greek, Ω (omega) representing long /o/, was derived by opening up the bottom of the ◯. Greek of course also had to adapt symbols for sounds that existed in Greek but not in Phoenician. Thus *X* (chi) and Φ (phi) were added to represent the aspirated /kh/ and /ph/, respectively; and the sound sequences /ks/ and /ps/ came to be represented as the single symbols Ξ and Ψ.

Starting in the first millennium BC, some Semitic writing systems adapted consonants for the representation of long vowels; this practice was not common in Phoenician however. Thus *'āleph* came to be used to represent long /a/, *yōdh* to represent long /i/, and *wāw* to represent long /u/. This practice is still found in Arabic and Hebrew today. These so-called *matres lectionis* or 'mothers of reading' were introduced into Semitic writing systems starting as early as the ninth century BC. Over the course of time, ways were invented of writing all vowels—not just the long vowels represented by the matres lectionis—using a set of dots or points. Anyone who studied Hebrew for their bar mitzvah is familiar with the dots (*niqqud*) that are used in Hebrew texts. Arabic uses a similar set of diacritics, as does Syriac. Actually, Syriac has two different systems depending upon whether one is considering Western or Eastern Syriac. In the Western system the vowel diacritics are derived from Greek, an interesting reimportation of what were originally Phoenician consonant symbols. (See Figure 3.7.) The vowel diacritics were added in large measure to preserve the correct pronunciations of religious texts. While Semitic speakers have no problem reading text that does not mark vowels—the normal situation in Arabic and Hebrew newspapers, for example—there is still the potential for variation in the pronunciation of the vowels (as well as the consonants) if the speaker speaks a dialect other than the standard variety. Complicating things further, the Arabic of the Quran and the Hebrew of the Bible do not represent the language of modern-day speakers, and for many centuries Hebrew was not spoken at all as anyone's

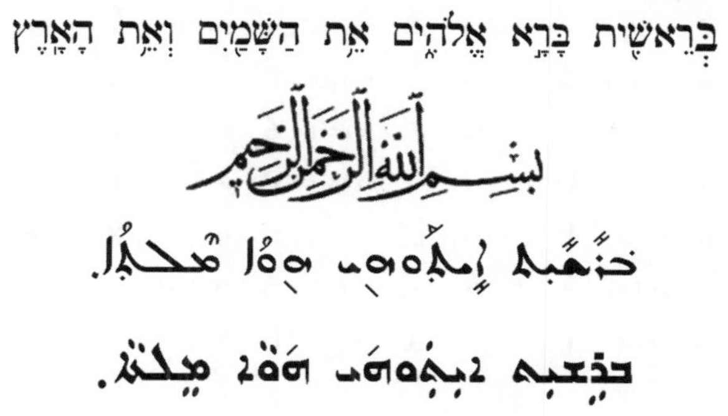

בְּרֵאשִׁית בָּרָא אֱלֹהִים אֵת הַשָּׁמַיִם וְאֵת הָאָרֶץ

بِسْمِ اللهِ الرَّحْمٰنِ الرَّحِيمِ

ܚܲܒ݂ܝܼܒ݂ܐ ܐܸܡܵܟ݂ܘܼ ܘܝܼܗܵܘܘܼ ܫܚܠܝܼܦܵܐ.

ܕܝܼܥܵܒ݂ܗ ܝܼܘܘܿܝܼ ܐܵܗ ܩܕ݂ܝܼܫܵܐ.

FIGURE 3.7 Diacritized text in Hebrew, Arabic, Western Syriac, and Eastern Syriac

Note: Greek-derived diacritics in Western Syriac. In addition to vowel points, the Hebrew example also includes *cantillation* diacritics, which indicate the manner of chanting the text.

Source: Syriac images created by Gareth Hughes, and distributed under the GNU Free Documentation License.

native language, but rather was only learned as a liturgical language by students in religious schools. For these reasons, vowel diacritics were introduced; the Masoretic system still in use for Hebrew appeared around the seventh century AD.

The idea of marking vowels with diacritics was adopted quite late in Semitic writing systems. But in one offshoot of Semitic, the *alphasyllabary* systems that are in use in India, the mechanism was developed early. The sources of Brahmi—the precursor of modern South Asian and Southeast Asian writing systems, including Devanagari, Tamil, Telugu, Kannada, Malayalam, Sinhala, Thai, Khmer, Lao, Burmese, and Javanese—are not uncontroversial, but the most plausible account has the system developing around the third century BC under influence from Aramaic writing. Aramaic was the language of administration in the Persian empire, which at the time extended as far east as India. Aramaic script was not only used for Aramaic itself, but was adapted to many of the Persian languages. And it was probably under this influence that the Buddhist King Aśoka the Great (304–232 BC) devised the Brahmi script and used it to promulgate the Aśokan edicts (laws) in Pali, a Middle Indic language derived ultimately from Sanksrit. The system of Brahmi is elegant, and has been preserved in its basic construction— though with massive variation in *outer form* (to use a term coined by the father of the modern study of writing systems, Ignace Gelb, to refer to the overt shapes of symbols)—right up to the present day Brahmi-derived scripts.

Figure 3.8 shows the basic consonant symbols of Brahmi, and illustrates how diacritics are used to indicate vowels. Every consonant has an *inherent*

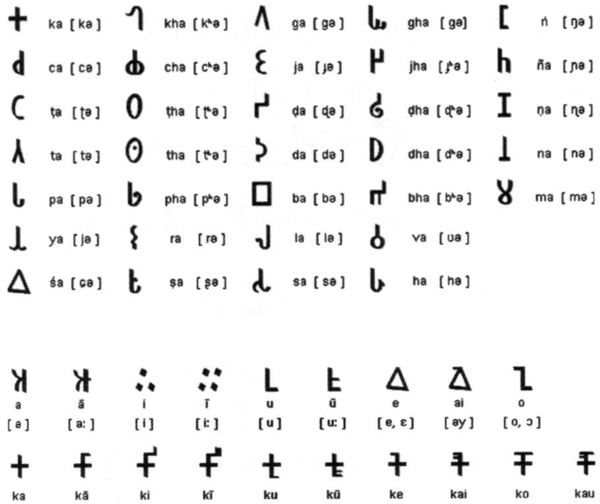

✝ ka [kə]	**ꓺ** kha [kʰə]	**Λ** ga [gə]	**ꓡ** gha [gə]	**[** ṅ [ŋə]
ꓷ ca [cə]	**ꞗ** cha [cʰə]	**Ɛ** ja [ɟə]	**ꓮ** jha [ɟə]	**ɦ** ña [ɲə]
ꓚ ṭa [ʈə]	**O** ṭha [ʈʰə]	**ꓒ** ḍa [ɖə]	**ꞡ** ḍha [ɖʰə]	**I** ṇa [ɳə]
ꓥ ta [tə]	**O** tha [tʰə]	**�** da [də]	**D** dha [dʰə]	**ꓕ** na [nə]
ꓡ pa [pə]	**ꓐ** pha [pʰə]	**□** ba [bə]	**ꓒ** bha [bʰə]	**ꓕ** ma [mə]
ꓞ ya [jə]	**{** ra [rə]	**ꓩ** la [lə]	**ꝋ** va [ʋə]	
Δ śa [cə]	**ꓦ** ṣa [ʂə]	**ꝋ** sa [sə]	**ꓶ** ha [hə]	

ꓨ	**ꓨ**	**∴**	**∴∴**	**L**	**Ḻ**	**Δ**	**Δ**	**ꓨ**
a	ā	i	ī	u	ū	e	ai	o
[ə]	[a:]	[i]	[i:]	[u]	[u:]	[e, ɛ]	[əy]	[o, ɔ]

✝	**ꓑ**	**ꓒ**	**ꓒ**	**✝**	**Ḻ**	**ꓕ**	**ꓕ**	**ꓕ**
ka	kā	ki	kī	ku	kū	ke	kai	ko	kau

FIGURE 3.8 Brahmi script

Note: The consonant symbols with the inherent vowel /a/ are shown above. Next are shown the independent vowels—those that are used in a syllable that has no initial consonant. Finally the vowel diacritics with consonant /k/.

Source: from Simon Ager, 'Brahmi Alphabet', in 'Omniglot—writing systems and languages of the world', www.omniglot.com, accessed 3 February 2008, used with permission.

vowel, which is usually something like /a/ or /ə/ in the various languages that use Brahmi-derived scripts. (In Hindi, for example it is /ə/; in Kannada it is /a/.) It is termed inherent because the consonant is interpreted as being followed by that vowel *unless* there is some other vowel symbol that overrides the inherent vowel, or there is an explicit cancellation of the vowel by a special diacritic (known as *virama* in Devanagari, and by various names for other scripts). As can be seen in Figure 3.8, other vowels are indicated by one or more strokes attached to the main consonant symbol in different locations. Figure 3.9 shows an example of text from Aśoka's 6th Pillar Edict.

Some examples of the syllables /ka/, /ki/, /kaa/, /ke/, /ko/ are shown in Figure 3.10 in Brahmi and three daughter scripts. What is striking about these examples is that although the outer form of the symbols looks quite different, the *inner form*—by which Gelb meant the abstract structure of a script—is the same in all of these cases. In particular, while the form of the diacritic for /aa/ and /e/ differ substantially between Brahmi and the three daughter scripts, in all cases /o/ is a composite of /aa/ and /e/.

The Brahmi-derived systems are termed *alphasyllabaries* because they have properties of alphabets in that both consonants and vowels are

FIGURE 3.9 Fragment of Aśoka's 6th Pillar Edict

explicitly represented (except for the inherent vowel), as well as properties of syllabaries, since the symbols are not arranged linearly, but rather chunked together into syllables. It is important to realize that they are *not* syllabaries, though one does sometimes see this claimed. The difference between the Indian alphasyllabaries and true syllabaries is clear enough: in a syllabary, if I have two syllables /ki/ and /ku/, these will correspond to two distinct symbols. Furthermore, there will be no way to break these symbols down into anything that corresponds to the /k/, /i/, or /u/. This is not the case in an alphasyllabary, where one can in general clearly break down the syllable symbols into components that represent the vowels and components that represent the consonants. If you compare the structure of the various syllables starting with /k/ in Brahmi with the set of syllables starting with /k/ in Linear B, this difference will become immediately apparent.

The third example of a full alphabetic system developed from Semitic, is the Ethiopic (or *Ge'ez*) script, which first appeared around the fifth century BC. In this early version Ethiopic, like its Semitic precursor, only represented consonants. Around the fourth century AD the script started indicating vowels with diacritics.[24] Though it was developed quite independently of Brahmi the

	Brahmi	Devanagari	Kannada	Tamil
ka	+	क	ಠ	க
ki	⨎	कि	ಠಿ	கி
kaa	⨏	का	ಠಾ	கா
ke	⨨	के	ಠೆ	கெ
ko	⨪	को	ಠೊ	கொ

FIGURE 3.10 /ka/, /ki/, /kaa/, /ke/, /ko/ in Brahmi and three Brahmi-derived scripts

Note: /ka/ is the basic symbol, with all others involving that symbol plus diacritics. In all of the scripts, /o/ is composed of the diacritics for /aa/ and /e/.

two systems are remarkably similar in design. As with Brahmi, it had a Semitic precursor, and as with Brahmi it developed a system where the basic conson-ant symbols represent by default the consonant with an inherent vowel (/æ/ in Amharic), and other vowels are indicated by adding diacritic marks to the consonant (Figure 3.11).

There is another interesting commonality between Brahmi-derived scripts and the Ethiopic script, which is also shared with Greek, but contrasts with the Semitic precursors, relating to the direction of writing. If we go back to Egyptian, we find that it could in principle be written either left-to-right or right-to-left. Vertical arrangements were also common, but within

Name	IPA	ä / æ	u / u:	i / i:	a / a:	e / e:	ə / ə	o / o:	wa / wa	yä / jæ
hoy	h	ሀ	ሁ	ሂ	ሃ	ሄ	ህ	ሆ		
läwe	l	ለ	ሉ	ሊ	ላ	ሌ	ል	ሎ	ሏ	
ḥäwṭ	ḥ	ሐ	ሑ	ሒ	ሓ	ሔ	ሕ	ሖ	ሗ	
may	m	መ	ሙ	ሚ	ማ	ሜ	ም	ሞ	ሟ	ፙ
säwt	ś	ሠ	ሡ	ሢ	ሣ	ሤ	ሥ	ሦ	ሧ	
re's	r	ረ	ሩ	ሪ	ራ	ሬ	ር	ሮ	ሯ	ፘ
śat	ś	ሰ	ሱ	ሲ	ሳ	ሴ	ስ	ሶ	ሷ	
ḳaf	ḳ	ቀ	ቁ	ቂ	ቃ	ቄ	ቅ	ቆ	ቋ	
bet	b	በ	ቡ	ቢ	ባ	ቤ	ብ	ቦ	ቧ	
täwe	t	ተ	ቱ	ቲ	ታ	ቴ	ት	ቶ	ቷ	
ḥarm	ḫ	ኀ	ኁ	ኂ	ኃ	ኄ	ኅ	ኆ	ኈ	
nähas	n	ነ	ኑ	ኒ	ና	ኔ	ን	ኖ	ኗ	
'älf	'	አ	ኡ	ኢ	ኣ	ኤ	እ	ኦ	ኧ	

FIGURE 3.11 A portion of the Ethiopic script

Source: from Simon Ager, 'Ge'ez script', www.omniglot.com, accessed 3 February 2008, used with permission.

each column there were short lines of symbols that were to be read either left-to-right or right-to-left. In nearly all texts it is easy to tell the reading direction: the *glyphs* representing animals and people all face towards the beginning of the line and thus *opposite* to the direction of reading. While both directions were possible and even common on monumental inscriptions, in manuscripts the typical order was right-to-left, and the handwritten styles hieratic and demotic were exclusively right-to-left. The early Sinai semitic script, adopted the same reading direction as Egyptian, presumably inspired by the Egyptian preference for right-to-left writing, and as everyone knows the right-to-left direction was maintained in modern descendants such as Hebrew and Arabic.

But something interesting happened when Semitic consonantal scripts were borrowed and adapted to become alphabets or alphasyllabaries, representing vowels: the direction flipped. It did not happen immediately. When the Greeks first adapted Phoenician writing they, like the Phoenicians, wrote from right to left, but the system soon shifted (around 700 BC) to a back-and-forth mode of writing (right-to-left one line, left-to-right the next, flipping the characters as the direction shifts). This style, called *boustrophedon*—literally, the 'turning of the ox'—was used for a few hundred years, being adopted into Etruscan and Early Latin until finally the Latin (and Greek) systems settled down into the left-to-right system we know today.[25]

If this switch of directionality were just an isolated occurrence in Greek writing and its descendants, nothing much would need to be said, but in fact the same thing happened—evidently independently—in India as part of the development of Brahmi, and in Ethiopia with the development of the Ethiopic script. Both scripts had Semitic precursors as we saw, and both went through an initial right-to-left phase before switching to being written left-to-right. What is notable here is that all three cases involve the adaptation of a consonantal writing system into one that represents both vowels and consonants (though as we saw, Indian and Ethiopian scripts represent vowels in a rather different way from the way they are represented in Greek and its descendants). Is there something about representing vowels that makes left-to-right reading (or writing) more natural? Is there something about consonantal systems that sits more comfortably with a right-to-left reading direction?

It has been speculated that the difference may have to do with the way the brain processes information, and specifically the way the two hemispheres of the brain process information.[26] Many people are familiar with the basic differences that have been attributed to the two hemispheres: the right hemisphere is more *holistic* and better at making connections between concepts from possibly very different areas; whereas the left hemisphere is more *analytic*, better at problem solving, but at the same time less 'creative' than the right hemisphere. Stating things thus surely oversimplifies the situation, but there is a core of truth nonetheless. What is certainly known is that each of our eyes is divided into two visual fields. The right visual field of each eye is processed in the occipital cortex at the back of the *left* hemisphere, and the left visual field is processed in the occipital cortex of the *right* hemisphere. When you read you move your eyes in little jumps called *saccades*, following the direction of reading. If you are reading, say, Spanish, new material comes into view in the right visual field, and thus projects ultimately onto the left hemisphere. In contrast, if you are reading Arabic, then new material in the text will come into view in the left visual field, and this in turn projects onto the right hemisphere. This much is certainly true. What remains is to link this obvious psychophysical fact about the low-level information processing of left-to-right versus right-to-left scripts with the putative differences between how the two hemispheres process information. It is certainly true that reading Arabic requires more 'holistic' knowledge than reading Spanish: as an Arabic reader, you have to fill in a lot of information for each word from your general knowledge of the language, and your knowledge of the particular context in which the word occurs. Reading Spanish, in contrast, requires less such holistic knowledge, but might be seen to require more analytical knowledge since you need to figure out how the word sounds from the little symbols that represent the different components of the sound. So the idea that has been proposed is that consonantal scripts have a natural bias to be read right-to-left since this allows the reader to take advantage of their right hemisphere's holistic processing capabilities. On the other hand, a full alphabetic system might show some advantage by being processed in the left hemisphere, and thus being written and read in the direction left-to-right.

V crs, th fct tht u cn rd ths Nglsh sntnc whr I hv tkn out mst v th vwls mns tht ths cnnt b an abslt rstrctn.

And indeed, as we just saw, Greek, Brahmi, and Ethiopic took a while—several hundred years in the case of Greek—to settle down to a left-to-right reading direction. Contrariwise, the Yiddish writing system, which is an adaptation of the Hebrew alphabet to writing Yiddish, a language derived from German, is actually a full alphabet. In Yiddish, consonantal symbols from Hebrew have been adapted to write vowels. But Yiddish did not flip its direction from right-to-left to left-to-right upon becoming an alphabet.

So, if there is any truth in the neuropsychological explanation for why scripts have the direction they do, it can only represent a weak bias. But weak biases can have powerful effects with large populations over hundreds of years.

3.3.1 *Hangul*

The Korean segmental writing, Hangul (Korean 한글), was invented by King Sejong the Great and promulgated in 1446 in a document entitled *Hunmin Jeong-eum* 'The Proper Sounds for the Education of the People' (Hangul 훈민정음, Chinese 訓民正音). Sejong was legendary for being devoted to his people and undertook a number of projects to increase the welfare of the population in Korea. Among these were a book of 'best practices' in agricultural technology published in a farmers' handbook entitled *Nongsa Jikseol* (농사직설, 農事直說, 'Explanation of Farming Matters'), and an equitable taxation system that made tax rates dependent upon agricultural and economic conditions. But his most famous contribution was the *Hunmin Jeong-eum*, whose motivation is explained by its opening paragraph (Figure 3.12):

國之語音,異乎中國,與文字不相流通,故愚民,有所欲言,
而終不得伸其情者,多矣.予,爲此憫然,新制二十八字,欲
使人人易習,便於日用矣.

The speech of our country differs from that of China, and the Chinese characters do not match it well. So the simple folk, if they want to communicate, often cannot do so. This has saddened me, and thus I have created twenty-eight letters. I wish that people should learn the letters so that they can conveniently use them every day.

The first premise, that Chinese writing was not adapted well to Korean, was to a large degree an understatement of Korean literacy problems at the time. While Korean was (with difficulty) written in Chinese characters—there was a system called *hyangchal* that was similar to Japanese *man'yō-gana*[27]—in fact most documents were not written in Korean at all, but rather in classical Chinese; indeed, the *Hunmin Jeong-eum* itself was written in Chinese. In order to become literate in Korea, one not only had to learn a complex script, but also a whole new language. No wonder it was difficult for uneducated people to read and write. The system guaranteed that only a small percentage of the population could afford to become literate, since the time involved in learning a new language along with its writing system was signficant. Sejong proposed to break through this barrier by offering a simpler solution. His solution was in the form of a segmental alphabet well-suited for representing Korean sounds. The twenty-eight letters that he introduces in the opening text each represents a consonant or vowel of

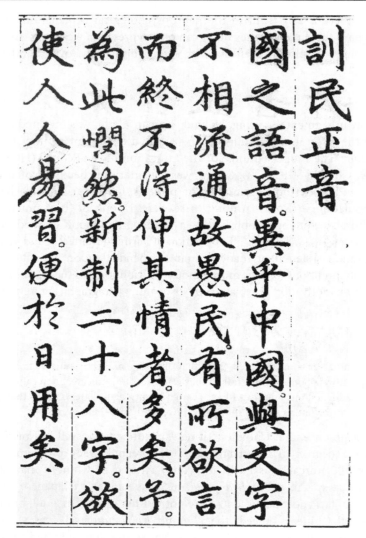

FIGURE 3.12 The opening of *Hunmin Jeong-eum*

Korean, with some additional diacritics to represent tonal accent (which was a feature of Korean at the time).

Hangul is often described as the world's most scientifically well-designed script, due to the way in which the letter shapes were chosen. The basic shapes of the symbols were iconic for the manner in which the sounds were made.

Lip sounds such as 'm', 'p', and 'b', shared the shape ㅁ, a stylized picture of the mouth (and not coincidentally the same shape as the Chinese character 口 *kǒu* 'mouth'). Sounds made with contact with the teeth (or more properly the alveolar ridge) such as 's', 'sh', and 'j' and 'ch', shared the shape ㅅ, representing the teeth. The tongue tip contact for sounds like 'l/r', 'n', 'd', and 't' was ㄴ representing a raised tongue tip. The 'k', 'g' series involving contact beween the tongue body and the velum involved ㄱ, schematically representing the tongue for that position (Figure 3.13). Finally 'throat' sounds, including 'ng', 'h', and an unpronounced consonant used for syllables that begin (and in the original system end) with a vowel, contained a cross-section of the throat represented by a circle ㅇ.

The vowel symbols used components that were iconic of the earth (a horizontal bar) and humankind (a vertical bar), with dots to differentiate the different vowels. In modern Korean the basic vowel shapes are:

Horizontal	ㅡ	eu
	ㅗ	o
	ㅜ	u
	ㅛ	yo
	ㅠ	yu
Vertical	ㅣ	i
	ㅓ	eo
	ㅏ	a
	ㅕ	yeo
	ㅑ	ya

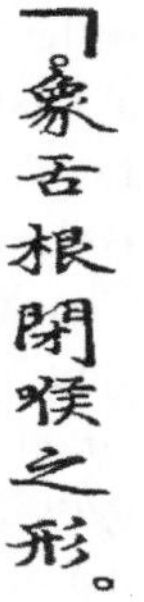
ㄱ象舌根閉喉之形。

FIGURE 3.13 Sejong's explanation of the shapes of the *g* symbol in the supplement to the *Hunmin Jeong-eum*

Note: The text reads: "ㄱ depicts the tongue root closing the throat".

FIGURE 3.14 The original shapes of some Hangul symbols, and their modern
equivalents

Note the consistent use of a second stroke to indicate a vowel with 'y' onglide.
The vowels 'ae' (as the vowel in 'cat') and 'e', are written as a combination of
the 'i' symbol and other vowels in a way that is reminiscent of the representation of some vowels in Brahmi. Again note the use of the extra stroke for a
'y' onglide.

    ae   ├ + │   ㅐ
    yae   ㅒ
    e   ┤ + │   ㅔ
    ye   ㅖ

Figure 3.14 shows the original shapes for a few consonants and vowels, along
with their modern (printed) form. The modern form evolved as a result of
writing with a brush—just as the more angular shapes of the original Chinese
characters prior to the Han Dynasty changed into their modern more fluid
shapes.

Where Sejong came by his ideas for the design of Hangul is not known.
Certainly the shapes themselves must have been developed by Sejong and his
advisors, since the text makes it clear that they had the articulatory phonetic
basis as described above. Some of the phonetic categories were derived from
traditional Chinese phonology. Thus the concept of the initial sound and the
places of articulation—牙音 *yáyīn* 'back tooth sound' (velar), 舌音 *shéyīn*
'tongue sound' (apical), 脣音 *chúnyīn* 'lip sound', 齒音 *chǐyīn* 'front tooth
sound' (dental/alveolar), and 喉音 *hóuyīn* 'throat sound' (Figure 3.15) are
straight from the Chinese 五音 *wǔyīn* 'five sounds' of one thousand years
prior to Sejong. But the vowels are characterized as being the 'middle sounds'
(中聲 *zhōngshēng*) of characters, and this seems to be an innovation (Figure 3.16).
Chinese phonology viewed characters as being composed of initials and finals,

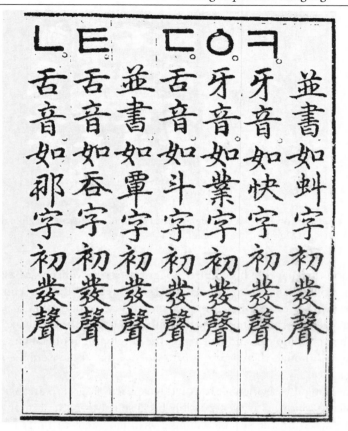

FIGURE 3.15 Some of the consonant descriptions in *Hunmin Jeong-eum*: from right to left, *k, ng, d, t, n*

Note: below each Hangul symbol is a description in Chinese that explains what type of consonant it is, and defines the pronunciation in terms of the initial consonant of a particular Chinese character. Thus for ⊏ *d* we have: 'tongue sound, like the initial of the character 斗 *dŏu*'.

where the final included the vowel and everything following it: a syllable like *ban* was divided into two parts *b-* and *-an*. Where Sejong got the idea of segmenting out the vowel is unclear. The notion of a *segment* must have been known, since there had been contact with India and Indian phonology through the importation of Buddhism. And the 'Phags-pa script was definitely known in Korea: during the thirteenth and fourteenth centuries, Korea, like much of the rest of East Asia, was ruled by the Mongols. Kublai Khan commissioned the Tibetan Grand Lama 'Phags-pa to design an alphabet for

FIGURE 3.16 The vowel ㅜ *(w)u* as defined in *Hunmin Jeong-eum*: 'ㅜ, like the middle sound of *kwun*' (Mandarin *jūn* 'nobleman')

the various languages of his empire. 'Phags-pa's script, which was based on the Tibetan alphasyllabary, was imported to Korea in 1273.[28] Korean scholars, who were trained to read Chinese, simply ignored it, but the notion of segmental writing at least became known via this importation. So the influence of Indian and Tibetan phonology and writing on the development of Hangul cannot be ruled out,[29] though there is no direct evidence that these were the source of Sejong's ideas.

Since Hangul is segmental, it would have been natural to arrange symbols in a linear fashion. However, possibly because it was natural in any case for scholars raised on the syllabic Chinese writing system to think in terms of syllables, the symbols were instead arranged in syllable blocks.[30] Syllables are divided into an optional initial consonant, an optional onglide ('w' or 'y'), an obligatory vowel, and one or two optional final consonants. In modern Hangul, if the final consonant is missing, then the final symbol in the syllable is the vowel, but the initial consonant, if absent, is written with ㅇ as a placeholder. The rules of combination are simple. The initial consonant combines left-to-right with a vertical vowel, top-to-bottom with a horizontal vowel. The final consonants are written underneath, left to right. Consider the syllables *kkeulh* and *manh*. The basic components are ㄲ 'kk' (which is one of the three so-called 'emphatic' consonants, written double, but counting phonologically as a single consonant), — 'eu', ㄹ 'l', and ㅎ 'h'. Since — is a horizontal vowel, and following the rules outlined above, the resulting combination is 끓. For *manh* the basic symbols are ㅁ 'm', ㅏ 'a', ㄴ 'n', and ㅎ 'h'. ㅏ is a vertical vowel, and so the resulting form is 맍. For the syllable *a*, there is no consonant onset, so one must start the syllable with ㅇ to give the result 아. The 'y' onglide is written as an extra stroke as part of the vowel, as we saw above, but a 'w' onglide is written with either ㅗ 'o' or ㅜ 'u', depending upon what the following vowel is. With a 'w' glide, the following vowel is always in any case a vertical vowel, so that, following the rules above, the 'w' is written below the consonant, and the vowel is to the right. Thus for 'gwa' we have 과, and for 'gweo' we have 궈.

The articulatory phonetic basis for the design of the symbols of Hangul is impressive and virtually unique, yet it is easy to overstress its importance in the day-to-day function of Hangul. Sampson (1985) classifies Hangul as the world's only 'featural' script, by which he means that the basic symbols of the script do not denote segments but rather features of segments, such as 'labial' or 'velar'. Thus, the fact that the velar series ㄱ 'g', ㄲ 'kk', ㅋ 'kh' all share a common shape is taken to mean that the ㄱ really denotes the feature 'velar', the doubling represents the feature 'fortis' (pronounced with extra strength) and the additional stroke for 'kh' represents the puff of air of aspiration. There is no question that this is part of the design of the system, and furthermore it is explicitly taught as part of the system when Hangul is introduced. But the phonetic featural aspect is something that is promptly forgotten: ㅋ just becomes, in the reader's mind, the symbol for 'k', and while its shape is in fact not arbitrary (unlike the English 'k'), it might as well be. The featural aspects of the script have little psychological immediacy.

On the other hand, the fact that the symbols represent segments is very apparent to all Korean readers. The difference here is simply one of productivity. The basic set of Korean written segments has not changed much since the fifteenth century, and therefore one is never called upon to invent new segmental symbols out of the basic featural symbols provided. Therefore it is effectively simpler just to learn the symbols as unanalyzable forms. The fact that the featural symbols are not always completely transparent in modern Hangul merely reinforces this. Thus compare the relative transparency of the plain (e.g. 'b') and aspirated (e.g. 'p') consonants below. As will be seen, the extra stroke of the aspirated form is not indicated consistently across all the cases:

b	ㅂ	p	ㅍ
d	ㄷ	t	ㅌ
g	ㄱ	k	ㅋ
j	ㅈ	ch	ㅊ

On the other hand, Korean readers and writers must deal with various combinations of letters into syllable blocks on a daily basis. This reinforces those segmental symbols as the basic building blocks of the script. In its everyday function, Hangul is not a featural script at all, but rather a very intelligently designed alphabet.

The literati did not take kindly to Sejong's invention, and for centuries Hangul was denigrated as the script of the ill-educated, not real writing. This was hardly surprising. In traditional Korean society, education and literacy was a privilege, and it is natural for people who have privilege not to want to cede that privilege to others. With the twentieth century, and mass education and virtually full literacy in South Korea, Hangul has completely supplanted Chinese-based writing. And while most Koreans still learn Chinese characters,[31] they also rarely use them and easily forget them. The situation is thus very different from that in Japan, where *kanji* are still an obligatory part of the writing system.

3.4 A summary

The writing systems that have developed over the course of the last five millennia have taken on a variety of different forms. The shapes of the basic glyphs range from highly pictographic as in Egyptian or Mayan, to abstract, as in the Greek or Latin alphabet. The styles can be 'linear' as in Linear B, or cursive as in Arabic. The ways in which the glyphs are combined differs also, with purely linear (uniformly left-to-right, or right-to-left, or top-to-bottom) arrangements being found in some (e.g. Latin, Greek, Linear B, *kana*); to others, such as Hangul, or the alphasyllabaries of India, where vowels and consonants are combined in a non-linear fashion into syllables. Yet despite these wide differences in outer form, there are remarkably few options for what writing systems can represent. All true writing systems represent sound. This is true even in those writing systems, like Chinese, or Egyptian or Mayan or Sumerian, that represent a large amount of semantic information as well. As for the sound representation itself, writing systems have a choice between representing syllables or representing segments. There is a fair amount of variation in how complete or accurate the representations are. Some, like Linear B, are poor representations of the language they encode. Others, like the Semitic writing systems, are accurate, but not complete—in that some information (in the case of Semitic, many of the vowels)—is simply missing.

It should strike you as interesting that, with four attested independently developed writing traditions, and the scores of systems that developed directly from, or under influence from the three Old World systems, there have been so few options for representing language in writing. Evidently humans are restricted in what they can easily perceive in spoken language in such a way that sounds or some combinations of sounds form a natural basis for a representational system; whereas, for example, semantic features (whatever those might be) are simply not accessible with anything like the same facility. Indeed, as we saw in the last chapter, conscious attempts to break free of those bonds, as Charles Bliss tried to do, have not been particularly successful.

3.5 Epilogue: writing implements and outer form

In our discussion of writing we have focused on how writing encodes language, but we have said little about the implements of writing—how writing was produced. Clearly the instrument and the medium has had a profound effect on the form of scripts. The cuneiform scripts of Mesopotamia had the shape they did because of the form of the stylus that was used to impress them on clay. This shape was retained even when the script was used in stone carvings. Similarly, Chinese characters have the shapes they do because for over two thousand years they have been written with a brush.

The scripts of north and south India differ in shape in part because of the writing medium. In particular, southern scripts such as Kannada, Telugu, Malayalam, or Sinhalese tend to be rounded relative to northern scripts such as Devanagari or Bengali. Palm leaves incised with a stylus were a popular medium in South India, and palm leaves tear more easily with straight strokes. In the North, palm leaves were also used, but were written

मानव अधिकारों की सार्वभौम घोषणा

মানবাধিকারের সার্বজনীন ঘোষণাপত্র

ಮಾನವ ಬಾಧ್ಯತೆಗಳ ಸಾರ್ವತ್ರಿಕ ಪ್ರಕಟನೆ ಪ್ರಸ್ತಾವನೆ

മനുഷ്യാവകാശങ്ങളെക്കുറിക്കുന്ന പൊതുപ്രവ്യാപനം

FIGURE 3.17 The title of the 1948 Universal Declaration of Human Rights in four Indian languages. From top to bottom: Hindi, Bengali, Kannada, Malayalam

Note: these illustrate two northern (Devanagari, Bengali) and two southern (Kannada, Malayalam) scripts.

Source: translations from http://gii2.nagaokaut.ac.jp/gii/lopdiary.php?itemid=480.

FIGURE 3.18 *Richard Sproat* in Nastaliq script

Note: The glyphs represent my name as follows. First of all, note that most vowels are not represented, so that the spelling of my name in Nastaliq would be rendered in Latin script as 'rchrd sprwt' (the 'w' representing the long /o/ sound of 'oa'). Starting in the *lower* right-hand corner, the single comma-like glyph is the 'r'. The next ligature to the left, consisting of an eye followed by another comma, and including the three dots below the eye, are the sequence 'chr'. Following that is a glyph that looks like a quotation mark with a little 'b' above it. That represents the 'd'. The following complex ligature, including the three dots represents the sequence 'spr'. The quotation-mark like glyph after that is the 'w'. Finally, at the top, the shallow bowl with the little 'b' above it is the final 't' of *Sproat*. Its placement at the top is done purely for esthetic reasons—in everyday use of the Nastaliq script, as in newspapers, one would expect this to occur after the 'w'.

Source: work of master calligrapher Syed Jamil-ur-Rehman.

on with pens. Hence northern scripts tend to be more angular, southern scripts more rounded. Figure 3.17 shows a sample of two northern and two southern Brahmi-derived scripts; note the more rounded form of the southern scripts.

In many Asian cultures (besides Hindu culture in India), calligraphy is associated with religion. In Islamic culture, depiction of living things is proscribed, so calligraphic religious texts occupy an important position in the visual arts. Many styles of Arabic-based scripts have been developed. Among the most elaborate version is the *nastaliq* script that is not only a calligraphic style, but is also used as the standard version of Arabic script to write Urdu. Figure 3.18 shows my name written in Nastaliq script, the work of a master calligrapher from a family of master calligraphers in Lahore, Pakistan. An example of decorative script from the Masjid Wazir Khan in Lahore is shown in Figure 3.19.

For Chinese, a number of character styles have developed over the millennia. The Seal Script, which became standardized in the Qin Dynasty (221–206 BC), is still used for decorative functions (such as personal 'chops' or seals). Brush styles include *lishu* (Clerical Script), the semi-cursive *xingshu* ('Running' Script), and the highly cursive *caoshu* (Grass Script). See Figure 3.20 for examples of these and other styles.

FIGURE 3.19 Ornamental Arabic script, Masjid Wazir Khan, Lahore, Pakistan

FIGURE 3.20 Chinese calligraphic styles: Small Seal, Clerical, *kaishu*, Running, Grass

Source: from Florian Coulmas, 1996, *Blackwell Encyclopedia of Writing Systems*, p. 63, Figure 7, used with permission.

FIGURE 3.21 A famous instance of Mao Zedong's (*caoshu*) calligraphy 向雷锋同志学习 'Learn from Comrade Lei Feng'

Note: In juxtaposing traditional Chinese penmanship with Marxist propaganda, this is surely an extreme example of the combination of opposites.

Education in China was traditionally synonymous with good calligraphy: a person who could not write well was considered ill educated. As a result, it was common for Chinese leaders to also have good handwriting. Mao Zedong was an avid practitioner of classical Chinese literary arts, including calligraphy (Figure 3.21)—ironic given his attempts to destroy Chinese culture during the Cultural Revolution.

4

Decipherment

The Latin script I am using to convey these words has a long history. It evolved through the Middle Ages from an earlier and shorter alphabet used by the Romans to write their language. The Romans in turn had adopted and adapted, via the Etruscans, a variant of the alphabet used by the Greeks, who had learned to write from the Phoenicians. The Phoenicians could trace their script's lineage back to the earliest Semitic scripts of the Sinai. And these early inhabitants of the Sinai were likely influenced in the design of their script by the literate Egyptian civilization to the west. Inevitably some of the links in such a long chain will have become obscured by the passage of time, and their nature will need to be reconstructed. Thus the exact sense in which Egyptian might have served as a model for Semitic scripts—as a consonantal writing system—could not be known until Egyptian could be read again in the nineteenth century. This process of rediscovery—decipherment—is the topic of this chapter.

As with any quest of discovery that ultimately ends in unlocking a door into the previously unknown, there is something inherently romantic about decipherment. When one deciphers an ancient writing system, one provides a key to a culture and people that may previously have been completely unknown, or only known through the histories and legends of others. Our image of the decipherer is often one of a lone genius struggling for years, poring over ancient texts, assimilating information from many disparate sources to crack a seemingly impenetrable code; and then a spark of inspiration comes and everything begins to fall into place.

Like most caricatures there is both truth and falsehood to this image. Geniuses have certainly been a factor: Thomas Young and Jean-François Champollion for Egyptian, Henry Creswicke Rawlinson for Babylonian, and Michael Ventris for Linear B, all made their mark on the history of code-breaking (see Figure 4.1). Examination of a wide variety of texts, knowledge of a broad set of languages and cultures and the willingness to consider many sources of potential evidence also played a role. Rigorous pursuit of a careful methodology was also a factor, and sparks of inspiration

FIGURE 4.1 Five famous decipherers: Thomas Young (1773–1829); Georg Friedrich Grotefend (1775–1853); Jean-François Champollion (1790–1832); Henry Creswicke Rawlinson (1810–95); Michael Ventris (1922–56)

Source: Ventris photograph from "The Ventris Papers", http://sas-space.sas.ac.uk/dspace/bitstream/10065/330/1/Ventris_11+06_erepository+(2).pdf.

were often key to eventually cracking the code. But these were never sufficient on their own.

Indeed, one of the most common misconceptions among the many would-be decipherers who are even now plying their trade on the Internet is that a lone (self-styled) genius with a preconceived belief about an undeciphered set of symbols, who appears to have made some progress towards his or her goal, must necessarily be on the right track. Often such people are quite earnest, and some produce volumes of work in support of their hypotheses. Unfortunately, most such work leads nowhere except for an honorable mention in the annals of *pseudo-decipherment*.

There are a few very simple reasons for this. First, geniuses aside, all cases of real decipherment have been a team effort, with discoveries made by a community of scholars. These scholars may not necessarily agree with one another, but each of them provides crucial evidence without which the eventual success could not have happened.

Second, decipherment is not just about ideas. One of the issues that fast becomes apparent is that there is no shortage of ideas, indeed quite the reverse. Michael Ventris, the main decipherer of the Mycenaean Greek Linear B writing system, had a notion that Linear B must represent Etruscan and pursued this idea right up to the time that the evidence for it being Greek became too overwhelming to ignore. The problem is invariably one of eliminating ideas, not generating them.

And finally, a proposal for a decipherment is a scientific hypothesis, and like any scientific hypothesis, it stands or falls on verification. And this verification can really only take one form: if your decipherment is correct, then it must be possible for other people to use it to come up with sensible interpretations of documents that you have never seen. If the only person who knows how to apply your system is you, then you have achieved nothing.

This final point is really the most crucial and is something that must be borne in mind whenever one reads of a decipherment proposal—for example in the popular press. There is the question of whether the proposed decipherment has been validated, and indeed whether it can ever *hope* to be validated; because in some cases the evidence is simply too scanty to allow one to come up with a testable solution.

The stories of individual feats of decipherment have often been told. The British writer Andrew Robinson devoted discussion in his book *The Story of Writing* (2006b) to the decipherment of Egyptian, Babylonian (and other cuneiform scripts), and Linear B; his book *Lost Languages* (2009) deals with undeciphered scripts; and he wrote biographies of Michael Ventris (*The Man Who Deciphered Linear B* (2002)) and Thomas Young (*The Last Man Who Knew Everything* (2006a)). Richard Parkinson, a curator at the British Museum, devoted an extensive discussion to the decipherment of Egyptian in his book *Cracking Codes* (1999), and Maurice Pope's book *The Story of Decipherment* (1999) devotes detailed discussions to the successful decipherment of a number of scripts.

In this chapter we focus instead on the *methodology* of decipherment, drawing on these and other classic cases as examples of how decipherment frequently proceeds and how it is verified. The latter point is not as trivial as it sounds. We are used to thinking of successful cases of decipherment in terms of the end-state, when the whole system is understood. Thus for Egyptian,

James Allen (2000: 9) notes that "[e]xcept for the most obscure words, hieroglyphic texts can be read today almost as easily as those of any other known language." But it was not always so. When Champollion made his decisive discovery (to which we return below) that native Egyptian words could be written phonetically, scholars were obviously far from being able to read much of anything written in Egyptian.

We will start our discussion of the methodology of decipherment not with cases of successful decipherment but rather with cases of *pseudo-decipherment*—decoding ancient texts in ways that convince the decoder, but largely fail to convince anyone else. This may seem an odd place to start, but I think the reasons for doing this will quickly become apparent.

4.1 Pseudo-decipherment

Sometimes the easiest way to explain something is to start with an example of what that thing is not. Pseudo-decipherment, the 'near enemy' of decipherment, is a good starting point for this discussion, since while pseudo-decipherment often bears the trappings of true decipherment, it fails to be decipherment for the simple reason that it does not produce a *verifiable* decoding of an ancient text, or even a portion thereof.

Consider the case of the artifact that is probably the most notorious in this regard, the Phaistos Disk. Illustrated in Figure 4.2, this unique artifact turned

FIGURE 4.2 The Phaistos disk

Source: From http://en.wikipedia.org/wiki/File:Crete_-_Phaistos_disk_-_side_A.JPG, available under the Creative Commons Attribution ShareAlike 3.0.

up in the Italian excavations at Phaistos, Crete, on 3 July 1908.[1] It is generally assumed to date to the nineteenth century BC, and therefore to belong to the Late Minoan period, though because of its uniqueness, ever since its discovery there have been those who have doubted that it was originally from Crete. The Disk is 16 cm in diameter, about 2 cm thick, made of clay, and *stamped* on both sides with symbols from an otherwise unknown 45-glyph pictographic symbol set. The use of stamps makes it the world's oldest printed document. The text consisting of 241 symbols running in spirals from the outside in on both sides, and is segmented with lines into 61 segments. These segments might have represented small phrases or words. The disk was apparently baked purposely, an unusual practice for ancient clay documents.

The artifact is so unusual that there have been suggestions that it is in fact a hoax. Most recently, Jerome Eisenberg, an art dealer and authority on art forgery, has argued[2] that a number of the characteristics of the disk, including various inconsistencies in the style, as well as a mix of exquisite and shoddy work in the manufacture, are consistent with its being a fake. Only a thermo-luminescence test will decide the matter, something the Museum at Heraklion, Crete, refuses to allow.

But from the point of view of the present discussion, it is immaterial whether the disk is a genuine ancient artifact or a modern forgery, since for the past hundred years there have been various attempts to interpret the meaning of the strange text. Some people have argued that it was not a text at all (one suggestion has it being a kind of board game[3]) but the majority of people who have tried to interpret the text have assumed that it contains a linguistic message, and that we are therefore dealing with an ancient writing system.

If the text was a linguistic message, then the obvious first question would seem to be: what language was it written in? While this is indeed a valid question, it is important to bear in mind that assumptions about the under-lying language can both help us—for example by suggesting phonetic inter-pretations of some signs—but also hurt us by causing us to see evidence that is not there. Famously, for most of his work on the Cretan Linear B script, Michael Ventris did *not* assume that what he was trying to decode was Greek. Indeed, he believed that it was probably Etruscan, and published a paper to that effect in the *American Journal of Archaeology* in 1940. What is particularly interesting about this is that as a result of distributional analysis, Ventris surmised that the glyph ⊜ probably represented the word (actually suffix) for 'and'. On the basis of his belief that the underlying language was Etruscan, he assigned it the tentative reading -*me*. As it turned out, the correct syllabic value for this sign was -*qe*—which happens also to be the Mycenaean Greek word (suffix) for 'and'. In contrast, many people who have attempted to decipher the Disk clearly have a preconception of what the underlying language must be. For example, Sankarananda (1968) argues that the disk was written in some version of Sanskrit, yet it is clear that his conclusion was reached from a starting point where that goal was presupposed. A similar situation apparently holds for Rjabchikov's (1999) argument that it represents a 'Slavonic dialect'.

Determining reading direction is a second issue. In some cases this is made obvious from physical properties of the text: texts where the left edge is well aligned and the right edge is irregular are good indications that the reading direction is left to right. If it looks as if elements have been crowded into the left-hand edge, because the scribe ran out of space, then it probably runs from right to left. Evidence that points to one symbol having been laid down before another, perhaps because the symbols overlap, can also give clues.[4] If symbols flip direction when the text breaks a line, then a boustrophedon style is indicated. For the Disk, it is generally assumed that the text reads from the outside in, and therefore, given the direction of the spirals, ran from right to left. While this seems somehow natural, it should be realized that there is not a lot of evidence for it.

The next important issue involves getting some clues as to possible readings for some of the glyphs: as with the children's game 'hangman', the task becomes easier once one has some initial guesses for some of the symbols. If one has a bilingual text, then of course this problem becomes much simpler: the key to cracking Egyptian started with the bilingual Rosetta Stone. But a bilingual text is not necessary, as Ventris's decipherment of Linear B shows, provided one can get some initial clues. Where do such clues come from?

In principle they can come from a variety of sources. If the script is reasonably pictographic, and one has a reasonable set of guesses as to possible underlying languages, one might assume that the phonetic values of some symbols are related in some way to the word for the thing the picture represents. It is known that ancient scripts made use of two such mechanisms—the *rebus* and *acrophonic* principles, which we already introduced in Chapter 1. But these principles are not as easy to apply as one might think, and there is much danger of false leads—with false leads being virtually guaranteed if one is wrong in one's guess about the underlying language. Even if one is right about the language, there is the issue of how to interpret the pictures. The figure of a crested head in profile ☙, the most common glyph on the Disk, is surely a picture of a head, but it is also a picture of a soldier or, as many have argued, a Philistine (who wore helmets that looked like this). The running boy glyph ☙ could represent a boy (as argued by Faucounau 1975), or perhaps it represents 'run'; or how about 'child', 'pace', 'race'...?

The other way in which one can guess as to the value of some signs is by finding signs in other scripts that are apparently related. This too is a minefield. If we can be reasonably sure that scripts *are* related, then we may be on safe ground. For example, it is fairly certain that Linear B was derived from Linear A, so it is a reasonable guess that similar signs probably had similar phonetic values.[5] A similar argument holds of Etruscan: we do not know much about the Etruscan language, but since the Etruscan alphabet was derived from Greek and was transferred by them to the Romans, we have a pretty good idea about how the written words were pronounced. But similarities can also provide false leads. The most obvious example of where this principle would lead one seriously astray is Cherokee. Many of Sequoyah's symbols look like English letters for the simple reason that they *are* English letters—assigned a very different phonetic value from their values in English.

In the case of the Disk it is hard to find convincing evidence from other scripts because there is not that much overlap between the signs on the Disk and the signs in known systems. The shield glyph ⊙ is somewhat reminiscent of the ⊖ *qe* glyph in Linear B and might in theory be related; in Fischer's pseudo-decipherment,[6] this similarity plays a role. Some of the symbols are similar to glyphs found in Luwian, which have caused some people to assume an Anatolian origin for the artifact. But on the whole the evidence is thin. One issue to be particularly worried about in making guesses about the interpretation of symbols is to avoid falling into the trap of *chance* similarities of symbols. A good case of this is the work of the Massey brothers,[7] available on the Web at http://home.att.net/~phaistosdisk/mystery.PDF. In their work they relate the Disk's symbols to a script they call Proto-Byblic. Thus in the discussion of one of the Disk's symbols, the fish, they start by recounting Arthur Evans's tracing of the history of the Linear A and B symbols down from the Cretan hieroglyphic character (Figure 4.3). They then go on to state:

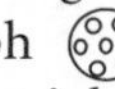

FIGURE 4.3 Cretan hieroglyph (left) and Linear A/B fish glyphs

That final Linear B character, with the value /mi/, thus developed from a hieroglyphic fish character identical to the Phaistos Disk character 🐟 which compares to the character in Proto-Byblic 🐟, which Dhorme gave the value /m₃/.

Well, maybe, but one has to ask the obvious question: how many ways are there to draw a fish? Most if not all ancient symbol systems have a fish glyph: the Chinese and Egyptian writing systems, as well as the Indus Valley symbol systems, all have fish glyphs and, in their original forms, they looked, unsurprisingly, rather similar. Form tells us little a priori, and it is very easy to be misled by apparent similarities.

It also helps to have some idea about the kind of text represented. Is it a list of possessions? A seal with an owner's name? A bill of sale? A letter? A proclamation? An epic? A prayer? Or a love poem? Sometimes the physical layout of the documents can give one a clue. In the case of Linear B the almost tabular arrangement of items (Figure 4.4), with pictograms that look like pictures of different kinds of commodities and symbols that look as if they must be numbers, made it very clear that we must be dealing with some kind of accounting text.

In the case of the Disk, because of its unusual form, it is harder to say what kind of text is most likely: disks with spiral text are not so common (the other

FIGURE 4.4 A Linear B tablet showing a clear tabular arrangement of accounts

famous example is the Etruscan Magliano disk). Many translations of the text—for example Fischer's and Faucounau's—have it as a type of proclamation: in Faucounau's case, it is a boast, in Fischer's a call to arms. Interestingly, the Massey brothers argue that it is, like Linear B, an accounting document, with some of the words being numbers, and others being names of commodities. A priori this seems highly unlikely: why would one pick such a curious form for something as mundane as an account of goods? And there is an additional problem with this interpretation: in ancient documents (especially accounting documents) numbers are *hardly ever* written as words and nearly always written with numerical symbols. Thus in Linear B one never sees numbers written out as words (*twenty four*), but rather always sees them written out using number symbols (*24*). Similarly in Sumerian and Egyptian numbers are written as numerals, not as words: in Egyptian it is exceedingly rare to find numbers written out, and in many cases we can only reconstruct their probable pronunciation from Coptic.[8]

Other clues to a decipherment involve internal analysis of the structure of sign sequences, which may point to linguistic properties that can be correlated with those of putative underlying languages. As we will see, in Linear B, Kober's 'triplets' suggested a language that marked different forms of related words with different endings—and as an important side product, suggested which syllabic symbols might share the same initial consonant, and which syllabic symbols might share the same vowel. Finnish Indologist Asko Parpola, in his work on the Indus Valley symbols (1994: 94–7), has presented arguments that the most common symbol in the Indus corpus, the 'jar' symbol ⊺∪, is probably a suffix (possibly a possessive marker), since it occurs at the end of strings. Furthermore, having argued that the underlying language is Dravidian, he has identified this symbol with a Dravidian possessive marker on the basis of its frequency. On the Disk, it has been suggested that the head-plus-shield ⬡⊙ sequence that is so common on Side A might be some sort of morphological prefix, suggesting in turn a language that has prefixal morphology. But of course this presumes that the items contained in the 61 segments are words, and what if they are not?

However, particularly for texts such as the Disk which are not part of a bilingual document or a larger body of texts in the same script, there is a concern that is at once orthogonal to all of the issues we have just discussed, but at the same time critical to any attempt at decipherment. Simply put, do we have enough text to work with? Is there sufficient text that one could develop one's proposed decipherment on one portion of the text, and then test the decipherment on another portion to see if it makes sense? If the answer is 'yes', then we have a hope of producing a decipherment that is *verifiable*. If not, then there is no hope and the correct answer is not even to try to decipher in the first place. As we will see, all successful decipherments succeeded precisely because the hypotheses could be *independently* verified on texts that were separate from the texts on which the hypothesized decipherment was developed.

In the case of the Disk, the answer is that there is not enough text. The text contains only 241 symbols, and while this may seem like a lot, given the uncertainties about what kind of symbol system it is (is it an alphabet, a syllabary, some kind of mixed system?), what the language (or languages) is, what type of document it is, there are simply too many possible interpretations. The sheer number of published decipherments, each of which was evidently compelling to the decipherer, attests to the fact that it is possible to interpret this text in many different ways. This point relates to the notion of *unicity*, developed by Claude Shannon (1949) in the context of code-breaking: Given a cipher that has a known property (e.g. an alphabetic substitution cipher), and an enciphered text in a known language, what is the minimum amount of text that is needed for there to be a unique decryption of the text? Shannon showed that this notion had a precise mathematical expression. But the Disk's non-unicity was long understood even without Shannon's mathematical formulation. Perhaps the best statement of this is due to John Chadwick, co-decipherer of Linear B:[9]

> My own view, shared by all serious scholars, is that the Disk is undecipherable so long as it remains an isolated document. Only a large increase in the number of inscriptions will permit real progress towards a decipherment. Meanwhile, we must curb our impatience, and admit that if King Minos himself were to reveal to someone in a dream the true interpretation, it would be quite impossible for him to convince anyone else that his was the one and only possible solution.

We can hardly expect that the level-headed judgment of a scholar like Chadwick will prevent enthusiastic amateurs from convincing themselves that they have finally cracked a mystery that no one else had been able to solve. Perhaps a convincing demonstration, via dating, that the Disk is after all a hoax will finally drive the nail into the coffin of such attempts, but even this seems doubtful. But at least one can hope that while there will always be a few people who are absolutely sure that they have provided a solution to an effectively unsolvable problem, most of the rest of the world will know better.

4.2 True decipherment

One of the reasons that pseudo-decipherers are often so convinced that they are on the right track is that they are able to point with pride at their methodology.

Steven Roger Fischer, in his book *Glyphbreaker*,[10] takes great pains to emphasize how careful he was about not making too many assumptions during his
attempt to decipher the Phaistos Disk. Indeed, many of the techniques that
have led people astray in decipherment work *are* valid techniques. All cases of
true decipherment have, at some stage, involved guesses at what the underlying
language must be, usually with minimal evidence. Many cases have involved
guesses about the readings of glyphs, based on what they seem to depict, or
apparent similarities to glyphs in known scripts. All true decipherment work
has made use of some amount of structural analysis of the available texts.

But this is hardly surprising, since these techniques are nothing more than
tools. As with any tools one needs two things in order to achieve a good
result: the right skills, and the right raw materials. Put the same tools in my
hands or the hands of an Amish master cabinetmaker, and the resulting
product will be very different. Give the Amish cabinetmaker the pith of a
date palm, and he will produce a far inferior product to what he could
produce if you gave him oak planks. If what you are trying to decipher is not
a linguistic symbol system, then no amount of good techniques will help
you. If the text you are working with is short, and there is no way to verify
your solution against independent data, then good methodology is simply
wasted.

But let us now look at how the tools of decipherment have been put to
proper use.

4.2.1 *Linguistic or non-linguistic?*

Before one embarks upon a decipherment there are a couple of initial
questions that must be asked about one's texts. The first, obviously, is whether
the archaeological find is genuine. For texts that involve dozens or hundreds
or thousands of examples, one can usually be reasonably sure, but isolates,
such as the Phaistos Disk, or near-isolates such as the recent tablets discovered
at Jiroft, Iran (Figure 4.5),[11] should always be suspect until one can get
definitive evidence of their date.

The next question, after the question of authenticity, is whether or not the
symbols in question are really a script. As we discussed in Chapter 2, there
have been many symbol systems invented over the course of the millennia,
and not all of them are writing in the sense we adopt here. One cannot simply
assume that a set of symbols, arranged in a more or less linear fashion, is
writing. A good example of this can be found in the Assyrian bas relief shown
in Figure 4.6. The pictograms arranged in a diagonal line shown in this figure
are not writing—they are symbols for deities, in particular the major deities of
the King Aššurnaṣirpal II (ninth century BC), also depicted here. But they

FIGURE 4.5 A recently discovered inscription from Jiroft, Iran

Note: While this has been claimed by some to represent one of the earliest forms of writing, others are doubtful of its authenticity.

might be mistaken for writing by someone who assumes that any sequence of symbols so arranged must be a script.

Sometimes healthy skepticism can turn out to be misplaced: when cuneiform inscriptions from Persia were first published in Europe, many people believed they were purely decorative. It was even proposed they were the impressions of birds' feet on the wet clay. This mistaken view was encouraged by the first published drawings, which seemed to show the patterns to be more repetitive than real cuneiform texts are.

If one finds long texts, that can often be taken as an indication that the symbol system was writing, though even here one must be cautious. There are systems, such as the symbology used by the Naxi in China, which are not writing in the normal sense of the word. Naxi texts (Figure 4.7) consist of a set of mnemonic cues in the form of pictograms, which help a trained reader recover a text.[12] Imagine a recounting of *Little Red Riding Hood* that uses pictures of a little girl in a red cape, a basket of food, a grandmother in a sickbed, a wolf, some hunters, and a house in the forest to remind the reader of the relevant portions of the story. Naxi more or less works this way. Naxi texts convey a message, a message that is obviously expressible in language. But they do not encode language directly. A well-known case of an undeciphered symbol system that may also fall into this category is the *rongorongo* of Easter Island. The texts are long, and this has been one reason that has convinced many that the system was true writing. But, as we shall detail further in the next chapter,

FIGURE 4.6 The linearly arranged symbols of the major deities of Aššurnaṣirpal II

Source: From http://upload.wikimedia.org/wikipedia/commons/8/87/Ashurnasirpal_II_stela_british_mu-seam.jpg, released under the GNU Free Documentation License, Version 1.2.

there is remarkably little evidence that this was the case. Writing implies that there should be long texts; long texts do not necessarily imply one has writing.

Perhaps the best indication one can hope for that one is dealing with a linguistic system is if one finds a bilingual text, where the other text is in a language one knows. Given the layout of the Rosetta Stone, there could be

FIGURE 4.7 Sample Naxi text
Source: From the Library of Congress http://www.loc.gov.

little doubt that the Greek and the Egyptian texts (in the two forms of
hieroglyphic and demotic) conveyed the same message. While it was still in
theory possible that Egyptian was some sort of Naxi-like mnemonic system
that was being interpreted into Greek, a study of the number of symbols in the
Egyptian text by Champollion (1821) established that there were too many for
it to be a purely 'ideographic' script. Furthermore, once the alignment
between the personal names in the Greek text and the Egyptian cartouches
had been made, and it became clear that there were phonetic correspondences
between the two, the indications were good that one was dealing with a real
writing system. More on this point in Section 4.2.3.

4.2.2 *The underlying language*

Decipherment is the discovery of the relationship between a set of written
symbols and a particular language. Obviously, then, one needs to have some
idea about what the underlying language is, and without that information,
not much progress can be made. Indeed, there are ancient scripts where we
are pretty certain of the mapping between the language and the symbols, but

where too little is known about the language to make much sense of most texts. One example is Etruscan. Since Etruscan used a variant of the Greek alphabet, there is little doubt about the pronunciations of words. But very little Etruscan can be read because the language was an isolate—a language not known to be related to any other—and what we can read is largely what can be gleaned from bilingual texts with Etruscan and some other language, such as Latin. Another example is the Minoan language that underlies Linear A. Since Linear B is a descendant of Linear A, and we know the readings of Linear B glyphs, one can make reasonable guesses as to the readings of Linear A. And since, like Mycenaean Greek texts, many Minoan texts were accounting documents, one can even guess as to the meanings of some of the words. But again, the Minoan language was an isolate, and so the majority of the texts cannot be read. John Younger at the University of Kansas keeps a repository of Linear A texts at http://people.ku.edu/~jyounger/LinearA/ for anyone who wishes to try their hand at interpreting them.

Clearly if we are dealing with an unknown script, then knowledge of the underlying language becomes critical, so inevitably the decipherer makes an educated guess on the language at some stage during the process.

In some cases this is obvious. In the case of the Easter Island *rongorongo* texts, assuming these were in fact writing in the normal sense, it is reasonably certain what the language must have been. Easter Island was colonized by Polynesians at some point during the 9th century AD and, pace the thoroughly discredited theories of Thor Heyerdahl about Peruvian origins for some of the Easter Islanders (1958), there was apparently no contact between Easter Island and the outside world until Dutch mariners under the command of Jacob Rogge-veen encountered the island on Easter Sunday, 1722. The language therefore must have been Rapanui, which still survives and is spoken by about 4,500 people on the island, though in a form which is now heavily influenced by Tahitian. Similarly, in the case of Mayan, it was clear that the ancient Mayans spoke a language related to the dozens of Mayan languages still spoken.

In other cases one cannot be so sure. In the case of Egyptian, there were reasonable *guesses* that the language was the ancestor of Coptic, the language used in the Egyptian Christian church, but there was no guarantee that this was correct, and it was not until progress was made on the decipherment that this conclusion became unavoidable. And, from that point forward, scholars could use Coptic as an additional source of hypotheses on the interpretations of Ancient Egyptian words.

For Linear B there was no way to know that it was Greek, and indeed there was much scholarly belief, influenced mostly by the personal views of Arthur Evans (who first discovered the Linear A and B tablets, and excavated the palace at Knossos), that it *could not be* Greek. Only when apparently Greek words, such as the words for 'boy(s)' (*ko-wo* in Linear B) and 'girl(s)' (*ko-wa*), started to show up did this conclusion become inevitable, and then Greek could be used as evidence for the further decipherment.

In other cases we simply have no way of knowing. In the case of the Indus Valley symbols, assuming they were a writing system, some scholars such as Asko Parpola or Iravatham Mahadevan have argued the language was Dravidian, since the Dravidians clearly inhabited the Indian subcontinent prior to the migration of the Aryans from the North. But there is really no evidence that the Dravidians ever occupied the Indus Valley, and the presence of a modern Dravidian language, Brahui, in that area (evidence that is often cited by Parpola) is probably a red herring since at least some scholars believe that Brahui speakers were relatively recent immigrants.[13] And so we simply cannot know what language the Indus Valley peoples spoke, if indeed there *was* a single language: as suggested in Farmer *et al.* (2004), there may be every reason to believe that the Indian subcontinent was as multilingual then as it is now, and there could easily have been several languages, possibly from different language families, spoken in the region.

Even once one has a reasonable idea about the language underlying an ancient script, one must realize that languages change over time and space and one cannot assume that the *form* of the language will be the same as the one that one is already familiar with. In general, decipherment is not merely the discovery of a mapping of unknown symbols to a known language, but rather the discovery of a mapping of unknown symbols to a language that may only partially be known. Usually one also has to reconstruct the language. So, the Mycenaean language of Linear B was spoken about six hundred years prior to the earliest previously known form of Greek, the Homeric language of the *Iliad* and the *Odyssey*. Languages can change a lot in six hundred years, as the following excerpt from Chaucer's 'Miller's Tale' (*The Canterbury Tales*, written between the late 1380s and 1400) shows:

> Whilom ther was dwellynge at Oxenford
> A riche gnof, that gestes heeld to bord,
> And of his craft he was a carpenter.
> With hym ther was dwellynge a poure scoler,
> Hadde lerned art, but al his fantasye
> Was turned for to lerne astrologye,
> And koude a certeyn of conclusiouns,
> To demen by interrogaciouns,
> If that men asked hym in certain houres
> Whan that men sholde have droghte or elles shoures,

> Or if men asked hym what sholde bifalle
> Of every thyng; I may nat rekene hem alle.

In the case of Mycenaean Greek, the differences from later Greek included changes in the sounds, as well as changes in the syntax, about which we will have more to say below. Also, as we have discussed already in the previous chapter, Linear B was a rather poor way of writing Greek, since the basic CV syllabary did not allow for a direct way of writing the complex syllables of Greek. As part of his decipherment, Ventris therefore had to rediscover this encoding method; the initial skepticism that some scholars had about his achievement was based in part on what seemed like egregious assumptions about the way in which Greek was represented.

Of course there have been cases of successful decipherment of a script for a language where the language itself was previously unknown in any form. The most famous case of this is Sumerian. However, this was possible only because of the rather fortunate fact that the cuneiform-based writing system that the Sumerians invented was adopted by later users, including the Akkadians, the Assyrians, and the Persians. There were important differences between all these versions, but enough in common that one could trace back from the later 'easier' cases to the ultimate unknown case of Sumerian. And this is exactly what happened. Grotefend's decipherment of Ancient Persian, which we will discuss below, was the starting point. Historical stages of Persian were well-known from many sources, and the decipherment of Persian cuneiform was largely a matter of fitting a partially known language to a new script. The much more complicated writing system of the Babylonians, cracked by Henry Creswicke Rawlinson, was aided by this previous solution to Persian, and also by the fact that Babylonian (Akkadian) was a Semitic language, and much could be gleaned from knowledge of other Semitic languages.

For Sumerian, decipherers were fortunate since, once they knew Akkadian, there were multiple keys to the earlier Sumerian language in the form of bilingual texts and school texts that listed Sumerian forms. Sumerian survived as the language of administration in the Akkadian empire, and was used as a written language long after it ceased to function as a spoken language. Thus, Akkadians who wanted to become literate in Sumerian had to learn it, and so grammars were necessary, many of which still exist.

The wide use of cuneiform and the special status of Sumerian in the Akkadian empire thus made it possible to decipher the language of the first people to invent writing. But Sumerian is not related to any known language:

it is an isolate. If the Sumerians had been the only ones to use cuneiform-based writing, and if that art had died with them, it is doubtful that Sumerian could ever have been deciphered.

4.2.3 *Bilingual texts and names*

The best situation one can hope for in decipherment work is to find a bilingual or multilingual text, where one or more of the languages are ones that are already familiar. One is rarely so lucky, but there have been a number of instances including most famously the Rosetta Stone, but also including bilingual texts in languages of Mesopotamia, that allowed one to trace back from Persian to Sumerian.

Even with bilingual texts there is much uncertainty. When scholars first started working on the Rosetta Stone, there were widespread misconceptions about the nature of Egyptian writing, including the idea that it was largely an 'ideographic' script. As we have already noted, symbol counts on the Egyptian portions of the Stone made this seem unlikely, but the conclusion that the script was mostly phonetic—which we now know to be true—was not something that was immediately dispelled by the bilingual text.

What bilingual texts allow one to do, of course, is search for patterns that repeat across the different languages. If the word for 'king' appears multiple times in one language, then there is a good chance that it appears a similar number of times in the other language, and in approximately the same positions in the text. Even a reader who does not know Chinese should have no trouble finding the word (in this case a single character) that means 'God' in the Chinese version of the following text. For those who do know Chinese, you might try your hand at the equivalent Korean text (though be forewarned that the word for 'God' is missing from one of the sentences.)

- And God said, Let there be light: and there was light.
- And God saw the light, that it was good: and God divided the light from the darkness.
- And God called the light Day, and the darkness he called Night. And the evening and the morning were the first day.
- And God said, Let there be a firmament in the midst of the waters, and let it divide the waters from the waters.
- 神說、要有光、就有了光。
- 神看光是好的、就把光暗分開了。
- 神稱光為晝、稱暗為夜．有晚上、有早晨、這是頭一日。
- 神說、諸水之間要有空氣、將水分為上下。

- 하나님이 가라사대 빛이 있으라 하시매 빛이 있었고.
- 그 빛이 하나님의 보시기에 좋았더라 하나님이 빛과 어두움을 나누사.
- 빛을 낮이라 칭하시고 어두움을 밤이라 칭하시니라 저녁이 되며 아침이 되니 이는 첫째 날이니라.
- 하나님이 가라사대 물 가운데 궁창이 있어 물과 물로 나뉘게 하리라 하시고.

Such words that can be found across texts serve as islands of relative certainty. One class of words in particular that has proved critical in the decipherment of many ancient writing systems are names, personal and place names in particular. This has been true for example in the decipherment of Persian cuneiform, Egyptian hieroglyphs, and Linear B. There are a couple of reasons for this. First, proper names may be written in a distinctive fashion: in Egyptian, two of the pharoah's five names were written in *cartouches*, something that was guessed (by Jean-Jacques Barthélemy, in 1761) well before serious decipherment work began.

Second, and more generally, personal and place names are often the only words that are likely to be known via the medium of other languages. So, Persian kings such as Darius and Xerxes were long known from Greek sources, and this proved very helpful in the decipherment of Persian cuneiform texts where these names occurred, though obviously in their original Persian versions—*dārayavahuš* and *xšayāršā*—they were quite different in form. Cretan town names such as Knossos, Amnisos, and Phaistos were known from later sources and served as important stepping stones in Ventris's decipherment of Linear B. And of course, in the decipherment of Egyptian, it was a very useful fact that the Egyptians represented the Greek names of the kings and queens of the Ptolemy family by phonetically transcribing them into hieroglyphs, as this gave important evidence on the phonetic values of some elements.

Indeed, personal names in a text can often act as a surrogate for a bilingual text. To put this in a modern context, consider that in early September 2008, many people were focused on Hurricane Gustav, and what damage it might inflict upon the US oil industry in the Gulf of Mexico, or on the city of New Orleans, which three years previously had been devastated by Hurricane Katrina. Not surprisingly, there was much discussion of this topic in the international news, and a Google search on the Chinese for 'Gustav'—古斯塔夫 *gǔsītǎfū*—turned up many news stories on this topic in Chinese online sources. Here there was no bilingual text: it simply seemed likely that this topic would be newsworthy enough to appear in Chinese-language newspapers, which is indeed what happened.

FIGURE 4.8 Inscriptions containing the names of Xerxes and Darius from Persepolis
Source: Robinson (2006*b*), used with permission.

In a similar vein, Georg Grotefend (1775–1853), a German high school teacher, expected, rightly, to find the names of Darius and Xerxes in an inscription from Persepolis.[14] Grotefend had already made the assumption that slanting wedges separating strings of glyphs in the cuneiform text were word dividers and that, since the length of the strings between the wedges (i.e. the number of glyphs) was typically rather large, it was most likely that Persian cuneiform was a largely alphabetic writing system. The inscription in question was carved on a doorway above two bas-relief figures, apparently representing kings. Two famous Persian kings from the period were Darius and his son Xerxes, and Grotefend reasoned that these might be the kings depicted. Furthermore, it was known from later versions of Persian that kings were referred to in rather formulaic style and it could be guessed that inscriptions might contain formulae such as: *X, great king, king of kings, son of Y...* (Robinson, 2006*b*: 74). In the two inscriptions in question (Figure 4.8) there was a group of signs in common (marked as '3' in the figure.) Since it was known that Xerxes was the son of Darius and that Darius was the son of Hystapes (who was not himself a king), Grotefend reasoned that the first inscription might read something like *Xerxes... son of Darius* and the second might read *Darius... son of Hystapes*. In that case the string labeled (1) would be the name *Xerxes*, the one labeled (3) would be *Darius*. And presumably the one labeled (4) would be the name *Hystapes*. Note that the string labeled (4) in the second text is in the analogous position to the one labeled (3) in the first, with a very similar text separating both from (2). The names by which we know these kings came from the Greeks, but it was clear

FIGURE 4.9 Grotefend's transcriptions for *Xerxes* and *Darius*
Source: Robinson (2006*b*), used with permission.

that the Greek renditions of the names were not very good since Greek lacked many of the sounds of Persian. Grotefend therefore consulted the Hebrew and Avestan (later Persian) versions of the names. Since Avestan was most likely to be closely related to the language of the inscriptions, Grotefend based his guess of the Old Persian pronunciations on the Avestan forms: *darheuš* and *xšherše*. With these guesses he came up with the tentative transcriptions of the two names shown in Figure 4.9. The string labeled (2) was plausibly a title, since it appeared after both the names *Darius* and *Xerxes*. In Avestan the word for 'king' was *kšeio*—Modern Persian *shah*. This seemed to fit (Figure 4.10): from the two names Grotefend was already able to transcribe the sequence *x-š-e-h-?-?-h*, leaving only two new glyphs, which might therefore plausibly be *i* and *o*. What about the lower string labeled (4)? If that was *Hystapes*, it would have to fit with the original Persian form of that name. For this string, given the previous decipherments, Grotefend had *?-o-š-?-a-?-?*. In Avestan, the name was *goštasp*, which seemed to allow for a match to that pattern (Figure 4.11). The formulaic *great king, king of kings*, expected by Grotefend, does in fact occur in these inscriptions: note that in both texts, the word (2) occurs again twice a little later on in the text. As we now know, many of the signs in this system were syllabic, not alphabetic, and the full text of the second inscription reads (Robinson 2006*b*: 75):

da-a-ra-ya-va-u-š / xa-š-a-ya-θa-i-ya / va-za-ra-ka / xa-ša-a-ya-θa-i-ya / xa-ša-a-ya-θa-i-ya-a-na-a-ma / xa-ša-a-ya-θa-i-ya / da-ha-ya-u-na-a-ma / **vi-i-ša-ta-a-sa-pa**-ha-ya-a / pa-u-ša / ha-xa-a-ma-na-i-ša-i-ya / ha-ya / i-ma-ma / ta-ca-ra-ma / a-ku-u-na-u-ša

Darius, the great king, king of kings, king of countries, son of **Hystapes**, and Achaemenian, who built this palace.

FIGURE 4.10 Grotefend's transcription for *xšehioh* 'king'
Source: Robinson (2006*b*), used with permission.

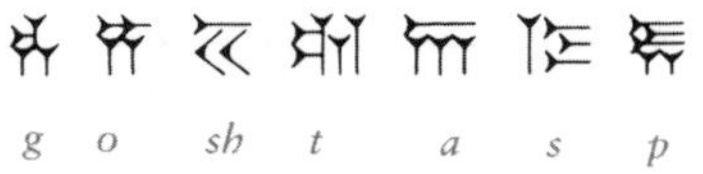

𒄖 𒄴 𒍝 𒀪 𒊭 𒉿 𒉽

g   o   sh   t   a   s   p

FIGURE 4.11 Grotefend's transcription for *Hystapes*
Source: Robinson (2006*b*), used with permission.

Grotefend was wrong in many of his assignments of symbol values, but he nonetheless provided the initial key to cracking cuneiform scripts, a key that went on, in modified forms, to open the doors of Akkadian, Hittite, and ultimately Sumerian. His process involved a number of inspired guesses: that the kings depicted were in fact the kings Darius and Xerxes, famous from history; that the later Persian formulaic references to kings would be found in these early inscriptions; that the language of the inscriptions was in fact Persian and that Avestan would serve as a reasonable key; that the system was segmental, or at least phonetic (as opposed to 'logographic' or 'ideographic'). Any of these guesses could have turned out to be wrong.

With the Rosetta Stone, and the important Bankes Obelisk, brought to England from Philae by William John Bankes), of course, people were on slightly safer ground. With Barthélemy's much earlier hypothesis that cartouches might contain royal names, it was possible to guess that the sequences in Figure 4.12 (from the hieroglyphic text—only one third of which had survived—on the Stone) and Figure 4.13 (from the Obelisk) might contain the names of Cleopatra (Greek: *kleopatra*) and Ptolemy (Greek: *ptolemaios*). Assuming you do not already know this, before reading on, it is worth looking at the cartouches and seeing if you can figure out which one is which, and which symbols probably have which values.

It will have helped to realize that *kleopatra* and *ptolemaios* share *p, o,* and *l*—though for *t* the Egyptians used different symbols in Cleopatra's and Ptolemy's names, and the symbol ⌒ that is used for *t* in *ptolemaios* is used with another function in *kleopatra*. In any event, Figure 4.12 is Ptolemy and Figure 4.13 Cleopatra.

Though the Bankes Obelisk contained both Greek and Egyptian texts, the texts were not, in fact, translations of each other. However, the two texts were sufficiently comparable that they both contained the names of Ptolemy and Cleopatra. For Ptolemy, therefore, it was possible to compare the versions of the name on the Obelisk and the Stone.

Using these sources of evidence, in 1816 Thomas Young correctly identified the 'Ptolemy' in a cartouche from the Stone and furthermore correctly

FIGURE 4.12 A cartouche from the Rosetta stone

identified the symbols for *p, t, m/ma, i, s*); unfortunately he also misidentified eight other symbols. (In 1821, Bankes himself correctly identified 'Cleopatra' on the Obelisk, though he did not propose any interpretation of the individual symbols in the cartouche.) Young also proposed (wrongly) that only foreign names were written in this alphabetic fashion. But with further refinements, and critical work by Champollion on texts from Abu Simbel (see below), by 1822 enough was known for Champollion to present his famous *Lettre à M. Dacier*, containing a list of hieroglyphic symbols and words (Figure 4.14).

Part of what added to the complexity of the task was that at least some occurrences of the cartouches contained material other than the name. The cartouche for Ptolemy actually reads: *Ptolemaios, may he be given life, beloved of Ptah*. The cartouche for Cleopatra contains a semasiogram—the small egg on the right-hand end in Figure 4.13, indicating a female name, plus the symbol ⌒ for *t*, representing the morphological feminine ending (which in Egyptian, coincidentally, would also have been pronounced as *a*, as in Greek.)

Names also figured prominently in the decipherment of Linear B, in this case place names. By early 1952, Michael Ventris had enough of the symbols decoded to be able to make out the name *ko-no-so* ⟨symbols⟩ evidently the rendition of *Knossos*. Another sequence was ⟨symbols⟩ *a-mi-? -so*: this seemed to correspond to the known placename *Amnisos*. Of course, place names themselves told Ventris nothing about the language underlying Linear B. However, the *ko* symbol was also used as the first syllable of two words that people had long suspected meant 'boy' ⟨symbols⟩ and 'girl' ⟨symbols⟩ : using the *ko* symbol from *ko-no-so* and other symbols that had been discovered, he was able to decode these words as *ko-wo* and *ko-wa*—very evidently spellings of early forms *korwos, korwa* of the later Greek words *koros* 'boy' and *korē* 'girl'.

FIGURE 4.13 A cartouche from the Bankes Obelisk

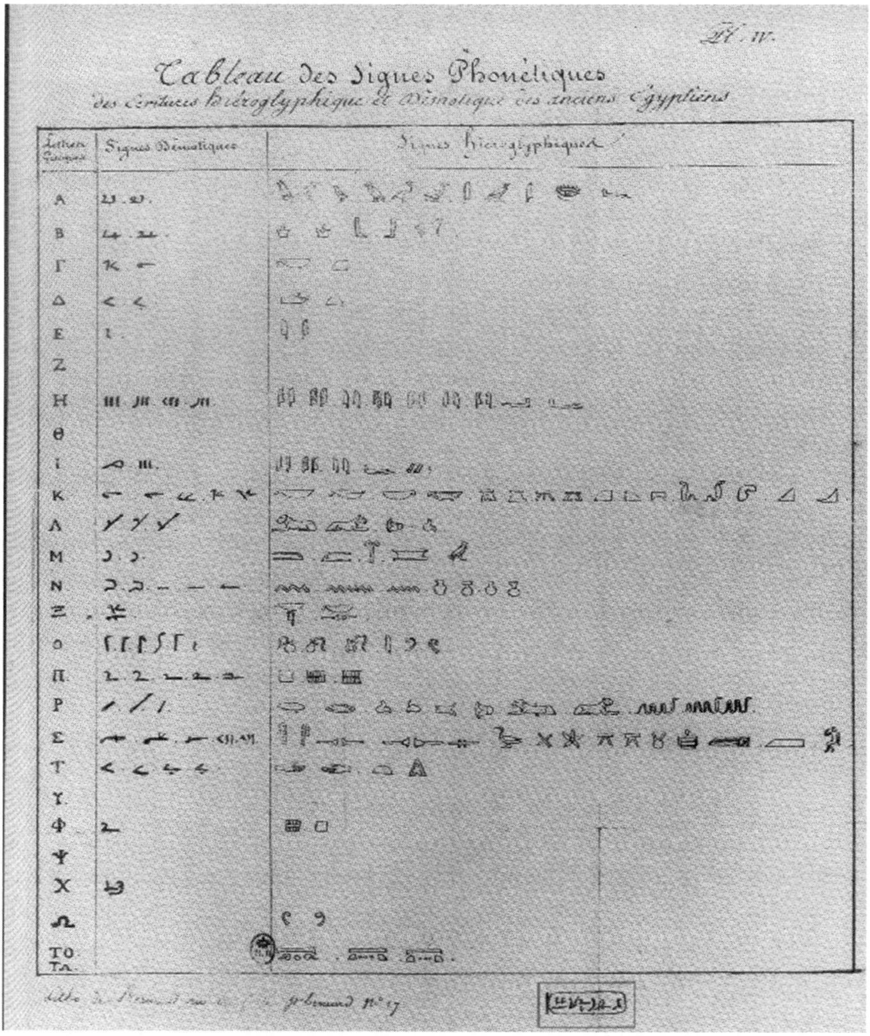

FIGURE 4.14 Champollion's *Tableau des Signes Phonétiques* from the *Lettre à M. Dacier* (1822)

4.2.4 *Structural analysis*

Language is full of recurring patterns. At the simplest level, we can consider simple distributions of elements. For example certain sounds will be more common in any given language than others. In English, the

/i/ sound in *tea* is far more common than the /ʒ/ sound of *plea<u>s</u>ure.* If we were trying to decode a phonetic script for English, we would certainly want to pay attention to the frequencies of symbols, since these would give a clue as to what the symbol would likely represent: in a segmental writing system, given that we have enough representative text, it is unlikely that the rarest sound would be encoded with the most frequently used symbol.

Other kinds of patterns also recur. In English, a common pattern is found in provenance adjectives like *Californian, Canadian, Mexican, European, African.* In a document that deals with places and their citizens, one would expect to find a lot of pairs of words where one word in the pair ends in *-an,* attached to some possibly modified form of the other word in the pair.

A case very much like this was at play in the decipherment of Linear B. Alice Kober, an American classicist who worked on the decipherment of Linear B from the early 1940s until her untimely death in 1950, discovered recurrent patterns of three words that seemed to be variants of one another in the Linear B texts. Two such patterns are shown in Figure 4.15. In each of the 'triplets', the three strings share a common prefix, two glyphs in the case of the first triplet, three in the case of the second. Kober reasoned, correctly as it turned out, that these might have been related words, which differed only in their endings. The second and third entries in each triplet end in the same glyphs, suggesting that these are probably equivalent morphological forms—just as, for example, *Canadian, Mexican,* and *African* are equivalent morphological forms.

Kober's analysis was useful because it suggested that whatever language underlay Linear B, it was probably one that used *suffixes* (rather than, say, prefixes) to produce morphological variants of words. This was perhaps not so surprising given where the language was spoken: all languages of the region have this property. But at least it made it less likely that the language was one that depended heavily on prefixation (e.g. various Berber languages, or Bantu languages of Africa).

FIGURE 4.15 Two sets of Alice Kober's Linear B 'triplets'

The other more immediate utility was that this structural analysis led to an important hypothesis about some of the glyphs themselves. It was already suspected that Linear B must be a CV syllabary. This assumption was motivated in part by the fact that the later Cypriot syllabary (deciphered in 1871 by George Smith on the basis of a Phoenician–Cypriot bilingual text), itself derived ultimately from Linear B, was of this type, and it was assumed that this was a general property of Aegean scripts—something that turned out to be true. Kober noted that if the script were of this type, then each of the elements represented in Figure 4.15 would be a CV (or possibly just a V if at the beginning of the word), and further that the first place in the triplets where the forms differ are probably cases where the C's are shared between glyphs, but the vowels differ. To see this, let us take the six forms in Figure 4.15 and represent them abstractly as in the following table. Here, we use C_i and V_i, for different values of i, to represent the unknown consonants and vowels. Since it was unclear whether the first glyph represented a CV or just a V, we put the C there in parentheses:

$$(C_1) \; V_1 \; C_2 \; V_2 \; C_3 \; V_3 \qquad (C_4) \; V_4 \; C_5 \; V_5 \; C_6 \; V_6 \; C_7 \; V_7$$
$$(C_1) \; V_1 \; C_2 \; V_2 \; C_8 \; V_8 \; C_9 \; V_9 \qquad (C_4) \; V_4 \; C_5 \; V_5 \; C_6 \; V_6 \; C_{10} \; V_{10} \; C_9 \; V_9$$
$$(C_1) \; V_1 \; C_2 \; V_2 \; C_8 \; V_8 \; C_{11} \; V_{11} \qquad (C_4) \; V_4 \; C_5 \; V_5 \; C_6 \; V_6 \; C_{10} \; V_{10} \; C_{11} \; V_{11}$$

Now, assuming that the words in the columns share the same beginnings, and that at least the words in the second and third rows share the same endings, a good hypothesis that would easily explain the data would be that the endings in the second and third rows comprise $V \, C_9 V_9$ and $V \, C_{11} V_{11}$, and the base everything preceding that. This also implies that V_3 and V_7 are the endings of the words in the first column. Then we can deduce the following equations:

1. $C_3 = C_8$
2. $C_7 = C_{10}$
3. $V_8 = V_{10}$

Thus 𝍐 must share the consonant with 𝍉 though differing in the vowel; and similarly for 𝍊 and 𝍋. Whereas 𝍉 must share the vowel with 𝍋, but differ in the consonant. This allows us to set up the following table, where symbols in the same row share a consonant and symbols in the same column share a vowel:

$$\top \quad \wedge$$
$$/\!\!\!\wedge \quad \vdash\!\!?$$

If we further assume that both words in the first row end in the same vowel (i.e. $V_3 = V_7$), then we can collapse this table further as follows:

All of this turned out to be correct. In fact, as we now know, the correct transcription for the two sets of triplets is as follows, where we have underlined the morphological suffixes involved in the alternation:

ru ki t<u>o</u>   a mi ni s<u>o</u>
ru ki ti <u>jo</u>   a mi ni si <u>jo</u>
ru ki ti <u>ja</u>   a mi ni si <u>ja</u>

(Note that 'j' here represents a 'y' sound as in 'you'.) In normalized spelling reflecting something close to the actual pronunciations these corresponded to:

lukt<u>os</u>   amnis<u>os</u>
lukt<u>ijos</u>   amnis<u>ijos</u>
lukt<u>ija</u>   amnis<u>ija</u>

In these forms it is possible to see the Cretan place names *Luktos* and *Amnisos*, and two pairs of provenance adjectives one in the masculine gender (*-ijos*) referring to a man from those places and the other in the feminine (*-ija*) referring to a woman.

Ventris's most fundamental contribution was his extension of Kober's method to the entire set of glyphs for Linear B in the form of his famous 'grid' (Figure 4.16). This consisted of a wooden frame representing a table, each of the cells of which contained a hook on which could be hung one symbol. The rows represented symbols that Ventris believed on distributional grounds started with the same consonant. The columns were for symbols that ended with the same vowel. It is important to realize that during the early stages of this analysis, there were very few of the symbols for which anyone had a reasonable clue as to the actual phonetic form, and Ventris was very conservative in his guesswork on this point. Ventris simply coded the symbols with pairs of letters. Nonetheless, on the basis of later known syllabaries, it was possible to guess at a few of the values. Indeed, Evans himself decoded the sequence ⊨+ (*po-ro*) next to the figure of a horse head as *po-lo* and noted its striking similarity to the Greek word *polos* for young horse (related to the English word *foal*); but Evans rejected this equivalence since he was strongly prejudiced against the idea that Linear B could have been Greek. As Ventris summarizes nicely in his posthumously published *Work Notes*,[15] a number of scholars had guessed that the glyph ⊢ *da* (Ventris' code AB) must have a value like *ta* or *da* (the symbols are the same in both Linear B and Cypriot); that ∩\ *ti* (Ventris AJ) was probably *ti* (these two are similar in the two scripts); and

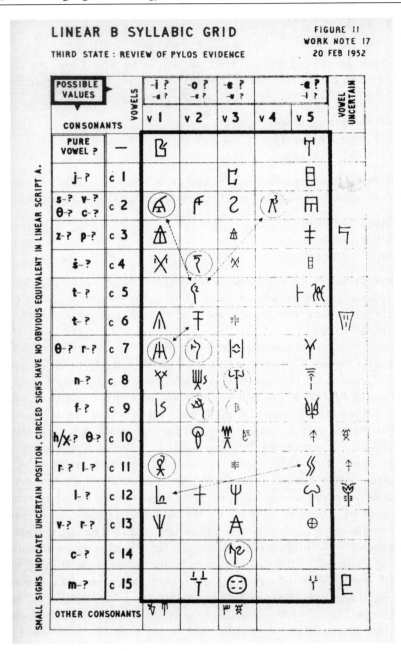

FIGURE 4.16 Ventris's 'grid'

that ≠ *pa* (Ventris AD) was probably *pa* (identical in the two scripts). But a number of the guesses were simply wrong: thus many scholars guessed something like *zo* for |₀ *ra* (Ventris EB) and *pu* or some syllable starting with *s* for 'ϒ *ru* (Ventris EH) (*pu* in Cypriot looks similar to *ru* in Linear B). Indeed, for the eighty-one symbols in Ventris's set, just five of the proposed readings which scholars largely agreed on turned out to be more or less correct.

Guesses about the interpretations of glyphs, even when one's evidence comes from a related known script, can be tricky. As we shall detail further below, Champollion made a bold leap in assuming that the Egyptian symbol ⊙ actually represented the Sun, and that its pronunciation could be guessed at on the basis of Coptic. He turned out to be right. In a similar way, a few of the guesses for the values of Linear B symbols also turned out to be correct, and these combined with other guesses, and the logic underlying Ventris's grid, meant that once things started to fall into place the decipherment proceeded very rapidly.

But it is important to bear in mind that structural analysis and guesses about the values of glyphs only prove their worth when they lead to a solution. One of the common errors of pseudo-decipherers is to point to their seemingly logical and reasonable set of structural analyses and guesses as to the values of glyphs, and assume that because these analyses are reasonable-seeming, they must *ipso facto* be on the right track. But only solid verification can demonstrate this, the topic to which we now turn.

4.2.5 *Verification*

As we have already noted, a decipherment proposal is a scientific hypothesis, and as such there is only one way in which it can be taken seriously as a hypothesis, and that is if it passes the test of independent verification.

The best verification that can be had is remarkably similar to what modern computer speech and language researchers do when they have a model—say a speech recognition system—that they have constructed with some data, and they want to get an honest measure of how well the system will perform in the field. As we will see in Chapter 7, the standard approach is to test on unseen *held out* data. In the case of decipherment, the same principle applies: in order to verify a decipherment proposal, one *must* have an independent source of data against which to test the proposed decipherment. Even better, if someone other than the original decipherer can apply the proposal to data the decipherer could not have seen, then we can be very sure that the decipherment is valid.

Now, in general, any correct conclusion that follows from the decipherment, and that is something the decipherers themselves could not have known, counts as confirmation. When Michael Ventris first wrote on 13 July 1952 in reply to a communication from John Chadwick about his decipherment of Linear B into early Greek, he expressed concern about a number of features. Ventris's decipherment already had a large measure of plausibility since one of the properties of this early Greek dialect was the presence of a /q/ sound in places where later Greek dialects had /p/ or /t/. Thus the word for horse, which in the later Attic language of Athens was *hippos*, showed up as *i-qo* in the Linear B tablets. The suffixed conjunction 'and', which in Attic was -*te*, appeared as -*qe* in the tablets. But it was already surmised by scholars that Greek of such an early date must have had this sound in these places; indeed comparison between Greek and related languages, such as Latin, more or less forced that conclusion. In the particular examples at hand, the Latin words are *equus* 'horse' and -*que* 'and'. Mycenaean Greek was a lot more like Latin than later Greek in this regard.

But there were other curious features. One of these, which Ventris noted in the letter to Chadwick, was the lack of definite articles. Attic Greek had articles, and these articles have been preserved for the past 2,500 years, and remain as a feature of Modern Greek. Ventris, like any English public-school trained boy of his generation, had studied Classical Greek. He was therefore puzzled by the lack of articles in this much earlier language that was none-theless clearly Greek. For Chadwick, who was an expert on early Greek dialects, this was not a problem. For, as he noted:

... there was no reason to be bothered by the absence of the definite article; philolo-gists had anticipated its absence in the early stages of the language.[16]

This and a number of other points that Ventris could not have known, but Chadwick did, served to convince Chadwick that Ventris must be on the right track.

For Linear B, the held-out corpus came from new excavations at Mycenae by the American archaeologist Carl Blegen. Blegen had been the original discoverer of Linear B tablets at Pylos on the mainland in 1939.[17] Prior to that time, Linear B had only been found in Crete, which lent credence to Arthur Evans' contention that they represented the language of the non-Greek Minoan civilization. After Blegen's discoveries, this idea suddenly seemed less likely—though Evans was apparently still right about Linear A being uniquely Minoan. Blegen continued to find tablets and in 1953, around the time of Ventris's announcement, Blegen discovered a new hoard of tablets at Pylos. Knowing of Ventris's proposal, he was able to apply the phonetic values that Ventris had come up with for the signs and quickly realized that the system worked. One of his tablets contained a catalog of various kinds of containers (Figure 4.17), including a three-legged bowl known from later Greek sources as *tripodes* (this is the plural form), and a bowl with four handles, which were known as 'ears' (later Greek *ous*). The containers themselves were depicted with pictograms on the tablet, and next to each of these was a sequence of Linear B glyphs, evidently the names of the depicted objects. Using Ventris's values, Blegen was able to discover that the tripod 𐀴𐀪𐀡𐀆 was *ti ri po de*, and that the four-eared vessel was 𐀤𐀵𐀫𐀸 *qe to ro we*. The first was obviously the Linear B rendition of the Greek word *tripodes*. The second is only slightly harder to interpret: the *ro we* sequence is evidently the portion meaning 'ear'—*ous*—plus an *r* that was presumably part of a previous morpheme. The first portion *qe to (r)* must mean 'four', giving the whole meaning as 'four eared', appropriate for this vessel. Attic Greek for 'four' was *tetra*, but this was a case where the earlier form must have had a 'q'—note Latin *quattuor* 'four'—so *qe to (r)* was clearly the right form. If someone other than the decipherer can use the values and read a new text in a way that makes sense, that is clear confirmation.

Even better if several people can use the decipherment independently of each other and come up with a solution on a new text that makes it clear that the solution must be correct. Such a case was the decipherment of Babylonian by Henry Creswicke Rawlinson (1850–51). Like many ancient 'mixed' systems, Babylonian writing was baroque. There were many ways to write the same sound, and each glyph could have multiple interpretations, as logograms, semasiograms, or various phonograms. Such fluid interpretations are a reality—Modern Japanese writing is an excellent example—yet they are a bugbear for the decipherer not only because the complexity makes it difficult to find the solution, but because it is also difficult to convince others that one is right. Clearly if I am attempting to decipher a new script and I claim that each glyph may have multiple interpretations, one's first reaction *should be*

FIGURE 4.17 Some containers from a list on a tablet found by Carl Blegen; a tripod and a *qetorowe* 'four-eared' vessel

suspicion: by making enough assumptions of this kind, I can fit any text to any preconceived notion that I may have about what it says.

Thus, in the mid-nineteenth century, people were generally skeptical that Babylonian had been deciphered. In 1857 the Royal Asiatic Society received a letter from W. H. Fox Talbot containing a sealed translation of a text from the reign of Tiglath Pileser I (Middle Assyrian period, 1114–1076 BC), along with a request to keep the translation sealed until Rawlinson had completed his translation, which Rawlinson had promised would be completed soon.[18] Talbot proposed that the two translations should then be compared, and if they were sufficiently similar, then this would convince people that the decipherment of Babylonian was a success.

Rawlinson not only agreed with this proposal, but suggested that two further scholars—Edward Hincks and Jules Oppert—be asked to provide translations, again independently of Talbot's and Rawlinson's own translations. When the four translations were examined by a specially appointed committee, it was found that the translations were so similar that there was no doubt that the decipherment was real. The following sample passages, quoted in Couture (1984), illustrate this:

Rawlinson: Then I went on to the country of Comukha, which was disobedient and witheld the tribute and offerings due to Ashur my lord.

Talbot: Then I advanced against Kummikhi, a land of the unbelievers who had refused to pay taxes and tribute unto Ashur, my lord.

Hincks: At that time I went to a disaffected part of Cummukh, which has withheld the tribute by weight and tale belonging to Assur, my lord.

Oppert: In these days I went to the people of Dummukh, the enemy who owed tribute and gifts to the god Asur, my lord.

Of course, one does not have to have achieved a more or less complete decipherment, as in the case of Linear B or Babylonian, in order to have verification that what one has so far is reasonable. After all, it is useful to know if one is on the right track. A good case in point comes from the decipherment of Egyptian. Thomas Young and Jean-François Champollion had already provided phonetic values for a number of symbols, but there were a number of questions that could not be answered by the cartouches containing Greek names. First of all, the Ptolemaic cartouches provided no evidence on a crucial question: while Greek words were clearly written phonetically, what about native words? It seemed entirely possible that Egyptian was primarily 'ideographic', except for cases where a word had to be transcribed phonetically. Second, because the names were Greek, they give us no insights about the underlying language. Many people suspected that Coptic was the descendant of Egyptian: after all, where else would the language have come from? But without a key into the ancient Egyptian vocabulary, one could not be sure.

Champollion's inspired guesswork (1822) on the cartouche from an inscription from Abu Simbel provided answers to both these questions, and provided further confirmation for the work that had already been done. A version of this cartouche is shown in Figure 4.18; the figure is here flipped from its original right-to-left orientation. The symbols labeled (3) and (4) were already known from the Rosetta Stone to represent 's'. The first symbol, (1), seemed to be a depiction of the sun; in this version of the cartouche it is represented as the head-piece of the falcon-headed version of the Sun god. Suppose, reasoned Champollion, Egyptian really was the ancestor of Coptic, and suppose the word for sun in Egyptian was therefore something like the Coptic word *re*. With two out of the three symbols decoded in this way, one could already see the skeleton of a name appearing: *r_ss*. Champollion reasoned that the name might be *Ramses*, known from Greek sources as *Ramesses*. He therefore proposed *m* as a reading for the middle symbol. In fact this was wrong: the reading is *ms*, rather than *m*, with the first *s* (3) acting as a so-called 'phonetic complement' for the *ms*. Subsequent decoding of the name of *Thothmosis*, which contained symbols 2 and 3, and an initial pictogram of an ibis, known to be a symbol for the god Thoth, provided further confirmation. Further confirmation still came from the Rosetta Stone, where symbol (2) was found to be aligned with the Greek word *genethlia* 'birthday': Champollion knew that the Coptic word for 'birth' was *mīse*, confirming the *m*—in fact *ms*—reading for this glyph.[19]

With the decoding of Ramses' and Thothmosis' names, Champollion was able to establish three important points. First, the work up to that point was apparently on the right track, since previously decoded symbols played a role

FIGURE 4.18 A cartouche from Abu Simbel

in deciphering this cartouche. Second, the Egyptians apparently did write their own language phonetically, not just names of foreigners; indeed, as we now know, *most* of the beautiful pictographic symbols one sees on Egyptian monumental texts have the rather mundane function of representing sounds. Third, Egyptian was apparently the ancestor of Coptic. Both of these latter points were extremely useful as the decipherment work progressed.

Of course, even though it seemed to make sense, Champollion's guess could have been wrong: at the time, most of the system was unknown and it could have turned out, on further investigation, that this cartouche did not represent the name of Ramses. This brings us to one last crucial point about decipherment, and that is that in all cases of real decipherment, the work progressed as it built upon previous work. In some cases, as with Linear B or Babylonian, the work was done largely by one scholar in the course of a few years of work. In others, as in the case of Egyptian, or Mayan, it involved many decades of work by dozens of scholars. But in either case things did not stand still.

This is one reason to be skeptical of claims by Asko Parpola and colleagues in Helsinki that they have provided the keys to a decipherment of the Indus symbol set. It now seems doubtful that the Indus symbols (used between 2600 and 2000 BC in the Indus Valley, in modern-day Pakistan and India) were part of a true writing system in any case.[20] But putting that issue to one side, and assuming for the sake of argument that they do represent true writing, the basic problem with Parpola's claims involves time. Starting in the 1960s and continuing into the 1970s, Parpola and colleagues provided electronic encodings of the available texts, and did various structural analyses of the symbol distributions using computational techniques. This computational work was carried out in collaboration with the well-known computational linguist Kimmo Koskenniemi, and made use of some methods due originally to Zellig Harris (Noam Chomsky's advisor at the University of Pennsylvania), variants of which are still used today. Parpola's hypothesis was that the underlying language was Dravidian, a language family that today is almost exclusively found in South India, and represented by major languages such as Tamil, Malayalam, Kannada, and Telugu. Parpola (though not necessarily other Indologists) assumes that Dravidian languages were more widely spoken in South Asia in the third millenium BC. As we have already noted, based on its frequency and distribution, Parpola surmised that the 'jar' symbol ⎰⎱ was probably a suffix, possibly a possessive marker in particular, but what he is most famous for is the 'fish' series, illustrated in Table 4.1. The words for 'fish' and 'star' were similar in early Dravidian, both having pronunciations like *mīn*. Parpola suggested that the fish symbol, which is common in the Indus

TABLE 4.1: A portion of Parpola's Indus "fish" series, showing various modified forms of the basic fish glyph, and Parpola's interpretations of these

Signs		Dravidian gloss	Literal meaning	Translation
夰	fish	mīn	star	star
夰	roof+fish	mey/may mīn	black star	Saturn
夰	halving fish	pacu mīn	green star	Mercury
夰 ‖	space fish	vel(l)i mīn	white star	Venus
夰 ♨	figtree fish	vata mīn	north star	north star
夰 ⦀	six fish	caru mīn	six star	Pleiades

inscriptions (it is the fourth most common sign) might be so common precisely because many of the texts referred to stars. Furthermore, some of the combinations in which the fish symbol found itself seemed compelling. There is one that looks like a fish with a Vietnamese hat (second row in Table 4.1), which might perhaps be a roof. The word for 'roof' (reconstructed by Parpola as *mey*, though other sources have *vey*) was similar to the word for 'black' (*may*), and Parpola suggested that this roofed fish might represent 'black star'—a Tamil name for Saturn. A few other combinations with interesting associations of this kind were found.

On the face of it this would seem to be much like Champollion's decoding of Ramses, but there are a couple of important differences. First of all, we knew all along that there were Egyptian kings named Ramses: the name is famous from history. In contrast, we do not know that the Indus Valley people called Saturn the 'black star' (even if they *were* Dravidian speakers): the fact that one finds this expression in Tamil is probably of little use, given the 2,000-year gulf between the Indus civilization and the first records of Tamil in the second century BC.[21] Also, because of the cartouche, it was known that the text inside must represent a name, and so a word like *Ramses* is clearly appropriate. On the Indus seals there is no indication at all that suggests that the interpretation 'Saturn' is right: there are no drawings of stars, nothing that would indicate an astronomical theme other than Parpola's own arguments.

The second important difference is that there has been no follow-up. The Helsinki team famously claimed to have cracked the Indus code in papers published in 1969 and 1970.[22] Since that time, while Parpola has continued to work on the problem (publishing a comprehensive volume in Parpola 1994), and has proposed decipherments for a couple more symbols, there has essentially been no progress.

If Farmer, Witzel, and I were right in our paper cited in note 20, this is because the Indus Valley symbols were not writing, and therefore any attempt to decipher them by normal linguistic decipherment techniques is bound to fail. But in any case, the work on Indus decipherment is a good example of what one does *not* find in successful decipherment work.[23]

Writing, Literacy, and Society

Anyone who is reading this book possesses an ability that for millennia was something never attained by the vast bulk of humanity, and was rather reserved for the elite few. Literacy was initially the purview of a class of technicians—scribes—who were trained in the use of the technology. In many cultures, over time, it broadened its coverage so that one did not specifically have to be trained as a scribe in order to know how to read and write. Nevertheless, it was a skill that was severely restricted in that access to literacy depended upon access to more general education, something that was simply not available to most people.

In the modern world, literacy is of course far more widespread. Needless to say, there are still pockets of illiteracy: in India, for example, 26.6 percent of the male population and 52.2 percent of the female population was illiterate as of 2007.[1] Yet for large parts of the world, literacy is more or less taken for granted.

What literacy means, its effect on thought and society, and the factors that lead to improved literacy, are the subject of this chapter. As we will see, for something that is so taken for granted, and is so much a part of our modern thinking that it is one of the basic indicators of a country's development, there is much that is unclear about literacy. Anthropologists and historians debate its role in the development of thought and culture. And language policy makers try to increase literacy by re-engineering writing systems to make them easier to learn. There is little consensus on these issues, though we will try to argue here that at least some of the common assumptions about literacy are off the mark.

5.1 What is 'literacy'?

What do we mean when we say that a person is literate? And what do we mean when we say that a society is literate? The answer to these questions will likely seem obvious. A literate society, after all, is a society where there are writing systems for the language or languages spoken by the people who are members of that society. And someone who is literate is simply someone who knows how to read and write.[2] But these simple definitions mask a whole set of complexities that have to be considered before we can understand the social impact of literacy.

The first question that has to be asked of a literate society is which language it is literate in? For literacy for many people does not mean literacy in one's own language. For many centuries, Korean literati were literate not in Korean, but in Classical Chinese, a language that nobody spoke natively.[3] In a similar vein, literacy in medieval Europe frequently meant literacy in Latin. Even today, many people are literate in languages that are not their first language; as one example, while there are standards for writing the Andean language Quechua, hardly any Quechua are literate in their own language; literacy for Quechua speakers effectively means literacy in Spanish.[4] In such a situation, learning to read and write no longer merely refers to learning to map symbols to the units of one's language. Instead, in order to be considered literate, one must also learn a different language. This situation frequently perpetuates itself, especially when the number of literate people is small. The Korean literati who had mastered Classical Chinese had little interest in switching to Hangul, when it was promulgated by King Sejong in 1446. Being literate was both a product of and a guarantor of privilege, and it is rare that a privileged class will give up their privileges. As a result, they deprecated literacy in Hangul, and in effect refused to consider it to be proper literacy.

This brings us to the second critical issue with literacy, namely the size and function of the literate population. In principle a society could allow all of its members to be literate, but economic pressures make this an unrealistic goal for many. But there have been many societies where the class of literates has been effectively engineered from the top level so that only a very few members of the society become literate. This was the situation in Egypt, early Mesopotamia, Mycenae, and in early China, where literacy was the province of scribes. In China, writing began with the inscriptions on turtle shells and cattle scapulae, recording the divinations of diviners, the prognostications of the king, and an assessment of whether the predictions were correct.[5] The scribes who recorded the divinations may have been separate from either the diviners or the monarch. The Mycenaean Greek scribes who used Linear B to record the economic affairs of the administration were a similar class of technicians. The closest analog we have today is probably the court stenographer.

In such societies, writing is viewed as a purely technical means to the end of recording a particular kind of event. As far as we know, the first writing in Shang dynasty China was never used for any other purpose than to record the results of divinations. To the best of our knowledge, the Mycenaeans never thought to extend the use of Linear B beyond its purely administrative function: the 'contemporary account of the Trojan war' that scholars had hoped Ventris's decipherment might eventually lead them to was never forthcoming, evidently because it was never written. One upshot of this is that a society may be literate, but still retain strong vestiges of an 'oral' society for the simple reason that writing has failed to penetrate into the fabric of society as a whole. Only when writing has permeated further: when it is used to write not only accounts, or divinations, but also laws, histories, agricultural and technological techniques, and belles lettres; only then is a society really and truly literate.

But even in societies that are literate in this sense may have limits on who may gain access. Ancient Athens, often touted in the scholarly discussions of literacy that we will examine further below as a society where democratic ideals were borne of widespread literacy, was anything but egalitarian. As Harris argues at length in *Ancient Literacy* (1989), while we have little direct evidence for the actual rate of literacy in classical times, it is nonetheless clear that it would not have been very high. Probably far less than one-tenth of the entire population of fifth-century Attica would have had significant literacy— though, perhaps surprisingly, among the literate would have been a few slaves, taught to read and write for the purpose of reading to their masters, or for clerical work. It is worthwhile remembering in any case that as a 'democracy', Ancient Athens had more in common with countries like Kuwait with its huge immigrant worker population and a small number of citizens, than it did with modern democracies of the kind we are familiar with.

A final issue with literacy is the type of materials used for writing. Clearly some materials are easier to manage than others. A standard joke in Goscinny and Uderzo's classic *Asterix* comics has all correspondence among the Romans and the Gauls inscribed on marble: the letter carrier at the beginning of *Asterix and the Normans* is depicted as lugging a huge sack full of marble slabs; the Roman soldiers are required to file reports in triplicate, meaning that they must be chipped with a hammer and chisel onto three slabs of marble. Clearly no society where functional literacy depended upon such a bulky material ever existed, hence the joke. Clay is clearly an improvement over stone, and in Mesopotamia, clay was the main material on which text was written: it fixed the wedge-shaped form of the script, so that even when writing was carved into rock, it still took the form made by the stylus on clay. Yet clay is obviously far from ideal as a writing medium: it is messy to work with, it can be broken, and it is hard to carry around. Certainly writing was very important in Mesopotamia and served many functions: writing was used not only for accounts (its original purpose), but for laws, dedications, histories, religious devotions, stories, and letters between citizens. This is testament to the fact that while clay was not ideal, it was probably good enough. But it is clear that the functions of literacy were limited. It was simply not possible to carry around documents with hundreds of pages' worth of text in the form of clay tablets. As argued by comparative historian Steve Farmer and colleagues,[6] this only became possible with lightweight materials—papyrus, bamboo strips, cloth, vellum, and paper—and it is only with such materials that we see a real explosion of the consequences of literate society.

5.2 The social impact of writing and literacy

Technology has a way of changing the way people live. Two hundred years ago, when sailing vessels were the only way of traversing the Atlantic, a scientist in New York would need a very strong motivation indeed to attend a scientific congress in Paris. Even one hundred years ago, when steam vessels had reduced the Atlantic crossing to about a week, attending such a meeting would have been both time-consuming and expensive. Nowadays, of course, it is simply a matter of taking a seven-hour flight. Furthermore, with technologies such as videoconferencing, or Skype, one can even attend the meeting without being physically present. Clearly technology can have a profound effect on life and society.

The effect of writing and literacy has been similarly deep. For literacy has the power to change the way people think and act. If there is one thing that is clear about writing, it is that it has the potential to create a permanent record of ideas. Of course that does not mean that those ideas cannot become distorted, a point to which we will return at various places below. But oral cultures *must* depend literally on word of mouth, as well as prodigious feats of memory on the part of people who want to maintain the traditions and lore of the society. As a result, the collective memory forgets. Writing allows people to preserve their traditions and history—or at least a sanctioned version thereof—for indefinite periods of time without requiring any more than the ability to read and interpret. Writing is often viewed as being more authoritative than speech. In many religions, in particular those of the Judeo-Islamic type, *scripture*—the written form of what is purported to be God's Word—is considered absolute and unmodifiable: as we already saw in Chapter 3, the introduction of vowel diacritics in Hebrew, Aramaic, and Arabic was motivated in large measure in order to 'fix' the written text.

But despite the effect that writing clearly has on a society that possesses it, it has been fashionable in some branches of cultural anthropology to downplay the difference between literate and oral cultures and to analyze the culture and thought of oral cultures in terms that have their origin in our own lettered culture. Perhaps most famous of these is the relativistic view of Claude Lévi-Strauss (1970) that placed 'cold' ('wild') and 'hot' ('domesticated') cultures on a par.

One of the best-known counterarguments to this view of oral cultures was presented by Jack Goody in *The Domestication of the Savage Mind.*[7] Writing, insofar as it represents speech, is essentially linear, with the time dimension of speech being replaced with a spatial dimension in writing. But writing is done on a two dimensional surface, and this introduces a degree of freedom that is hard to replicate in speech. This property of the surface allows for constructs such as tables, which have no ready counterpart in speech, as well as lists. Of course it is possible to list things in spoken language, but the permanence of writing allows one to construct much larger lists, and the two-dimensional aspect allows one to clearly delineate the elements of the list. Thus as Goody explains, in literate cultures from the Egyptians and Sumerians onwards, one finds lists of all kinds of things, such as types of plants, cures for various diseases, and lists of grammatical forms of the language. And this in turn leads to new ways of thinking about the world, encouraging the development of taxonomies that are far more sophisticated than one finds in oral cultures.

An even stronger example is the table, something that is extremely hard to imagine in speech, but comes readily when one has two dimensions at one's disposal, and where the eye can jump around in the table and assimilate the relationships between entities implied by the rows and columns.[8] Tables by their very nature present analyses of data. The rows represent one kind of feature, the columns another. For example, a table that deals with human development in various countries might have, as the rows, the various countries being treated, and as the columns the various economic or social factors being considered. As Goody notes, once one has a table, it is incumbent upon one to fill all the slots in the table: if there is a column that represents the GDP (Gross Domestic Product) of a country, then it is expected that every row will have a number corresponding to the value of the GDP for the country in question. Of course, one may be missing data for that particular variable for that particular country: in that case, one has to indicate in the table that the datum is missing, or else substitute some other appropriate value, such as the GDP from a previous year, with a note to that effect. Thus tables force an ordered way of thinking about phenomena, one that is far less clearly forced in oral societies, which lack such constructs.

Indeed, Goody argues that in contrast to literate societies, oral societies have none of these analytical tools at their disposal. In oral cultures, all communication is necessarily by word of mouth. This means that 'history' as it is recorded in oral societies can only be transmitted by stories that are handed down from generation to generation and memorized. But these stories are mutable. An example from Goody and Watt (1968), a precursor to Goody's book, illustrates this point:

> The state of Gonja in northern Ghana is divided into a number of divisional chiefdoms, certain of which are recognized as providing in turn the ruler of the whole nation. When asked to explain their system the Gonja recount how the founder of the state, Ndewura Japka, came down from the Niger Bend in search of gold, conquered the indigenous inhabitants of the area and enthroned himself as chief of the state and his sons as rulers of its territorial divisions. At his death the divisional chiefs succeeded to the paramountcy in turn. When the details of this story were first recorded at the turn of the present century, at the time the British were extending their control over the area, Jakpa was said to have begotten seven sons, this corresponding to the number of divisions whose heads were eligible for the supreme office by virtue of their descent from the founder of the particular chiefdom. But at the same time as the British had arrived, two of the seven divisions disappeared, one being deliberately incorporated in a neighbouring division because its rulers had supported a Mandingo invader, Samori, and another because of some boundary changes introduced by the British administration. Sixty years later, when the myths of state were again recorded, Jakpa was credited with only five sons and no mention was made of the founders of the two divisions which had since disappeared from the political map.

Thus, in a very important way, oral societies, such as the Gonja, are focused on the 'here and now'; all history is subservient to the needs of explaining the current situation. By lacking written records, much less such constructs as lists or tables, it becomes harder for members of an oral society to think critically about their lore. Of course it is perfectly possible for such trans-mutations of history to happen in literate cultures too, and they frequently do. But literacy at least holds the possibility that, no matter what the 'official' version of history is, there may be surviving documents that tell a different story.

Goody and Watt (1968) argue that alphabetic literacy, in particular, was a key factor in the rise of analytical philosophy, science, and democracy in Ancient Greece. The benefits of literacy to analytical thinking will have a broader effect, the more members of society can participate in the process. On this model, alphabets are supposedly significantly easier to learn than syllab-aries or mixed semantic-phonetic systems such as Sumerian or Chinese, if only because the number of symbols to be learned is so much smaller. There is an up-front cost in that alphabets typically represent segmental phonemes, something we have suggested are somewhat unintuitive compared with syllables. So one must at least master the mapping between symbols and these unintuitive linguistic units. But once one has done that, and assuming the writing system in question is regular in its spelling–sound correspondence (which Ancient Greek was, though English obviously is not), then the system can fairly readily be learned. Thus, Goody and Watt argue, the introduction of alphabetic literacy in Greece was a catalyst to rapid changes in Greek thought, since it enabled widespread literacy, given that the system was quite easy to learn. Not only analytical thought about philosophy and science, but concepts of democracy also developed, in large measure because laws became accessible to a large number of people who could then debate the merits of those laws.

Of course, there are a couple of problems with Goody and Watt's arguments here. For one thing, it is easy to overstress the extent to which Athenian society *was* egalitarian, as we noted above, and hence how many people were actually literate. Secondly, as we shall argue below, there is no evidence to support the idea that script type has any influence on literacy rate.

The idea that it is alphabetic literacy in particular that is critical for creative thinking has been around for many years and has appeared in many guises. Moorhouse's *Triumph of the Alphabet*[9] was unequivocal in its praise for the cognitive benefits of the Greeks' invention. Various chapters in the De Kerckhove and Lumsden (1988) collection present arguments in favor of the alphabet as a facilitator of analytical thinking. Probably the most extreme view along these lines is expressed by William Hannas,[10] which we briefly saw in Chapter 3. For a short time, *The Writing on the Wall: How Asian Orthography Curbs Creativity* (2003) made a splash in the popular press, with a review in the *New York Times* and discussion in other forums. Hannas's basic thesis is that East Asia has a serious technological creativity gap with the West, and that the root cause of this is the writing systems in use in various East Asian countries, including China, Korea, and Japan. Accepting at face value Hannas's argument that East Asian countries are notable for lacking technological creativity,[11] one is naturally interested in understanding why this should be so. Why is it that a region of the world which produces some of the most creative minds, when educated abroad, is seemingly incapable of producing true innovation itself? Hannas's argument boils down to the thesis that East Asian writing, which is centered around the syllable, requires less analysis on the part of the learner than does an alphabet. When one learns an alphabet, one must analyze speech into a set of phonemes, units that are quite unintuitive and which illiterate speakers, or speakers of languages that use non-alphabetic scripts, tend not to be consciously aware of. When one learns Chinese characters, obviously there is a lot of memorization to do, but insofar as each character represents a phonological syllable, there is not a lot of actual analysis one has to do. Syllables, after all, are units of speech that even illiterate people are aware of, as we have pointed out already. So in learning a syllabic writing system, one is essentially learning to map a sequence of symbols one-for-one onto a sequence of syllables. No further analysis is required.

Hannas's claim is both shocking and intriguing. If he is right, then the simple remedy of enforcing romanization in Japan, Korea, and China would solve the problem. But one's gut feeling is that the story cannot be right. As I argued in a review of Hannas,[12] the use of syllabaries certainly requires analysis on the part of the would-be learner since, as we argued in Chapter 3, it is almost never the case that spoken syllables map in a trivial fashion to individual symbols in the syllabary. Furthermore, the main writing system of Korea, Hangul, is a segmental system. While the symbols are certainly organized into syllable blocks, it is hard to avoid the conclusion that Korean speakers learning to read must go through the same segmental analysis that learners of linear alphabetic scripts go through.

In any case, if indeed there is a creativity gap to be explained, there are some more obvious sources of it than the writing systems. The core of East Asian culture—what former Singapore Prime Minister Lee Kuan Yew liked to call 'Asian values'—stems from an ancient and politically expedient interpretation of the views traditionally ascribed to Confucius. These values include filial piety to one's parents and, by extension, to the state, and a blind observance of tradition. One by-product of 'Confucian' values is the traditional Asian education system, which centers not around developing an individual's creativity, but rather around memorizing accepted texts for later recitation. The Chinese expression for memorization, 背書 *bèi shū*—literally to 'turn one's back on the book'—sums this up rather nicely, for in traditional schooling one literally showed one's mastery of the material by turning one's back on the book and reciting from memory. This characterized education during Imperial times in China, where the student was prepared by rote learning for performance in the civil service examinations. The situation in traditional Korea and Japan was entirely similar. This also, of course, characterized education in medieval Europe; the practice was not unique to Asia. But the spread of printing using moveable type in Europe and the widespread availability of multiple Classical as well as contemporary sources that this afforded gradually eroded this authoritarian approach to education,[13] in a way that was not matched in East Asia. Much has changed over the past century in Asia, but memorization for the purposes of passing exams, and unquestioning respect for authority, still figure prominently in Asian society. None of this does much to spur on creativity. For creativity requires that one question the status quo, question why something is true—not merely accept it—and, yes, question authority. Societies that do not encourage such questioning will inevitably suffer in terms of creativity.

One suspects in the end that the *kind* of writing system one has is not a major factor in how technologically and scientifically creative one will be. After all, Chinese writing in principle allows for quite a bit of analysis: the semantic-phonetic structure of most characters invites the learner to use the information to guess the meanings of characters that they do not know and, often (in the case of native speakers), to match up a previously unknown character with a word that they already know from speech. Traditional teaching of writing in China does not make explicit mention of this structure, yet children who are able to do the analysis required to figure out the structure of characters also tend to be better readers.[14] Such analysis surely exercises the mental faculties in a way similar to that exercised by alphabetic writing. So, again, the problem is likely not with the writing system itself, but rather with the education system in which the teaching of reading and writing is embedded. As we will argue below for literacy, if you want to increase your country's technological creativity, toying with the writing system may not be the most natural place to start.

5.2.1 *Beyond Goody*

The work of Goody and his colleagues in the 1960s is among the first work to examine the role of literacy in shaping society. As with any pioneering work, the assertions were perhaps a bit too bold, and the shift between illiterate and literate culture is not as clear a phase transition as Goody implied. A more accurate understanding depicts the change instead as one of *multiple stages*, whose first leap certainly coincided with the advent of literacy, but where there were many subsequent leaps. A second leap that has been argued to be relevant is the kind of widespread and pervasive literacy that becomes easier to achieve when lightweight materials are used for the writing surface. In a paper that covers a wide range of issues related to exegetical thought, including the development of monotheism, Steve Farmer and his colleagues[15] have argued that these conditions lead over time to what they term *stratified* or *layered textual traditions*. Ancient written literature, whether it be the Chinese classics, or the Bible, or the works of Plato, invariably shows up in multiple versions with variations. One version of the text has a particular passage; another omits it and perhaps replaces it with another, possibly contradictory passage. In any complex compendium, such as the Bible, the version that we possess today has been through innumerable changes since the texts were first written. In the case of the Bible, there were many texts that never made it into later versions, and were discarded as heretical; the New Testament we know today, for instance, was decided by committee at the Council of Nicaea in AD 325,[16] though this was merely the culmination of three centuries of disputes about the authenticity of varying accounts. Anyone who believes that the Bible that has come down to us over more than two thousand years is the unadulterated word of God is deluding themselves. What we have instead is a text that has been worked and reworked over the millennia, much as a house that has undergone many phases of structural remodeling.

This layered structure to such texts comes at a price, since each generation of scholars feels the need to rationalize the often conflicting versions through exegesis of the available texts. But this exegesis in turn encourages a particular kind of correlative thinking, one that Farmer and colleagues argue derives ultimately from human neurobiology. Some of the kinds of correlative thinking outlined by Farmer, Henderson, and Witzel include:

- The assignment of supernatural beings from a variety of textual traditions to a variety of 'grades' of beings, resulting in theories such as those in the Christian tradition involving the different levels of angels and demons.
- Cyclical theories—such as the many reincarnations of the Buddha—arise from the attempt to reconcile different seemingly contradictory accounts by assigning them to different cycles.
- Concepts such as heaven and hell arise out of conflicting stories that are resolved by placing elements in a hierarchical fashion.

A late example of this trend discussed by Farmer et al. is the chart in Figure 5.1 from Robert Fludd's *Utriusque Cosmi maioris scilicet et minoris metaphysica, physica atque technica historia* (1617–21), which shows parallels between various physical and supernatural entities, and seeks to reconcile apparent contradictions between theories of these entities by putting them in an orderly arrangement. The columns represent classes of entities: divine beings, the sidereal world, minerals, stones, plants, trees, aquatic beings, birds, quadrupeds, and colors. The rows represent groups of entities from different groups that are somehow correlated. On the left of the chart are musical scales, which are also to be correlated with the elements in the rows. While the details of Fludd's chart are, from our perspective, obviously nonsense, the use of tables to elucidate parallels between different domains is clearly a property of real science. For example, as any electrical engineering student knows, the wave equations that describe the acoustic properties of uniform lossless tubes are identical to the equations for a lossless uniform electrical transmission line:[17]

Harmonia Mundi Sympathica, 10 Enneachordis totius naturæ Symphoniam exhibens.

Enneachor'ton I	Enneach. II	Enneach. III	Enneach. IV	Enneach. V	Enneach. VI	Enneach VII	Enneach VIII	Enneach IX	Enneach X
Mundus Archetyp. DEVS	Mundus Sidereus Cœl.Emp.	Mundus Mineralis	Lapides	Planta	Arbores	Aquatilia	Volucria	Quadrupedia	Colores varij
Seraphim	Firmamentum	Salia,ftellæ Minerales.	Aftrites	Herbæ & Flor.ftell.	Frutices Bacciferæ	Pifces ftellares	Gallina Pharaonis	Pardus	Diuerfi Colores
Cherubim	♄ Nete	Plumbum	Topazius	Hellebo-rus	Cypreffus	Tynnus	Bubo	Afinus, Vrfus	Fufcus
Troni	♃Paranete	Æs	Amethi-ftus	Betonica	Citrus	Acipenfer	Aquila	Elephas	Rofcus
Domina-tiones	♂Paramef.	Ferrum	Adamas	Abfynthiû	Quercus	Pfyphias	Falco Accipiter	Lupus	Flammeus
Virtutes	☼ Mefe	Aurum	Pyropus	Heliotrop-ium	Lotus,, Laurus	Delphinus	Gallus	Leo	Aureus
Poteftates	♀Lichanos	Stannum	Beryllus	Satyrum	Myrtus	Truta	Cygnus Columba	Ceruus	Viridis
Principatus	☿Parhypa.	Argentum Viuum	Achates Iafpis	Pæonia	Malulpu-nica	Caftor	Pfittacus	Canis	Cæruleus
Archangeli	☽Hypate	Argentum	Selenites Cryftallus	Lunaria	Colutea	Oftrea	Anates Anferes	Ælurus	Candidus
Angeli	Ter.c ûEle. Proslamb.	Sulphur	Magnes	Gramina	Frutices	Anguilla	Stru thio camelus	Infecta	Niger

FIGURE 5.1 Chart showing 'the sympathetic harmony of the world' from Robert Fludd's *Utriusque Cosmi maioris scilicet et minoris metaphysica, physica atque technica historia* (1617–21)

$$-\frac{\partial v}{\partial x} = L\frac{\partial i}{\partial t} \qquad (5.1)$$

$$-\frac{\partial i}{\partial x} = C\frac{\partial v}{\partial t} \qquad (5.2)$$

where v is voltage, i is current, L is inductance, and $C =$ capacitance. To underscore the analogies between the two domains, any textbook on digital signal processing will display a table like that in Table 5.1.[18] This example, needless to say, is a far cry from Fludd's fanciful cosmology, much less the primitive correlative analyses that came from early textual exegesis. But viewed from the broader perspective, one can see this as an endpoint in a system that started five thousand years ago when people first learned to correlate marks on a writing surface with words that came out of their mouths.

Returning to Goody's original analysis, it should be stressed that not all the benefits he described depend upon writing, strictly defined. After all, one can have tables, or lists, of symbols that are not part of a true writing system. What is critical is that the symbols allow one to represent entities, so that the arrangements into tables, lists, and so forth can be interpreted as defining

TABLE 5.1 An example of a modern correlative model: analogies between lossless tubes and lossless electrical transmission lines

Acoustics	Electricity
p: pressure	v: voltage
u: volume velocity	i: current
ρ / A: acoustic inductance	L: inductance
$A / (\rho c^2)$ acoustic capacitance	C: capacitance

Source: From Rabiner and Schafer (1978: 63, Table 3.3).

relationships between the entities. One example of a symbol system that seems to have been used in this way is the *rongorongo* of Easter Island (Rapanui). The *rongorongo* was a symbol system developed by the Easter Islanders themselves, and preserved in texts inscribed with sharks' teeth or obsidian on wood, mostly driftwood. While hundreds of texts apparently existed when they were first described by the French missionary Eyraud in 1856, only a handful survive today. Nobody knows how old the system is. Easter Island tradition has the system going back to the first settlers in the 800s, but Fischer (1997*b*) has argued that the islanders developed a symbol system after getting the idea of writing from Spanish visitors in 1770: the Spanish asked representatives of the islanders to 'sign' a treaty ceding the island to the king of Spain, and the islanders' 'signatures' involving a few symbols, some of which bear some resemblance to *rongorongo* symbols, are preserved in the treaty. Fischer's thesis has some plausibility since none of the eighteenth-century explorers—Roggeveen, Cook, or La Pérouse—reported on a symbol system in use by the islanders. The basic symbols of the system number in the hundreds according to the standard classification of Barthel (1958), though many scholars have argued that Barthel's symbols are decomposable into a simpler set. One side of one of the best preserved texts, the *Mamari* ('egg') tablet, is shown in Figure 5.2. The symbols are often anthropomorphic or zoomorphic, with one of the distinctive features being alternations between head and hand shapes as well as poses of the figures. Another curious feature is that texts were written in *reverse boustrophedon*: the text evidently began at the *bottom* of the tablet running from left to right. The next line reversed the direction, but instead of flipping the symbols across the vertical axis as in early European boustrophedon, the figures were rotated 180 degrees to upside down. In addition to the artifacts themselves, there is a fair amount of ethnographic evidence for the culture of *rongorongo*. The most extensive records were made by the British ethnographer Kathleen Routledge

FIGURE 5.2 Mamari Tablet

Source: Stéphen Chauvet, 1935, *L'Île de Pâques et ses mystères*, Editions Tel, Paris.

in her 1914–15 visit to Easter Island.[19] There she was able to interview a few of the islanders who were young boys during the mid-nineteenth century when the system was still in active use. They record ceremonies in which hundreds of '*rongorongo* men' from all over the Island took part in a competition presided over by the the 'king' (*ariki*). The participants were required to read from their tablets, and were rated on their performance.

Most scholars who have addressed the problem have assumed that *rongorongo* is writing, but in fact very little evidence exists that this was the case. Many scholars have proposed that the system consists of some sort of phonetic or mixed phonetic-semantic symbols (like Sumerian, Chinese, Egyptian, or Mayan). Yet despite serious work by a number of people over half a century, and the many papers that have been published that analyze the structure of the symbol system, there has been essentially no progress on actual decipherment. This is surprising if it was a real writing system, since on the face of it the conditions for decipherment would seem to be close to ideal. There is a fair amount of text (the corpus consists of about 12,000 glyphs in Barthel's coding of the texts, though there is also a lot of repetition of material across tablets); we know a lot about the language spoken by the ancient Easter Islanders; and through the early ethnographic studies, we even have some

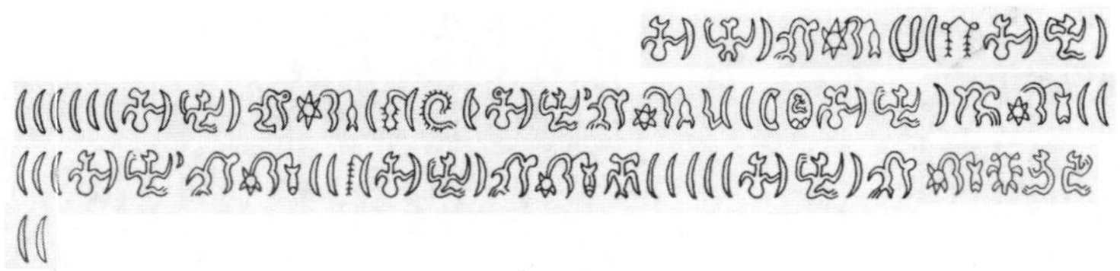

FIGURE 5.3 The calendar of the Mamari tablet

knowledge of the *rongorongo* chants. The ethnographer Alfred Métraux believed (though also without much evidence) that the system was a mnemonic system where particular symbols evoked ideas, or even whole stories, which would then be generated by the *rongorongo* chanter during his performance. Such systems do exist: the most famous case of a mnemonic system of this kind is that of the Naxi of southwest China, already mentioned in Chapter 4.

Indeed the one piece of text that has been clearly interpreted is a portion of the Mamari tablet, shown in Figure 5.3. The symbols, most of which look like crescent moons, clearly suggest something like a calendar, and Barthel was the first to suggest that this was what the sequence was. However it fell to the French scholar Jacques Guy, to demonstrate this.[20] He did this by comparing the sequence of moons and interspersed symbols with three versions of the Easter Island calendar recorded by ethnographers. He was able to show that the interspersed symbols, such as the central symbol indicating the full moon, clearly corresponded to the various 'named' nights in the old Rapanui calendar, and he was also able to propose interpretations for some of the symbols. The full moon, @, which on closer inspection looks a little like a small figure of a man sitting next to some cooking stones, corresponds to the Polynesian's 'cook in the Moon' (corresponding to our 'man in the Moon', or the Chinese 'rabbit in the Moon'). Guy also argues that the boxed figure sequences in Figure 5.3 were to be interpreted as instructions on when to add an extra night, depending on the apparent size of the moon: since the orbit of the moon is misaligned with the night–day cycle as well as the yearly cycle, a lunar calendar requires constant maintenance to keep it aligned with the seasons. The Easter Islanders were evidently adept at adding nights to their calendar when things got out of sync.

A calendar clearly represents a kind of list, and the Mamari calendar, following Guy's analysis, represented a fairly sophisticated symbolic representation of an algorithm for maintaining the lunar calendar. This clearly shows the benefit of a graphical system, but it does not in and of itself depend upon writing; once again, *rongorongo* has not been shown to be writing in the strict sense we have adopted here. What is critical here is only that the Easter Islanders were evidently adept at symbolizing ideas with graphical symbols. As Roy Harris (1995) has argued, writing, insofar as it is a form of graphical communication, shares with other forms of graphical communication the property of using two-dimensional space. Thus, it inherits tables and other graphical ways of organizing information from non-linguistic symbol systems. Whatever function those graphical devices have in these non-linguistic systems carry over in part or in whole to versions that involve true writing.

Of course, it remains true that without full writing, one will be limited in the sets of things that one can represent. The Easter Islanders could represent calendars. It is not clear that they would have been able to represent tables of medicines and their properties, or lists of grammatical forms of the Rapanui language. So, to extend the benefits of graphical representation, and thus to have a broad effect on the cognition of a society, Goody is still right: one needs writing.

In a sense none of this is surprising. We saw at the beginning of this book that Mesopotamian writing evolved out of a proto-writing system involving numbers and a few symbols for kinds of commodities. In neatly arranged tablets that represented commodities and their amounts, Mesopotamians invented the table before they invented full writing. Indeed, one might speculate that writing evolved in Mesopotamia in part *because* of the tabular representations of goods. Tables, as we have said, more or less force one to fill in the values for all the slots, or at least to explain why some value is missing. There is another thing they do: they invite other rows and columns. It is all very well if I can write the names of the animals, grains, oils, and cloth that I own and the amounts that I have. What if I am a merchant: might I not want to add a column indicating the name of the person(s) from whom I have purchased the items, or to whom I have sold them? Might it not be useful to have yet another column that indicates the place the items came from? And these in turn would put pressure on users of the system to invent ways to represent names of people and places. And this in turn would encourage the development of phonetic encoding, leading to full writing.

5.3 Increasing literacy in a society

Whatever one may conclude from the previous discussion of the role of literacy in shaping culture and thought, one cannot deny that the ability to read and write plays a fundamental role in most societies. It is hardly surprising then that one of the goals which many governments over the past few hundred years have set for themselves is the goal of enhancing literacy in their countries.

5.3.1 *Script engineering*

A common approach to increasing literacy is what might go under the term of *script engineering*. A famous case was the invention of Hangul by King Sejong, which we already examined. In this case, a wholly new script was invented that was intended to be simpler for the common people to learn than the traditional Chinese writing that was used in Korea, and continued to be used for many centuries after Sejong.

The mid 1990s witnessed spelling reforms for various European languages, notably German, Dutch, and French. The Dutch reform of 1995 involved many changes that were intended to make the spelling system more rational. One change that received a lot of attention from the public and linguists alike was the respelling of the so-called 'linking morpheme' in compounds, replacing an earlier set of principles that had themselves been put in place as part of the spelling reform of 1954. The linking morpheme in question is illustrated in the word *paardekracht* 'horsepower' (*paard* 'horse', *kracht* 'power'), spelled according to the 1954 convention, and highlighted in bold in the example. The 'e' here is pronounced as a schwa (ə). But it is also pronounced as a schwa when spelled 'en' as it would be in *paardenliefhebber* 'horse lover'. The motivation for the different spelling under the 1954 convention had to do with semantics. If the left-hand noun was interpreted as singular, it should be spelled 'e', if plural as 'en'. Note that 'en' is one of the ways in which Dutch nouns spell their plural forms, and while linguists would argue that the linking morpheme is really a separate thing from the plural marker, the fact that they may both be spelled as 'en' tends to associate the two in Dutch readers' minds. The idea in these particular examples is that horse lovers typically love more than just one horse, whereas horsepower refers to the power of one horse. But this is a tricky principle to apply in general, so the 1995 reform did away with all that and declared that the morpheme should be spelled 'en' if, and only if, the left-hand noun formed its plural exclusively in 'en'; otherwise it should be spelled as 'e'. One noun that forms its plural exclusively in *-en* is *paard*. For our two examples, this meant that now *both* would be spelled using 'en': *paardenliefhebber*, *paardenkracht*. This would perhaps be fine, except that the new system also allowed for systematic exceptions. One such exception: a plant name where the left-hand member is the name of an animal, an example being *paardebloem* 'dandelion' (literally 'horse flower'). By the general rule this should now have been spelled *paardenbloem*. But there are many such plant names in Dutch, and so to avoid having to change a lot of spellings in botanical texts, it was agreed to leave these spellings alone. Thus 'dandelion' is spelled *paardebloem*. There are several other exceptions to the general rule. As with any committee decision, a simple principle can easily become complicated by lists of special cases, so that the result is no simpler than the system being replaced. In the end, the *paardebloemregel* ('dandelion rule') caused enough consternation that in the subsequent reform of 2005, it was dropped. The correct spelling now is *paardenbloem*. In any case, it is highly unlikely that the kind of low-level fiddling exemplified by the Dutch reforms has any effect whatsoever on literacy.

Perhaps the most famous script reform aimed explicitly at increased literacy was the simplification of Chinese characters initiated under the Communist government of Mainland China starting in 1956. Chinese writing reform itself has a much longer history, dating back more than two thousand years when the First Emperor, Qin Shi Huang, standardized the Chinese script from a variety of regional variants in 219 BC, at the founding of the Qin dynasty.[21]

In its modern context, script reform in China started off with more or less concerted efforts to propose romanizations. Romanized versions of Chinese dated back to the sixteenth century, when the first Jesuit missionaries entered China and set about learning Chinese in order to negotiate with Ming Dynasty officials. But these romanizations were intended solely as a pedagogical aid to the missionaries themselves and to any other Westerner who would learn Chinese. The first attempts to develop romanized scripts for use by the Chinese themselves were by Protestant missionaries working in the provinces, who were usually interested in preaching to their converts not in standard Chinese, but in the local regional language. Since these local varieties of Chinese had no written version (learning to read Chinese meant learning to read a heavily classical version of the Standard), they were fertile ground for innovation. Indeed, many of these missionaries found that they could achieve great success in teaching literacy in their simple and phonemic romanization, with adults who had previously been illiterate learning to read and write in a very short amount of time. But even illiterates in China were aware that 'real' writing involved the traditional characters, and ultimately these schemes all failed since they ran afoul of Chinese traditions.

It was not until the fall of the Qing dynasty and the founding of the Republic of China in 1911 that serious attempts to *replace* the traditional script with romanized orthographies were proposed. There were a number of systems proposed—*Guoyeuh Romatzyh* or 'national language romanization' being merely the most famous—and a number of prominent figures were involved in the process. Among these were the great Chinese linguist Y. R. Chao (Zhao Yuanren) and the writer Lu Xun. But again, these systems never took off, and the most that came of them were alternative methods of romanizing Chinese for the benefit of foreign learners.

In 1935, a serious proposal was put forward to reform the Chinese script by simplifying characters.[22] The proposal did not fly, and was quickly forgotten: one of the reasons for the failure may have been the impending war with Japan. But it did serve as the inspiration for subsequent reforms. With the fall of the Republic on the mainland and the founding of the People's Republic of China in 1949 came a new interest in reform of the script. Mao had already told the American Journalist Edgar Snow in 1939 that he viewed romanization as inevitable. For a while it looked as if there would be a serious move in that direction. But then in 1956 came an edict that rather than replacing the script with a wholly new one based on the roman script, instead the traditional script would be streamlined by character simplification. As DeFrancis (1984) notes, while this move came with the claim that the Chinese government had tried romanization and that it had failed, there was in fact no evidence that romanization was ever seriously attempted. Perhaps Mao was ultimately convinced by the argument that though romanization might aid literacy, it would come at the cost of rendering older texts written in characters inaccessible to the majority of people. But as we will see later on, this is a price other societies have been willing to pay.

The simplification of the script consisted of two steps, namely the elimination of some characters, and the simplification of the stroke counts of others. But the authorities were apparently never really serious about character elimination. According to DeFrancis (1984: 260), out of the 10,000 characters that were part of the Chinese telegraphic standard, only 7 per cent were eliminated during the simplification process. Modern information technology gave the potential for a substantially more significant effect in this regard. Prior to Unicode, two basic standards were developed for encoding Chinese text electronically. The Big5 standard, variants of which are used in Taiwan and Hong Kong, was designed to encode traditional characters, and encodes about 13,000 characters. The GB-2312(1980) standard, widely used in the Mainland and Singapore, was designed for simplified characters, and had a much smaller set of used code points—only 6,763. Since one is effectively limited to the character code points provided by the encoding if one wants to store or transmit text in a standard, the upshot is that if one wants to use the Mainland standard, one has only half of the characters that are available if one uses the Taiwan standard.[23]

The second aspect of writing-system simplification was character simplification, which also involved two basic types. The first was the simplification of the whole character, for example the character 國 *guó* 'country' was replaced by 国; or 車 *chē* 'car' simplified to 车; or 馬 *mǎ* 'horse' simplified to 马; or 個 *gè* (a 'classifier' morpheme that must be used when counting particular kinds of objects) as 个. In many cases these simplified versions stemmed from traditionally accepted script variants derived from cursive writing styles.

The second type involved the simplification of the semantic or phonetic components of the characters. When such a component is a separate character, then any simplification of that separate character is usually also carried over to the character when it functions as a component. Thus 魚 *yú* 'fish', simplified to 鱼, also functions as a semantic component in the names of many kinds of fish, and appears in its simplified form. Compare the traditional form of the character 鯉 *lǐ* 'carp' with its simplified form 鲤; note that the 魚 component on the left-hand side replaces the four dots under the body of the fish (derived from the fish's fins and tail in the original pictograph—see Figure 3.1) with a single line, as in the full form of *yú*.

The 1956 simplification was augmented in 1964, and a further simplification was proposed in 1977, though this last simplification was soon retracted. According to DeFrancis, overall 2,238 characters and 54 character components were simplified.[24] This resulted in a fairly substantial reduction in the number of strokes that one has to write. DeFrancis reports an estimate on the basis of 250,000 characters of running text, that the average stroke count of the characters has been reduced from 9.15 to 7.67—a 16.1 per cent reduction.

Thus far things seem reasonable enough: at least the number of symbols was somewhat reduced and in principle the amount of work required to learn the system might seem to be less, given that there is an overall complexity reduction for the whole system. But of course the real question is whether simplification made any difference in the rates of literacy. To be sure, China's literacy rate has increased dramatically since 1949: according to Zhao and Baldauf (2008), and many other sources, the pre-1949 literacy rate in China was less than 20 per cent, whereas today it is over 90 per cent. But surely most if not all of this can be attributed to economic improvements in China over the past six decades, and in any case the literacy rate of Taiwan (where traditional characters are still used) is an even higher 96 per cent.[25]

Indeed, DeFrancis cites some evidence that suggests that until the early 1980s simplification did little to improve literacy—if by literacy we mean minimally the ability to read and write characters correctly. In 1982, there appeared tacked to lampposts around Tianjin the sign shown on the left in Figure 5.4. While the first two characters are correct and interpretable as *mǎchē* 'horsecart', the third character does not exist, and while the fourth and fifth do exist, they make no sense in the context: the combination means

FIGURE 5.4 DeFrancis's *horsecart* example. On the left, the characters that actually appeared; on the right the correct form of the characters.

"struggle". This sign caused some puzzlement, until it was realized that what was intended was the version on the right of Figure 5.4: 马车带粪兜 *mǎchē dài fèndōu* 'horsecart carry manure bags' (in traditional characters: 馬車帶糞兜)—an injunction to horsecart drivers to carry manure bags and pick up after their animals. The fourth character that was used was a homophone for the correct one, the fifth character a homophone except for a difference of tone. The third pseudo-character is broadly similar in form to the intended one, meaning that the author of the sign had simply forgotten how to write the character correctly. As DeFrancis points out, the writer was presumably someone in a position of some authority—likely a Party cadre, and therefore exactly the sort of person who should have benefited from the revolution in writing that character simplification was supposed to represent. The fact that three out of five reasonably common characters were miswritten suggests that simplification helped only marginally, if at all, with the task of learning to read and write Chinese.

Why did simplification fail? As I argue in my review of Zhao and Baldauf (2008):[26]

Simplification may have eliminated the numbers of strokes in quite a few characters, it may (in some cases) have improved the predictability of the 'phonetic' component, and it may further have resulted in the elimination of some characters. But it did not change the fundamental nature of the Chinese writing system. No matter how you look at it, learning to read and write Chinese is *work*: you simply have to memorize a lot of material. Certainly once you know a couple of thousand characters, learning the remainder that you are likely to need (between 5,000 and 7,000) becomes much easier. But it is that initial step of learning the first couple of thousand that is hard, and simplification did nothing to address that issue.

Given that character simplification did little to improve literacy, it is worth revisiting the question of why the Chinese government did not pursue a more radical reform—romanization, or some other phonetic system—that would at least have made the *initial* stages of learning to read and write easier (though in and of itself would probably not have done much to increase functional literacy). It is an obvious enough point that if there had been the will to make this step, it could have been implemented: Mao clearly had the power to enact exactly this reform had he chosen to do so.

The situation in China was in some ways rather parallel to the situation in Turkey in the 1920s after the fall of the Ottoman Empire. Mustafa Kemal ('Atatürk') implemented a series of reforms between 1920 and 1924 with the explicit goals of eliminating the traditional features of Turkish culture and aligning Turkey with the West. Among these were proscription traditional Turkish dress including the fez, and elimination of the unwieldly Arabic script-based writing system, replacing it with a highly phonemic Latin-based system; Figure 5.5 shows Kemal teaching the new script in 1928. This reform did come at a price: it meant that older documents written before the reform became inaccessible to people who had not learned the older script. This remains a problem today for Turkish historians who do not know the original script, and cannot read Ottoman-era documents, unless someone has gone to the trouble of transcribing them into the new orthography.

Obviously this concern—cutting off the literate population from the past—did figure in the Chinese decision not to pursue romanization. Also, it is clear that China was not particularly interested in aligning with the West and, after the early limited period of friendship, was not interested in aligning culturally with the Soviet Union either (and thus cyrillization would not have been an option). Still, there remain some glaring inconsistencies here. While Mao himself clearly loved the classics, and was in addition a master calligrapher, there were a number of periods, most notably the Cultural Revolution, when study of the old literature was not permitted. So, as a practical matter, it would probably have made little difference had the script been reformed, since nobody was reading the classics anyway. And the Western origin of the Latin script was surely a red herring also. After all, China had ostensibly adopted Marxism-Leninism as its political model, a wholly

FIGURE 5.5 Mustafa Kemal teaching the new Latinized Turkish orthography, 1928

Western political system, despite attempts by the PRC to give it an Asian face. And had the Latin script still remained a problem, they could have invented a native phonemic script—as had already been done with *zhuyin fuhao*, the phonemic script invented during the early Republic and still used in Taiwan to teach children to read characters. So the reasons for avoiding total elimination of the old writing system do not ring particularly true given the political context at the time that reforms were being proposed.

5.3.2 *What really contributes to literacy?*

So if simplifying a script does not automatically lead to higher literacy, what does?

William Harris's excellent study of *Ancient Literacy* (1989) makes what in hindsight should be an obvious point: no matter how simple a script may be, unless there is a motivation to learn to read and write, people will generally not do it. The motivations may be various. According to Aristotle, there were four basic functions for literacy: 'moneymaking, household management, instruction, and civic activities'.[27] While one might add many other reasons to Aristotle's list, his are at least reasonable motivations, but again individuals have to feel, or be taught, the motivations, and they have to have an opportunity to learn to be literate. There needs to be sufficient time for education, and an infrastructure for ensuring that. People who believe that making a script simple will solve illiteracy forget that literacy is much more than merely learning a couple of dozen symbols from an alphabet. Functional literacy—in any writing system—takes years of practice. There has to be the economic foundation to support this.

In fact, it is remarkably simple to make the case that literacy is a product of economics and, indeed, has little or nothing to do with the complexity of the writing system in use in a country.

The United Nations Development Programme (http://hdr.undp.org/) publishes annual reports on 340 development indicators for 174 countries. These include economic indicators such as the per capita gross domestic product, and the percentage of people living on under $4 a day; health care factors such as the per capita expenditure on health care; environmental factors such as the use of renewable energy sources; and social factors, such as education levels and the level of adult literacy. Since these data are all readily available, it is easy to answer the question of what factors correlate best with adult literacy.

First of all we need to say something about what is meant by literacy in this discussion, since it has a rather more specific definition than the one we have heretofore been assuming. To some extent this varies from country to country. Thus, according to the UNDP's primer on *Measuring Human Development*,[28] a person is considered literate in Morocco if they can read and write a simple statement about their life; whereas Macedonia adopts the more bureaucratic definition that someone is considered literate if they have completed schooling at least through grade 4. The UNDP bases its definition on that of UNESCO, which is similar to that used in Morocco: an adult, aged 15 or above, is considered literate 'if she or he can read and write well enough to understand a simple statement related to her or his daily life'.[29] Even with this simple definition, there are certainly complicating factors. As we noted already, in many parts of the world, being literate means effectively being literate in a language other than the one that one speaks at home. For example, this is true in many parts of China, where one learns to read and write the national standard Mandarin in school, rather than one's own local language. It is also true in the Arabic-speaking world, where written Arabic is a quite different language from the various regional colloquial dialects. In such cases, one not only has to learn to use the symbols that are part of the writing system, but one must also learn a second language.

Many economic factors correlate with literacy, so defined. In what follows we will use a standard measure of correlation—Pearson's coefficient—to show relationship between two variables, where the second variable is always the percentage of adults (defined as people over 15) who are literate according to the above definition. A perfect correlation has value 1.0; a perfect *negative* correlation has value –1.0—negative, meaning that as one variable increases in value, the other decreases. If two variables are completely uncorrelated the Pearson's coefficient is 0. It is exceedingly rare in real examples to find perfect correlation or perfect lack of correlation so in practice one considers the strength of the correlation: a correlation above 0.6 (or below –0.6 for negative correlation) would certainly be considered to be pretty strong.

A variety of indicators and their correlation with adult literacy are given in Table 5.2. Not surprisingly there is a good correlation between the percentage of children who reach fifth grade, and the level of adult literacy, though note here that this indicator was computed only for those children who at least entered first grade. There is a good *negative* correlation with the percentage of people employed in agriculture: the more people employed in agriculture in a country, the lower the literacy rate, not surprising given the intense manual labor required in most agricultural societies. Health factors such as nutrition (children under height or weight), and the quality of care of the mother and infant at birth also correlate—the latter very strongly. Attendance of skilled health professionals at birth is more normally associated with maternal health, but it surely correlates in any case more widely with the quality of health care in the country. Furthermore, causality may feed in both directions: as suggested by Bor (2005), a literate population makes the dissemination of health-care information easier and more effective. Figure 5.6 plots the correlation between the percentage of births attended by skilled health personnel and adult literacy.

Returning to Table 5.2, one factor that does *not* correlate with literacy is the complexity of the script. To get the data for script type, I considered, for each country, the script used by the dominant language(s), and then for each script I provided an estimate of the number of symbols that a user must learn in order to attain minimal mastery of the system. For most scripts these were based on the number of code points assigned to the basic symbols in Unicode (www.unicode.org); for scripts that include capitalization, I counted lower and upper case letters separately, since these both need to be learned, and in many cases the uppercase version of a letter is not simply a larger version of the lowercase letter. For Korean, the individual *letters* (*jamo*) were counted, rather than the combined Hangul syllable composites, since it is the *jamo* that are the basic units of the script. Similarly, for Ethiopic, I counted the basic consonant symbols and the vowel diacritics separately, rather than counting

TABLE 5.2 Development indicators and their Pearson's coefficient *R* of correlation with adult literacy rates

Indicator	R
% of children who started grade 1 and reached grade 5	0.57
% of population employed in agriculture	−0.62
% of children under height for age	−0.64
% of children under weight for age	−0.69
% of births attended by skilled health personnel	0.83
Contraceptive use	0.73
Complexity of script	0.09

the composites as single units. For Chinese and Japanese I based the estimates on commonly cited figures that for Chinese one needs about 5,000 characters, and for Japanese about 3,000; note that Japanese includes learning the two kana syllabaries, which together add about 150 symbols to the set. Obviously these counts are very rough: there are many languages that use the Latin, Cyrillic, and Arabic scripts, for example, and among these languages the number of symbols that are considered basic varies widely.[30] The figures therefore represent no more than a ballpark estimate of the number of symbols a user must learn (Table 5.3).

Script complexity, so defined, has almost no correlation with literacy. Of course, this crude definition of script complexity hardly tells the whole story. It is not just the number of symbols that one must learn, but also how they are used in the system, that makes a writing system harder or easier to learn. Spanish has slightly more letters than English in its alphabet, yet English is much harder to learn to read and write because of the highly complicated spelling rules of English compared with the very 'phonetic' writing system of Spanish. Japanese, while having fewer total symbols in common use than Chinese, is much harder to learn since, as we saw in a previous chapter, there is a highly complex mapping between the symbols in the script and the words of the language: characters with six or seven different context-dependent pronunciations are not unusual in Japanese. But note that if we were to improve our definition of complexity, the correlation would only be *worse* not better. Some of the countries with the highest levels of literacy, such as most of the countries of Western Europe, have old writing systems that, as with English, have accrued lots of irregularities that make learning to read and write a challenge. Apart from English, other such writing systems include French, Danish, and Swedish. On the other hand, some countries with the lowest levels of literacy are countries in Africa where, at least for the native

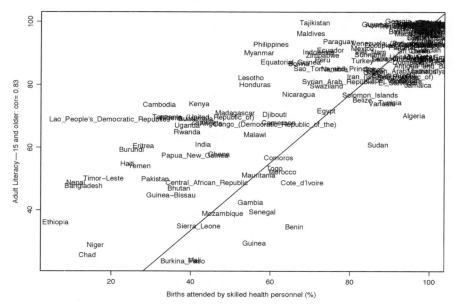

FIGURE 5.6 Adult literacy as a function of the percentage of births attended by a health-care professional

Note: Data points are shown with the country names. Also shown is the regression line for the data.

languages, the writing systems are much newer: in many cases, the languages are written in adaptations of the Latin alphabet, in ways that are highly 'phonetic' and thus in principle easy to learn.

None of this is to say that there is no difference between scripts and writing systems or that these differences have no effect. It obviously takes more effort to learn to read English, or Chinese, than it does to read Spanish. But it is easy to forget that literacy is more than just knowing a script and how it encodes your language. It also requires a command of the written genre: the style of written text, the types of topics discussed in writing (as opposed to speech), the grammar and vocabulary of written language—mastery of all these is critical to functional literacy, and these are things that must be learned in a formal setting, no matter what kind of writing system you happen to use. Imagine a speaker of Spanish, who has previously had no contact with written materials, and has just learned the letter-to-phoneme correspondences for Spanish; such a person is unlikely to find it easy to understand a passport application form. In any case, what these data do suggest, very strongly, is that if you are a government official charged with increasing literacy rates in your nation,

TABLE 5.3 Script complexities for a variety of scripts: the (rough) number of symbols that need to be mastered for full literacy in the script

Script	Number of symbols
Arabic	120
Armenian	75
Brahmi	70
Chinese	5,000
Cyrillic	65
Thaana	40
Ethiopic	40
Georgian	40
Greek	50
Hangul	40
Hebrew	30
Japanese	3,200
Roman	50

fiddling with the details of the script is probably not the best place to start. Far better to convince the Ministers of Economic Development and Health to do something about the economic well-being and health of the population.

And really, none of this should be surprising. As Harris (1989: 14) usefully reminds us:

The invention of a short but efficient alphabet by certain Phoenicians and Greeks made the tasks of learning to read and write almost as easy as they could be. However, as subsequent events have repeatedly shown, widespread diffusion of this knowledge does not by any means automatically follow; the history of Western culture passed through many centuries during which hardly anyone learned these skills although they are within the capacity of almost every five-year-old.

Widespread illiteracy in Western countries was a direct result of economic and social conditions, not the difficulty of the writing systems involved.

5.4 The literate oral culture

Genuine attempts to increase literacy, even ones that are flawed in their reasoning, are to be praised. For the benefits that literacy give to a society that possesses it, and in particular one that possesses it in a cheap and widespread form, are very clear.

But it is important to remember that the social benefits possible with literacy are by no means guaranteed by it. For as with any tool, writing can be misused. The social benefits that we have examined, such as the preservation of the past[31] and the removal of people's thoughts from the 'here and now', and the preservation of knowledge with the development of new modes of inquiry afforded by the ability to make critical comparisons among different ideas that are written down: all of these benefits depend upon the proper use of writing. It is perfectly possible to use written texts in a way that nullifies those benefits. Worse, precisely because the texts *are* written, people have a natural tendency to trust them, so the potential for abuse is strong indeed.

Of the various dystopic visions that sprouted in English literature in the mid-twentieth century, none is more poignant in this regard than Orwell's *Nineteen Eighty-four*. Oceania is literate, and most of the functioning of the society depends heavily upon literacy. And yet in many ways Oceania is a classic case of an oral society. First and foremost, the past is no longer preserved in any meaningful sense. Indeed, just the opposite is true:

Day by day and almost minute by minute the past was brought up to date. In this way every prediction made by the Party could be shown by documentary evidence to have been correct, nor was any item of news, or any expression of opinion, which conflicted with the needs of the moment, ever allowed to remain on record. All history was a palimpsest, scraped clean and reinscribed exactly as often as was necessary. In no case would it have been possible, once the deed was done, to prove that any falsification had taken place. (George Orwell, *Nineteen Eighty-four*, Part 1, ch. 4.)

In every sense this (ab)use of writing allows it to be used the way legend is used in purely oral societies, as documented by Goody and others: fabricated history serves to support the present.

Why end our account of the history of the social impact of writing with a work of fiction? Because, unfortunately, Orwell's account is less fictional than we might like to believe. For there are powerful political forces in many parts of the world that are not notably friendly to the benefits of literacy. Religious fundamentalism, and radical nationalism, are noteworthy for being unsympathetic to unbridled inquiry, to any questioning of the established dogma. For these movements, the past is of no interest, except the version of the past that they create for their own ends.

As Steven Pinker has argued,[32] the classic notion of the 'noble savage' is dead: there is nothing inherently more moral about humans in their 'wild' state than in their civilized state. For example, Pinker has the following observation on the !Kung San (2002: 56):

The !Kung San of the Kalahari have been described by Elizabeth Marshall Thomas as 'the harmless people' in a book with that title. But as soon as anthropologists camped out long enough to accumulate data, they discovered that the !Kung San have a murder rate higher than that of American inner cities. They learned as well that a group of the San had recently avenged a murder by sneaking into the killer's group and executing every man, woman and child as they slept.

One of the products of our civilization, namely widespread literacy, has the potential to bring us out of this wild state by offering us a set of tools with which we can evaluate our condition, and act in a manner that is both more human and more humane. But these benefits must be cultivated and maintained. Literacy itself will not stop us from slipping back to an 'oral culture', with all the dangers of short-term focus that this brings with it.

Of course, one could perhaps *imagine* oral cultures that are peace-loving, even if there is a dearth of evidence that such cultures ever existed. But, unfortunately, the agendas of many of the political and religious groups with a stake in eliminating the benefits of literacy do not suggest that the societies they have in mind would be particularly benign ones. And the realities of overpopulation, climate change, and dwindling resources do not present a recipe for the kind of vision of an 'innocent' society that one finds in Voltaire's description of El Dorado in *Candide*.

All of this suggests that if we succumb to the various forces afoot to tear down the benefits of five thousand years of writing technology, the result is unlikely to be pretty.

A Brief History of Mechanized Speech and Language Technology

For all its importance in the history of civilization, writing is a passive technology. Once created, written texts do not do much by themselves. We turn now to a different type of language and speech technology, namely machines that, to a greater or lesser extent, are *actively* engaged in the production or interpretation of speech or language. Much of the technology we will describe in the next few chapters, therefore, augments our abilities in a new kind of way, in that it involves mechanical (or electronic) devices that can mimic human abilities and participate more or less actively in human interactions. The present chapter starts this discussion by tracing the history of some of the modern technologies that we will discuss in depth in the following two chapters.

In his quest for victims of his inimitable satire, Jonathan Swift spared few people. *Gulliver's Travels*, possibly the greatest satirical work ever written, treated almost every aspect of humanity from political life all the way to the morals of humans in general. In the third book—*A Voyage to Laputa, Balnibarbi, Luggnagg, Glubbdubdrib, and Japan*—the target was philosophers and scientists. The centerpiece of this book is, of course, the flying island of Laputa, inhabited by a race of philosophers who are both literally and figuratively disconnected from the earth.

It was under the influence of these philosophers that a group of people from Balnibarbi, the land below Laputa, decided to develop academies of 'projectors', who would investigate scientific and philosophical problems ranging from architecture and agriculture to metaphysics. Since their understanding of Laputan science was at best imperfect, this led to the ruin of Balnibarbi, as more and more resources were poured into hopeless schemes for 'improving' all aspects of daily life, in various 'Academies' scattered around the country. Gulliver visits the main Academy in the capital city of

Lagado, where he encounters, among other things, what must be the world's first sketch of a language generation engine:

We crossed a Walk to the other Part of the Academy, where, as I have already said, the Projectors in speculative Learning resided.

The first Professor I saw was in a very large Room, with forty Pupils about him. After Salutation, observing me to look earnestly upon a Frame, which took up the greatest part of both the Length and Breadth of the Room, he said perhaps I might wonder to see him employed in a Project for improving speculative Knowledge by practical and mechanical Operations. But the World would soon be sensible of its Usefulness, and he flattered himself that a more noble exalted Thought never sprung in any other Man's Head. Every one knew how laborious the usual Method is of attaining to Arts and Sciences; whereas by his Contrivance, the most ignorant Person at a reasonable Charge, and with a little bodily Labour, may write Books in Philosophy, Poetry, Politicks, Law, Mathematicks and Theology, without the least Assistance from Genius or Study. He then led me to the Frame, about the Sides whereof all his Pupils stood in Ranks. It was twenty Foot Square, placed in the middle of the Room. The Superficies was composed of several bits of Wood, about the bigness of a Dye, but some larger than others. They were all linked together by slender Wires. These bits of Wood were covered on every Square with Paper pasted on them, and on these Papers were written all the Words of their Language, in their several Moods, Tenses, and Declensions, but without any Order. The Professor then desired me to observe, for he was going to set his Engine at Work. The Pupils at his Command took each of them hold of an Iron Handle, whereof there were fourty fixed round the Edges of the Frame, and giving them a sudden turn, the whole Disposition of the Words was entirely changed. He then commanded six and thirty of the Lads to read the several Lines softly as they appeared upon the Frame; and where they found three or four Words together that might make part of a Sentence, they dictated to the four remaining Boys who were Scribes. This Work was repeated three or four Times, and at every turn the Engine was so contrived that the Words shifted into new Places, as the Square bits of Wood moved upside down.

Six Hours a-day the young Students were employed in this Labour, and the Professor shewed me several Volumes in large Folio already collected, of broken Sentences, which he intended to piece together, and out of those rich Materials to give the World a compleat Body of all Arts and Sciences; which however might be still improved, and much expedited, if the Publick would raise a Fund for making and employing five hundred such Frames in Lagado, and oblige the Managers to contribute in common their several Collections.

He assured me, that this Invention had employed all his Thoughts from his Youth, that he had emptied the whole Vocabulary into his Frame, and made the strictest Computation of the general Proportion there is in Books between the Numbers of Particles, Nouns, and Verbs, and other Parts of Speech.

I made my humblest Acknowledgments to this illustrious Person for his great Communicativeness, and promised if ever I had the good Fortune to return to my

Native Country, that I would do him Justice, as the sole Inventer of this wonderful Machine; the Form and Contrivance of which I desired Leave to delineate upon Paper, as in the Figure here annexed [Figure 6.1]. I told him, although it were the Custom of our Learned in Europe to steal Inventions from each other, who had thereby at least this Advantage, that it became a Controversy which was the right Owner, yet I would take such Caution, that he should have the Honour entire without a Rival. (Jonathan Swift, *Gulliver's Travels*. Part III: A Voyage to Laputa, Balnibarbi, Luggnagg, Glubbdubdrib, and Japan, ch. V)

The exact inspiration for Swift's particular satire here may never be known, though, as suggested in a paper by John Shufelt,[1] it is presumably the case that he was satirizing the Royal Society for beliefs which were sometimes simultaneously misguided and pompous. There is no record in the annals of the Royal Society for the relevant portion of the eighteenth century for any discussion of mechanical devices for dealing with any aspect of language.

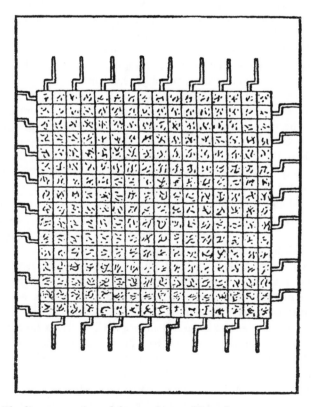

FIGURE 6.1 The literary engine of the Academy of Lagado

Yet the ideas must surely have been floating around, for it was later in the same century that the first serious attempts were made to produce speech-like sounds using machines.

6.1 Machines that produce speech

To understand the context for this work, it is important to realize that little was understood of acoustics—the science of sound production—in the eighteenth century. Of course, some aspects of sound had been understood at least since the Greeks, and there was a lot of interest in acoustics as it related to music, as evidence by the work on *well tempered* scales during this period. But it was not until the much later work of Helmholtz (1821–94) that we began to have a good understanding of how sound was produced in chambers and how the different shapes taken on by the human vocal tract relate to the sounds produced.

Still, some observations had been floating around. Isaac Newton observed in 1665 that one could produce a progression of vowel sounds using liquid poured into a flagon:

The filling of a very deepe flaggon with a constant streame of beere or water sounds ye vowells in this order w, u, ω, o, a, e, i, y.

We know now that this is because as the flaggon fills and the main *resonance* of the container thus becomes higher, it mimics the progression of the second formant (or resonance) of the vocal tract as the tongue positions itself for the vowels in the sequence that Newton described; see Chapter 7.[2]

The first description of a machine that could produce speech came in 1773 from Christian Gottlieb Kratzenstein, who was a professor of physiology at Copenhagen. He was able to produce vowel-like sounds using resonance tubes connected to organ pipes. A depiction of Kratzenstein's machine is given in Figure 6.2, from Thomas Young's *Natural Philosophy* (the same Thomas Young who figured prominently in the decipherment of Egyptian).

But the most extensive early work on producing speech was due to the Hungarian scientist Wolfgang Ritter von Kempelen (Kempelen Farkas Lovag was the Hungarian version of his name), who in 1791 published *Mechanismus der menschlichen Sprache, nebst der Beschreibung seiner sprechenden Maschine*—'Mechanism of Human Speech with the Description of his Speaking Machine'. An excellent history of von Kempelen's invention is given in Dudley and Tarnoczy (1950),[3] and we will be drawing on this history in the discussion here.

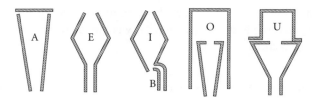

FIGURE 6.2 Professor Kratzenstein's vowel-producing resonance chambers
Source: from Thomas Young's *Natural Philosophy* (1845).

During the eighteenth century there was a surge of interest in mechanical devices of all kinds, but particularly in automata that mimicked living things. Advances in clockwork technology were in part responsible, and various ingenious devices were built, including fully working models of birds that would sing and flap their wings. Von Kempelen was already famous for his 'Mechanical Turk', a chess-playing automaton featuring a turbaned 'Turk' who played a strong game of chess against human opponents. The machine was really a Wizard of Oz device, since concealed inside the box behind which the Turk sat was a diminutive chess player, who tracked the moves on the board above him with magnets under the pieces, and who could move the puppet Turk by means of levers. Still, the device was a marvel of mechanical ingenuity.

Von Kempelen's interest in speech started in 1769. As Dudley and Tarnoczy note, it is not certain what initially sparked his interest, but it was likely a combination of a general interest in scientific matters plus a more specific desire to work on problems that might benefit people with disabilities, such as deaf-mutes. Be that as it may, von Kempelen started trying to devise machines that would mimic speech, and went through a number of iterations before homing in on his final design, the result of twenty years' work. His final machine, illustrated in Figure 6.3, consisted of a number of components including bellows for lungs, a 'mouth' made of rubber, a 'nose' with two nostrils (clearly visible in the figure, and which had to be covered unless a nasal sound such as /n/ was desired), and vocal chords simulated with an ivory reed. Unvoiced sounds such as /p/ or /k/ were produced by closing the opening of the mouth tightly with the hand. And the resonance properties of the 'mouth' could be controlled with the left hand covering the opening in various ways, and even placing the hand inside the 'mouth' in order to simulate the production of various vowel sounds. Using this device, von Kempelen was able to simulate most of the sounds needed for German.

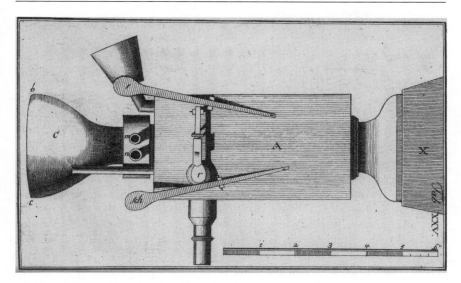

FIGURE 6.3 Von Kempelen's *sprechende Maschine*
Source: image courtesy of the University of Pennsylvania.

The following passage, from Dudley and Tarnoczy, is based on von Kempelen's own description of the operation of the machine. The markings refer to the marks in Figure 6.3 (bold face, and solidi surrounding phonetic symbols, added by me):

The operator rests his right arm on the bellows X and pumps it with an up-and-down motion, speech being produced on the down motion. The fingers of the right hand are set to operate the special consonant controls marked **r**, **sch**, **n**, **m**, and **s**. The left hand is placed palm inward before the opening **bc** of bell **C**. The vowels are produced by working the bellows with the right elbow while blocking the nostril-imitating tubes **m** and **n** by fingers of the right hand, with the left hand set in such position before **C** as listening and practice indicated best for the particular vowel being produced. For sound /a/ the hand is kept distant from the mouth opening; for /e/ the hand is hollowed slightly with its bottom edge against the mouth and its top edge about one inch away; for /o/ the top of the hollowed hand should be about one-half inch from the mouth; for /u/ the hand is held flat with the opening of the mouth reduced to a minimum short of stopping the reed vibration; but with the opening greater than for /i/; for /i/ the flat hand is placed tightly across the mouth opening and the index finger then crooked, so that there appears at the second knuckle a small opening, more air pressure being required for this vowel than for the others. He says the positions for other vowels such as the umlauts [front rounded vowels found in German but not English—RWS] are intermediate to the given positions and can easily be located with a small amount of practice.   (Dudley and Tarnoczy, 1950: 160)

After von Kempelen there were many other mechanical speaking machines. One, due to Joseph Faber, was exhibited in 1846 at the Egyptian Hall in Piccadilly, London. It was claimed to be an improvement on von Kempelen's device, and was demonstrated with ordinary conversation and whispered speech, and was also able to sing.

A particularly interesting description comes to us from Erasmus Darwin (1731–1802), Charles Darwin's grandfather:

I contrived a wooden mouth with lips of soft leather, and with a valve over the back part of it for nostrils, both which could be quickly opened or closed by the pressure of the fingers, the vocality was given by a silk ribbon about an inch long and a quarter of an inch wide stretched between two bits of smooth wood a little hollowed; so that when a gentle current of air from bellows was blown on the edge of the ribbon, it gave an agreeable tone, as it vibrated between the wooden sides, much like a human voice. This head pronounced the p, b, m, and the vowel a, with so great nicety as to deceive all who heard it unseen, when it pronounced the words mama, papa, map, and pam; and had a most plaintive tone, when the lips were gradually closed. My other occupations prevented me from proceeding in the further construction of this machine; which might have required but thirteen movements, as shown in the above analysis, unless some variety of musical note was to be added to the vocality produced in the larynx; all of which movements might communicate with the keys of a harpsichord or forte piano, and perform the song as well as the accompaniment; or which if built in a gigantic form, might speak so loud as to command an army or instruct a crowd.

(Erasmus Darwin, *Temple of Nature*, pp. 119–20)

The last proposal, to build a gigantic version of the device that could command a crowd, illustrates the fact that little was understood of acoustics in the eighteenth century. Darwin believed that the device, if built large, would be louder than the more domestic sized unit that he presumably built. That it surely would be, but another result of the large size would be that the resonances of the chamber would be too low, so that the result would not sound much like human speech.

During the eighteenth century, not only were there advances in our understanding of the acoustics of speech, but there were also fundamental discoveries in the study of language. In 1796 William Jones presented a paper demonstrating that Sanskrit, the sacred language of India, was related to Latin and Greek. This discovery of *Indo-European* (as Thomas Young later called the language family that included Latin, Celtic, Greek, Germanic, Indic, and Slavic, among others) laid the groundwork of the field of historical linguistics, which led eventually to modern work in linguistics, as well as providing insights into the history of humankind.

These eighteenth-century advances in speech and language studies led to an explosion of work in the nineteenth century. Notable work included that of Melville Bell (Alexander Graham Bell's father), who made significant contributions to the study of phonetics, including a phonetic transcription system that he called *Visible Speech*. Henry Sweet (the model for Henry Higgins in Shaw's *Pygmalion*) founded the modern study of phonetics. Meanwhile, Helmholtz developed the modern science of acoustics.

By the early twentieth century, advances in electrical engineering had made it possible to build electronic devices that could produce sound. One of the fundamental factors here is the analogy between lossless electrical transmission lines and acoustic tubes, so that acoustic (air) pressure is analogous to voltage, *volume velocity* (the amount of air flowing through a particular point over a particular time period) is analogous to current, and there are also acoustic analogs to inductance and capacitance; see again Table 5.1, and the surrounding discussion. This is totally familiar to any student of electrical engineering (any standard text in digital signal processing such as Rabiner and Schafer (1978) discusses it). Using these analogies, it is possible to build analog electrical circuits that mimic the behavior of a set of acoustic tubes coupled together—which is exactly what the human vocal apparatus is.

The most famous such device that dated from the first half of the twentieth century was Homer Dudley's *Voder* (for *VOice DEmonstratoR*). Dudley, a researcher at Bell Labs, had done fundamental work on the transmission of speech (one of the core interests of Bell Labs, since this was the research arm of the telephone company). The Voder was developed as a demonstration of what could be done with the technology of the day. It was exhibited at the 1939 World's Fair in New York and San Francisco. The Voder booth at the World's Fair is shown in Figure 6.4, and a schematic diagram of the Voder is given in Figure 6.5. As with von Kempelen's machine, the Voder required a skilled human operator, and a number of young women were trained at Bell Labs to operate the device over a period of between six months and a year. The operator had at her disposal a set of keys which controlled the synthetic resonances of the system that allowed it to simulate various sounds, a switch operated by the wrist that turned voicing (vocal chord vibration) on and off, and a foot pedal to control the pitch of the voice so that the Voder would not speak in a monotone. The Voder was evidently quite a success, drawing large crowds of spectators, and being interviewed on the radio.

The Voder was the first successful fully-electronic voice synthesizer, but of course it had the practical drawback that while it could produce very convincing-sounding speech, it required a skilled human operator to do it. It would not be until the 1950s that people started to investigate the automatic

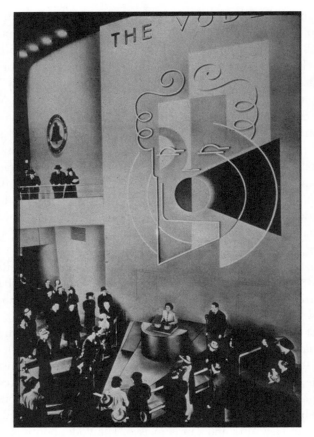

FIGURE 6.4 The Voder display at the 1939 World's Fair in New York City

production of speech sounds. An important figure in this later development was Gunnar Fant of the Royal Institute of Technology (Kungliga Tekniska Högskolan—KTH) in Stockholm. His 'Orator Verbis Electris' (OVE) formant synthesizer (1953) involved electronic circuitry which mimicked the acoustic properties of the vocal tract by separate formant resonators connected in series. We will take the story of speech synthesis on from here in Chapter 7.[4]

6.2 The mechanical treatment of text

For most of their history, mechanical and electronic devices for producing speech, while of great scientific value, and in some cases entertainment value,

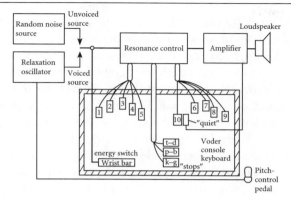

FIGURE 6.5 Dudley's Voder

had little practical use. This situation was not destined to change until the widespread deployment of speech technology within the past couple of decades.

The mechanical treatment of text was another matter entirely, and practical solutions to the problem of producing or representing text by mechanical or electronic means have had widespread utility.

The earliest such technology, of course, was printing, though it is difficult to decide where exactly one would place the transition between merely a glorified version of ordinary writing, and a full mechanical system.

Printing is one of those topics that almost everybody knows something about since, if nothing else, it is something that everyone learns in school: who has *not* heard of Gutenberg? Furthermore, there are a number of very good discussions of the salient points of the history of printing. A recent example is the discussion in Gnanadesikan (2008). I will therefore do no more than remind the reader of some of these points. It is my intention here to spend far more space on the history of two topics that get far less attention, namely typewriting and electronic encodings.

The earliest printing (on cloth), dating to around 220, involved carving the full text onto wood blocks. Possibly the oldest surviving example of a printed text on paper is a portion of the Dharani Sutra buried inside the Seokgatap stupa in Gyeongju, Korea, dated to the early eighth century AD.[5] Surely the most impressive surviving collection of woodblocks is the Korean Tripitaka, stored at Haein-sa in North Kyongsang province: carved between 1236 and 1251, they consist of 81,258 wood blocks, each measuring 65 by 24.5 by 6.6 centimeters, consisting of twenty-three lines of fourteen characters each—a total of over 26 million Chinese characters.[6]

Single wood blocks of course allowed for the mass production of text, but they still involved a lot of work to produce the original carvings. The method in effect treated the printed page as if it were a picture, as with a lithograph. A key insight—that writing, unlike arbitrary graphics, involves repeated units— led ultimately to moveable type, invented by Pi Sheng some time around 1040, and first made out of ceramic, later of metal. As was true later with type- writers, and again with electronic encodings, so it was true with printing that writing systems with smaller character sets had a distinct advantage. Thou- sands of distinct type blocks were needed for Chinese; just a few dozen for the Latin alphabet. It was presumably partly due to this that it was in the West— with Gutenberg's invention of the printing press (*c.* 1436)—that printing with moveable type became fully mechanized and comparatively cheap. In East Asia, moveable type printing remained expensive, and books continued to be produced using wood blocks for the mass market (Pratt, 2006: 144). The spread of printing, engendered in large part by the spread of literacy that printing itself helped fuel, led in turn to what was in effect a new class of scribes: typesetters. Critical in the development of printing was the develop- ment of appropriate lightweight materials for use as a printing surface. One can print on almost any material that is flat and will take the ink, but for practical purposes the material had to be strong, light, and cheap. Paper, one of the other famous Chinese inventions, was perfect in this regard. Paper was of course also critical for the widespread adoption of a technology that ultimately made it into the hands of far more people than printing ever did—typewriting, to which we now turn.

6.2.1 *The typewriter and its social impact*

In its mechanical form, high-quality printing was always the domain of specialist artisans. Printing presses were expensive bulky items, hardly suited for use, say, in the home. Typewriters changed this by providing a mechanical solution to writing that, while inferior in quality to professional printing, had the advantage that the machines were comparatively inexpensive, small, and sufficiently easy to use that, during their century-long history, millions of people would learn to use them.

In this section we briefly recount the invention of the typewriter; a curious but often ill-understood feature—the QWERTY layout for the Latin alphabet; and some of the social consequences of the adoption of the typewriter as a standard business tool.

6.2.1.1 *Christopher Latham Sholes*   In a somewhat whimsical book on the typewriter, Wershler-Henry (2005) notes that the history of typewriting can

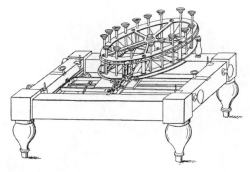

FIGURE 6.6 Thurber's 'patent printer'

fairly be traced back well into the seventeenth century, when William Petty was granted a patent (1647) for a version of the *pantograph*, a machine that linked several pens together so that the pens could all follow the writing movements of a human operator. Pantographs (Petty's was in fact *not* the first of these) were in a sense both the earliest copiers and the earliest writing machines. Thomas Jefferson was a great aficionado of pantographs.

Machines more akin to the modern typewriter, in that they involved keys and some form of type bar, started to appear in earnest in the early nineteenth century. What is often termed the 'first American typewriter' was developed by Charles Thurber (1843—Figure 6.6). The head of the royal Danish 'Deaf and Dumb' Institute (Døvstummeinstitut), Rasmus Malling Hansen, developed a 'writing ball' aimed at blind users, which figured a set of keys distributed over a ball, each of which activated a typebar; see Figure 6.7. Blind users could of course not see the resulting text, but the ball aided them at least in inputting text. Malling Hansen's invention may well have been one of the first of what we would now call Augmentative and Alternative Communication devices. A number of similar devices aimed at blind users were invented in the course of the nineteenth century.

But, while he was not the first to invent a typewriting machine, the person most associated with typewriting as we have come to know it was Christopher Latham Sholes (1819–90). Sholes was involved in many professions ranging from postmaster to state senator, and he was also an ardent abolitionist. He is best known, however as an inventor, and prior to his work on the typewriter he was involved in designing machines to consecutively number train tickets and book folios.[7]

FIGURE 6.7 One of Rasmus Malling Hansen's writing balls

Source: image © 2009 by Auction Team Breker, Cologne, Germany (www.Breker.com, and see also The International Rasmus Malling-Hansen Society http://www.malling-hansen.org), used with permission.

An interesting account of a precursor to Sholes's typewriter is given by Charles Weller, who knew Sholes personally.[8] Weller describes the first encounter with Sholes's new invention as follows (1918: 7–9):

Sometime during the month of July, 1867, while employed as chief operator in the office of the Western Union Telegraph Company in the city of Milwaukee, Wis., Mr. C. Latham Sholes, whom I had known for some years, called at the office and asked for a sheet of carbon paper, something which was rarely used in those days, except in making duplicate copies of Associated Press reports received by telegraph for the daily press.

Upon complying with his request he casually remarked that if I would call at his office the next day at about noon he would show me something that he thought would be interesting. Knowing that Mr. Sholes possessed a remarkable inventive genius, having been the first to conceive of the method of addressing newspapers by printing the names of subscribers on the margin, and having later invented a machine for paging blank books and the consecutive numbering of bank notes, I was prepared for an exhibition of something novel in this instance. Upon calling at his office the next day in the Federal building where he then occupied the government position of Collector

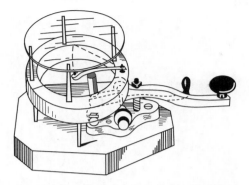

FIGURE 6.8 Sholes's original prototype for a typewriter key assembly based on a telegraph key
Source: from Weller (1918).

of the Port of Milwaukee, I found him in company with a gentleman explaining a little piece of mechanism on the table before them, the base of which consisted of a piece of pine board, above which, supported by wooden pegs was a ring rudely fashioned out of wood with a jack knife, on the edge of which was set four other pegs supporting a circular piece of glass; on the side of the ring was pivoted a small brass bar about two inches in length, on the upper end of which was cut the letter 'w.' Beneath this bar and on the wooden base was affixed an ordinary Morse telegraph 'key' arranged in such manner that by striking the round button end of the key a smart tap with the finger the type bar was quickly thrown up against the circular piece of glass above, striking it exactly in the center. By holding a piece of carbon paper with a thin piece of white paper against the piece of glass and moving it slowly with one hand while the key was being struck rapidly with the other hand, a regular and perfect line of w's was produced similar to this:

wwwwwwwwwwwwwww

Weller's illustration of the apparatus that Sholes was demonstating is shown in Figure 6.8.

Weller then went on to describe how Sholes developed a full typewriter with a piano keyboard (there had been other such piano-based typewriters by other inventors), which was patented by Sholes and his collaborators Carlos Glidden and Samuel W. Soule in 1868 (Figure 6.9). The piano keyboard as a model for input was, of course, a dead end, and in fact Sholes also had a patent on a full typewriting machine based on his telegraph key input system. The patent on that machine was actually filed earlier than the patent for the piano-keyboard machine, but for procedural reasons ended up being granted later.[9]

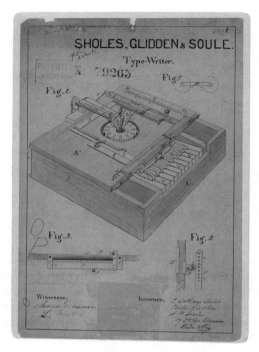

FIGURE 6.9 The Sholes, Glidden, and Soule typewriter based on a piano keyboard, 1868

Manufacture of the first machines was a tricky business since, obviously, machine shops had had little experience at building such delicate and exacting machinery. One of the results of this was that keys tended to jam relatively easily, a fact that led Sholes to consider how to design the keyboard layout to minimize the risk of jamming; we turn to that issue in the next section. Beyond machining, there were many other complications in the early days of typewriting. For example, Weller describes how typewriter ribbons were manufactured by purchasing lengths of silk ribbon, which were cut to size, dipped in ink, and left hanging over chairs to dry.

In 1873, Sholes had the decisive break that assured that his invention would become the first commercially successful typewriter. Remington and Sons, a firearms manufacturer based in Ilion, New York, which also had a side business in sewing machines, agreed to purchase the patent for Sholes's machine and start commercial production (Figure 6.10). While there were various modifications to the original design that were implemented in the course of Remington's refinements of the Sholes typewriter, one of the

A CONTRACT HAS BEEN MADE WITH THE IL-
ION ARMS MANUFACTORY OF THE REMINGTON'S AT ILION,
NEW YORK, FOR THE MANUFACTURE OF A THOUSAND MA-
CHINES, WHICH ARE NOW IN PROCESS AND PROGRESS OF
CONSTRUCTION. WE ARE MUCH ENCOURAGED WITH THE
PROSPECT OF THE VALUE OF THE THING IN VIEW OF ITS
UTILITY.

FIGURE 6.10 Sholes announcing, in a letter to Weller dated 30 April 1873, his contract
with Remington
Source: Weller (1918: 50).

things that was not changed was the keyboard layout, a topic to which we
now turn.

6.2.1.2 *The QWERTY Keyboard*   As Wershler-Henry[10] points out, the typewriter is dead. Yet Sholes's invention lives on in various ways. The term
'carriage return' makes as little sense to someone who has never seen a
typewriter with its cylindrical paper carriage as the term 'clockwise' would
make to someone who had never seen an analog clock face, yet the term has
become completely entrenched in our vocabulary for talking about typing.
Another and more important legacy is the QWERTY keyboard, universal in
every English-speaking country, indeed practically universal (with minor
local variations) in all countries where the Latin alphabet is used. Only the
French have a preferred keyboard with a significantly different—but still not
totally different—arrangement of keys.

An early Remington keyboard is shown in Figure 6.11. Some symbols we
have on modern keyboards were lacking: the digit zero was to be written with
a capital 'O', the digit one with 'l' (lower case 'L'), an '!' as an apostrophe
followed by a backspace followed by a period. Some symbols that are now
lacking were given keys of their own: the commonly used fractions. But the

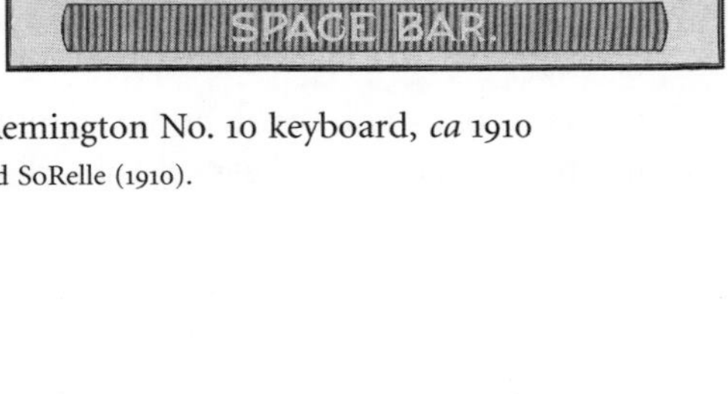

FIGURE 6.11 The Remington No. 10 keyboard, *ca* 1910
Source: from Cutler and SoRelle (1910).

keyboard is otherwise essentially the same as the keyboard I am using on my laptop to write this text.

There are two common misconceptions about QWERTY. One is that QWERTY is highly inefficient from the point of view of maximal typing effort (and hence speed) and that other arrangements are better; the usual contender for the most efficient keyboard is the Dvorak Simplified Keyboard, patented by ergonomics expert August Dvorak in 1936.

The second is that Sholes actually wanted an inefficient key arrangement and designed QWERTY for this purpose. Those of us old enough to have used a mechanical typewriter know that it was fairly common for the keys to jam. In the earliest models, with the relatively crude machining of the parts, jamming was a much more serious problem. Hence, it is claimed, Sholes designed his keyboard so as to slow down typing, thus minimizing the risk of jamming.

6.2.1.1 *Sholes's rationale for QWERTY*   Let us deal with this second issue first, since it is the historically prior of the two. In fact the story does get one thing right: QWERTY was a direct result of the key jamming problem. But Sholes's motivation for QWERTY was actually to enable typing that was as rapid as possible given the capabilities of the early machines. The design of QWERTY was rather clever, and depended upon corpus statistics, namely the relative frequency of letter pairs in English. Sholes's financial backer James Densmore had a brother Amos Densmore, who was a schoolteacher. Sholes asked Amos Densmore to compile a list of common English letter pairs (bigrams). If one does this exercise oneself on a sample of English text, one will end up with a table like the following, which lists the ten most frequent letter bigrams, with their counts, derived from the King James Bible:

th	189,406
he	153,362
an	90,152
nd	75,799
in	55,925
er	54,690
ha	52,187
re	48,998
of	44,124
or	41,882

If you examine this set of letter pairs and consider the layout of the QWERTY keyboard, you'll see that by and large the keys are not close to each other.

The only exceptions in this set are *r* and *e*, which are adjacent to each other on the keyboard. Of course we do not know what text Amos Densmore used to compute his list: if he used a short text that was very different in character from the King James Bible, then he might have arrived at rather different statistics. Still, as long as the text was at least ordinary prose, one can be fairly confident that *th* and *he* would have been at the top of the list, given the prevalence of the word *the*.

But in any case—and this is critical to understanding what Sholes did—the real issue is not where keys are, but where the typebars are relative to each other. The typebars on the earliest Remington models (the Remington 1, which was the Sholes–Glidden machine, and the slightly modified Remington 2) were by and large close together if the corresponding keys were close together.[11] More specifically, for any pair of keys adjacent in the top two or bottom two rows on the keyboard, the corresponding typebars were separated by the typebar for the key either above or below the two and in the middle. For example, the typebars for "g" and "h" are separated by the typebar for "b", and the typebar for "t" and "y" are separated by the typebar for "6". This pattern does not work as between the second and third rows, however: in the original models, the typebars were arranged in a circle, and struck upwards towards the carriage (so that the typist could not actually see what was just typed)—see Figure 6.12. The top half of the circle corresponded to the top two rows, the bottom half to the bottom two rows. The typebars for 'q' and 'a' are adjacent, but the typebars for 't' and 'h' are actually opposite one another. This in itself speaks to the cleverness of Sholes's design: the most common letter bigram in English has the keys close together for easy access, yet the chance of jamming is minimal since the typebars are maximally far apart. If Sholes were trying to slow down typing, why bother to have 't' and 'h' placed on the keyboard as they are? Figure 6.13 shows the typebar placements for the five most common English letter bigrams, 'th', 'he', 'an', 'nd', 'in', showing that in each case Sholes tried to space these far apart. The same holds for 'ha' (separated by nine intervening typebars), 'of' (fourteen intervening), and 'or' (nine intervening). Again, the only exception is 'er' (and of course 're'), which are separated by just one typebar.[12]

So far so good, but there is a slight problem with this analysis, which suggests that we do not after all really have a good answer for why Sholes chose the QWERTY arrangement—and that the common wisdom on this point is somewhat uncertain. According to historian Richard Current,[13] Sholes's original thought was to arrange the keys alphabetically. While this was not specifically stated, presumably this meant an arrangement that was left-to-right and top-to-bottom, so that 'a' was where 'q' is now, 'b'

FIGURE 6.12 A Remington 2 typewriter from 1895, which was similar to its predecessor, the Sholes–Glidden Remington 1

Note: the lower panel shows the machine with the carriage open to reveal the typebars.

Source: photos courtesy The Martin Howard Collection of Early Typewriters, www.antiquetypewriters.com

was where 'w' is, and so forth. Ergonomically this would not be a very good arrangement—for a touch typist—since it would place some common letters in awkward positions: 't' would be where 'z' is, and 'a' where 'q' is, so that both of these common letters would have to be typed with the left little finger. But what about the typebar clash problem? It turns out that from that point of view, the alphabetic arrangement is not so bad compared to QWERTY. One way to calculate a score for a keyboard arrangement on the original Sholes machine is, for each pair of letters, to multiply the typebar

FIGURE 6.13 From top to bottom and left to right: the typebar positions for 'th', 'he', 'an', 'nd', and 'in' on the Remington 2

Source: photos courtesy The Martin Howard Collection of Early Typewriters, www.antiquetypewriters.com.

distance for that pair by an amount proportional to the expected frequency of the letter pair.[14] Under this measure, a keyboard arrangement will get a high score if very common letter pairs are maximally far apart, which seems intuitively correct. The score for the QWERTY keyboard comes out to 12.26, that of the alphabetic keyboard a not-much-worse 12.14. A much better keyboard could have been achieved by swapping 'r' and 'm', for a score of 14.24. Given this analysis, we have to conclude that while Sholes surely did make an effort to minimize typebar clashing, the details of exactly what he did and why are still unclear.

Sholes evidently made no effort to put the commonly used letters on the home row, as they are in the Dvorak keyboard. Presumably it never even occurred to him to do this, for reasons that are rather clear. Optimizing the home row only makes a difference if you are a touch typist. The first touch typing competitions were reported in 1888,[15] a full fifteen years after Sholes sold his patent to Remington.

Given the statistical basis for QWERTY it is perhaps all the more remarkable that QWERTY is so widely used in non-English-speaking countries. After all, letter co-occurrence statistics do not carry over from one language to another; the sequence *th* is not nearly so common in German as it is in English.

6.2.1.2 *Is QWERTY so inefficient?*   This last point relates to the first issue we raised in the introduction of this section, namely the supposed inefficiency of QWERTY relative to other possible arrangements of keys—most notably Dvorak. Why, if it was so inefficient, did it nonetheless become the industry standard, spreading far beyond the English-speaking world?

This issue is discussed in a fascinating article by economists S. J. Liebowitz and Stephen E. Margolis.[16] QWERTY had been held up as an example of how an inferior product can nonetheless win out over competitors because of lack of co-ordination among users of the product. A standard example is Sony's Betamax standard for videotapes, which was widely recognized by experts as being a superior technology to VHS (which it actually pre-dated). But Betamax eventually lost in part because once a competitor had arisen and gained a larger market share, more and more users would be wary of buying Betamax machines, figuring that they might be the only ones to do so, which would eventually lead to tape distributors ceasing to distribute Betamax tapes (because there would be no market), which would mean that the users would be left holding a machine they couldn't use. A similar story was supposed to account for why QWERTY won out over competitors, and why an apparently superior technology (Dvorak) largely failed to replace it when it came along more than fifty years later.

FIGURE 6.14 Dvorak's Simplified Keyboard

Source: Dvorak et al. (1936), from Light and Anderson (1993), used with permission.

Liebowitz and Margolis challenge both assumptions underlying this view: that QWERTY *is* substantially inferior to Dvorak; and that QWERTY won early on because of fear of having an obsolete machine, as with Beta.

The inefficiency of QWERTY. The usual argument about the inefficiency of QWERTY notes that for typing English, QWERTY distributes typing unevenly between the hands, putting more burden on the left hand, it overloads the weaker fingers, and the home row is used less than one-third of the time, since the commonest letters are not found on the home row.

In response to these concerns, August Dvorak, an ergonomics expert, patented the Dvorak Simplified Keyboard (DSK)[17] (Figure 6.14), with the claim that it was vastly more efficient than QWERTY in terms of the amount of finger movement needed.

Subsequent research seemed to uphold this claim. The most often cited of these tests was a study conducted by the Navy and published in a 1944 report. Liebowitz and Margolis were able to get a copy of this report 'with difficulty'. The report included a set of studies. The first of these involved retraining fourteen Navy typists on Dvorak keyboards for two hours a day. After fifty-two hours, the typists were able to attain their old QWERTY speeds of 32 words per minute, and after a total of eighty-three hours, they were able to reach 56 words per minute, or a 75 per cent increase in speed. Yet as Liebowitz and Margolis (1990) noted, there was at least one problem with this study in that the subjects were evidently poor typists: their original rate was 32 words a minute, whereas the Navy's definition of 'competence' was 50 words a minute. If the same typists had received an additional thirty hours of training on QWERTY keyboards, might they not have also achieved equivalent rates? At the very least one has to wonder, if the point was to demonstrate a clear superiority of the DSK, why they did not start with skilled typists, and demonstrate an improvement for that group. There is another problem with the study in that the Navy's top ergonomics expert, who surely must have been involved, was not a disinterested party: he was Lieutenant Commander August Dvorak.

Liebowitz and Margolis go on to discuss later, more rigorous studies that show far less improvement (if any) from retraining on Dvorak keyboards: in one case, a paltry 2.6 per cent improvement was reported. Interestingly this accords with a computational model for optimizing keyboards worked out by Lissa Light and Peter Anderson (1993). Light and Anderson propose a 'cost' for a keyboard which can be broken down into three components:

- The relative frequency of every letter pair for English (or whatever language you want to optimize for), as we already discussed above.
- The 'travel times' between positions on the keyboard.
- The mapping of the letters to the keys.

The first and third of these are easy to compute. The second needs empirical data, as it is based on such considerations as the strength of the individual fingers. Light and Anderson base their estimates of travel times on previous work in human factors. They determine the cost of a given keyboard configuration as a sum, over every pair of letters, of the product of the frequency of the letter pair, and the travel time between the positions of the two letters. A lower cost is a more efficient keyboard. By this measure, QWERTY gets a cost of 1542, but Dvorak does not score much better: its cost is 1502. While it is hard to predict typing speed directly from these costs, the small difference is at least consistent with the small gains that Liebowitz and Margolis cite. In an estimate reported later in the paper based on letter pairs, Dvorak performed just 3.5 per cent better than QWERTY.

In contrast there are keyboards that, by Light and Anderson's metric, are *much* worse than QWERTY and there are ones that are better than DSK. The purpose of Light and Anderson's paper was to use a machine learning method known as *simulated annealing* to find an optimal keyboard in the space of all possible keyboards. There are too many keyboards to do an exhaustive search: even if we assume that letters are only mapped to keys that have letters on a QWERTY keyboard (note that this rule was *not* obeyed by DSK), there are about 4×10^{26} possible keyboard arrangements. Simulated annealing allows one to find good local optima, which are nonetheless not guaranteed to be the global optimum. Using this method, the best arrangement Light and Anderson were able to find is shown in Figure 6.15; it has a cost of 1428, with an 8 per cent better performance than QWERTY. The worst keyboard they report has a cost of 1754.

One factor in typing speed that is clearly important is that common letter sequences should involve alternating between the hands. Light and Anderson discuss this, and argue that for the first ten most common letter pairs, given their letter statistics, QWERTY scores only 5 out of 10 alternations, whereas

FIGURE 6.15 Light and Anderson's 1993 optimal keyboard for English, used with permission

Dvorak scores 8 out 10 (which coincidentally is the same number as their optimal keyboard scores). But when we perform the same computation on the pair list we derived above from the King James Bible, we see a rather different distribution:

Pair	QWERTY	DSK
th	Y	N
he	Y	Y
an	Y	Y
nd	Y	N
in	N	Y
er	N	Y
ha	Y	Y
re	N	Y
of	Y	Y
or	Y	Y

Here, QWERTY scores 7 out of 10, not much worse than Dvorak's 8 out of 10. Efficiency, then, will depend upon what type of text you are typing.

It is worth noting in passing that the standard Korean keyboard is a beautiful instance of the principle of hand alternation. In this keyboard, shown in Figure 6.16, the consonant symbols are all on the left and the vowel symbols on the right. (The reader may want to refer to Section 3.3.1.) Since Korean mostly alternates between consonants and vowels, this is a very nice arrangement.

Why did QWERTY win? So QWERTY is not as horrendously inefficient as is usually believed, but it is not notably efficient either. It is fair to say that it was probably well designed for Sholes's original purpose, but perhaps not ideally so. And Sholes's original purpose—the avoidance of jamming keys—would have quickly become less of an issue as the technology of typewriter manufacture became better understood.

So why did QWERTY win?

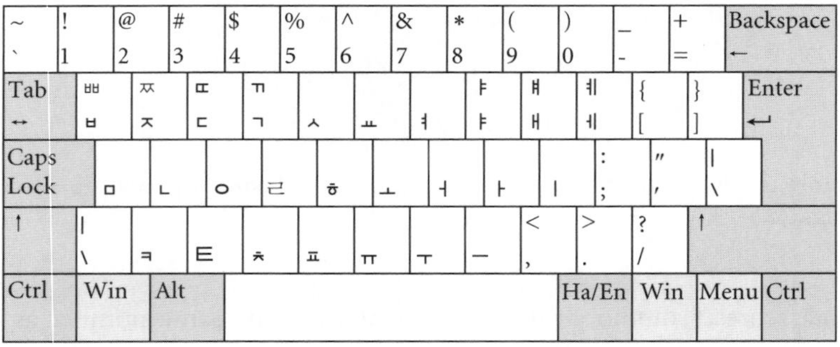

~ `	! 1	@ 2	# 3	$ 4	% 5	^ 6	& 7	* 8	(9	) 0	_ -	+ =	Backspace ←
Tab ↔	ㅃ ㅂ	ㅉ ㅈ	ㄸ ㄷ	ㄲ ㄱ	ㅅ	ㅛ	ㅕ	ㅑ	ㅐ ㅐ	ㅔ ㅔ	{ [	}]	Enter ↵
Caps Lock	ㅁ	ㄴ	ㅇ	ㄹ	ㅎ	ㅗ	ㅓ	ㅏ	ㅣ	: ;	" '	| \\	
↑	| \\	ㅋ	ㅌ	ㅊ	ㅍ	ㅠ	ㅜ	ㅡ	< ,	> .	? /	↑	
Ctrl	Win	Alt						Ha/En	Win	Menu	Ctrl		

FIGURE 6.16 The standard Korean keyboard

Not, Liebowitz and Margolis argue, because it became so dominant that people were afraid to buy alternatives, and manufacturers to make those alternatives. For one thing, as they point out, it was normal in the early days of typewriting for typewriter manufacturers to supply a trained operator with the purchase of a machine. After all, typing was still a novelty, and the early machines would have certainly required someone who was quite familiar with them to operate them. So it would have made little difference what arrangement of keys the manufacturer used. Standards were not particularly needed, and more importantly, if there were a key arrangement that obviously led to faster training and typing for the operators, it would have been in the manufacturers' interests to pursue them. According to Liebowitz and Margolis, this relationship between typists and typewriter manufacturers lasted as late as 1923 in that 'typewriter manufacturers operated placement services for typists and were an important source of operators' (1990: 19).

The dominance of QWERTY has been attributed to its success in early speed typing competitions, such as the one in Cincinnati on 25 July 1888, which was won by Frank McGurrin on a Remington QWERTY keyboard. Yet, as Liebowitz and Margolis note, there were other competitions where typists using non-QWERTY won. One might also be tempted to attribute QWERTY's success to the market dominance of Remington, a large arms manufacturer, that also manufactured sewing machines.[18] But this is not so clear either, as there were many manufacturers of typewriters in the early days, and Remington was not clearly dominant in the market.

Liebowitz and Margolis's study ultimately makes it clear that we do not really know why QWERTY became the standard. It was originally devised to address a technical issue with Sholes's early design, but that motivation quickly disappeared. It was not obviously inferior to any other available layout in any terms that could have been measured in the early typewriter period, nor was it clearly superior.

Since it became established though, it has withstood assaults from alternatives which, apparently, failed to be so overwhelmingly superior to QWERTY that people would simply have to adopt the new standard. Dvorak's keyboard failed, not because of the unreasonable dominance of an inferior standard, but because it was *not that much better*. There is another turn in the story of typing that Liebowitz and Margolis do not discuss, but which is rather telling in this regard, namely the development of computers. Today most if not all of us are familiar with computers, but of course this is a very recent phenomenon. The first time I ever used a computer was at my high school around 1976, when we had a single dumb terminal connected via a dial-up modem[19] that allowed us to call into a mainframe belonging to the San Diego City School system. The terminal had a QWERTY keyboard.

Why? If there was ever an opportunity for a shift, this would have been it: the world of computer operators was very small, and while many of them would have learned to type (as I had) on a QWERTY typewriter, they could easily have switched over to, say, Dvorak, if that was an obvious win. If nothing else, early computer geeks rather relished things that set them apart from the rest of humanity. Here was a targeted market that was for the most part separate from the market that was served by conventional typewriters. It was a situation ripe for *disruptive innovation*.[20] Yet it did not happen, presumably because there simply was no strong motivation: Dvorak did not solve a problem so much better than QWERTY that it was worth making the switch.

Today of course, most computer operating systems support key remapping: you can, if you so choose, map the keys any way you want, and with 4×10^{26} possibilities for remapping the alphabet keys alone, there are enough combinations that each person on earth could have 6.7×10^{16} all to him- or herself. And one can buy little stickers to place on the keys in case you forget your remapping. But very few people bother to do this. The most I ever do is remap the caps-lock and control keys, to move the control key (which I use a lot) to a position that is more comfortable for my left little finger. Again, at the end of the day, QWERTY is not so inferior a solution that it cries out for replacement.

6.2.1.3 *Typewriter girls*   Though many of the early notable typists were male, typing very soon became a largely female profession. By 1887, Rudyard Kipling wrote of the 'typewriter girls' that he encountered in San Francisco.[21] He evidently found their independence—their willingness to work earning 'as much as a hundred dollars a month' without any clear goal of eventually finding a husband—both exciting and, at the same time, puzzling and disturbing. In the latter view, Kipling was of course not alone. A study by Christopher Keep notes the common fear at the time that by working in business they would 'not only "unsex" themselves, but endanger that continuous transmission of cultural values from mother to children on which society depended.' Furthermore, many doubted that women were constitutionally up to the task: when the Young Women's Christian Association started typing classes for women in 1881 'there were fears that the female constitution was not equal to the rigors of an intensive six-month training program.'[22]

Despite these concerns, views on the appropriateness of this line of work for women changed to the point where the term 'typist' conjured up an image of a young woman seated behind a machine. By 1910, 80.6 per cent of typists were women; by 1930 that percentage had jumped to 95.6 per cent.[23] Part of the reason for this was surely economic: women could be hired more cheaply than men—often at half the cost. As Keep notes, in the nineteenth century and well into the twentieth century it was normal to make a distinction between 'individual' wages and 'family' wages. Men, it was assumed were supporting a family, or soon would be, and thus were paid at a higher ('family') rate than women who, it was assumed, would merely be supporting themselves until such time as they married and dropped out of the labor pool. If this were not enough, corporate job descriptions were restructured so that the former category of 'clerk' was split into tasks that required decision-making and those that were merely mechanical. Clerks who were in the former category—invariably men—had an opportunity to rise into management. Clerks of the latter category, such as typists, were in dead-end positions.[24] The social impact of these economic changes which the typewriter helped bring about were significant. Thousands of young women migrated to the cities to work in dead-end jobs for wages that were often meager. Victorian fiction, and as we saw, Kipling, tended to romanticize the 'typewriter girl' as being a new breed of woman, independent, self-sufficient, and self-assured. For most typists, the reality was rather less glamorous.[25]

The creation of a low-paid echelon of female workers in business and industry had ramifications that lasted well into the twentieth century and, many would probably argue, has not been fully eradicated today.

6.2.1.4 *Typing in other languages*   Two basic constraints on typewriters limited their ready adoption for some languages. They work best for scripts that have small character sets, since a large character set implies a large number of keys. And they work best for scripts that are strictly linear, since arrangements of symbols in other than a left-to-right (or right-to-left) fashion is technically challenging.

As a result, typewriters were easily adapted to some languages, but not to others. Relatively easy are any languages that use the Latin alphabet. Similarly such scripts as Greek, Cyrillic, or Armenian are quite straightforward, as is Hebrew, though obviously in that case the machine must be designed such that the carriage moves in the opposite direction to that of an English typewriter.

More problematic are languages where symbols are ligatured together (Arabic) or symbols are arranged in ways other than simply linearly, as in many Brahmi-derived scripts of India and Southeast Asia, or Korean Hangul. The basic symbol set for Hangul is very small, but the arrangement into syllable blocks is complicated, and so it was difficult to design a typewriter that could place the glyphs in appropriate positions. One invention along these lines was due to Pyung Woo Kong.[26] Kong's invention involved classifying the glyphs into initial consonants, vowels, intermediate vowels, and final consonants, which included double consonants in final position; and providing two different slots through which the typebars are guided. Figure 6.17 shows how the typewriter works. To type a syllable 왔 *wass* requires typing the symbols ㅇ, ㅏ, ㅗ and ㅆ (itself a double final ㅅ). The sequence followed is shown in the figure. First one types the initial consonant ㅇ (labeled 26a), whereby the typebar with that character is guided through the slot labeled 35 in the diagram. The platen (shown as a horizontal cylinder at the top of the diagram) is also moved one space to the left, bringing the area under slot 34, which is to the left of 35. Then the typist types ㅏ (26b), ㅗ (26c), and ㅆ (26d) in succession, whereby the corresponding typebars are guided through slot 34, and placed in the appropriate positions.[27] Kong's design was ingenious, but at the same time the complex mechanism of his machine underscored the limitations of typewriting technology when it came to scripts that were not strictly linear. The complexities of handling Korean prompted some people to propose linearizing Hangul.[28] Fortunately for Hangul, the relatively short period of typewriting was superseded by computers, where the rendering of elegant Hangul syllable blocks using a simple keyboard is no longer a problem.

When it came to languages with really large character sets such as Chinese or Japanese, typewriting broke down. Typewriters did exist for these languages, but they were huge devices with many thousands of pieces of type, operable only by trained specialists. Unlike typewriters

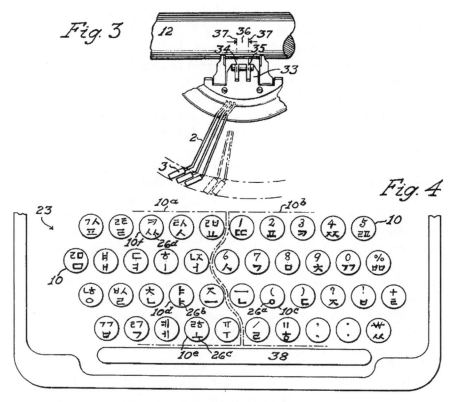

FIGURE 6.17 Pyung Woo Kong's Korean keyboard, US Patent 2,625,521

for English and many other languages, Chinese and Japanese typewriters never became household items. Figure 6.18 shows one such
device.

6.2.2 *Encodings: telegraphy to Unicode*

Well after the invention of printing, but before the invention of the first
commercially successful typewriters, text moved from the physical world
into an entirely new medium. The advent of electronic communication,
both via text and (by the telephone and later media) voice and video,
added a new dimension to the ways in which language technology augments
human abilities. The invention of writing made texts, in principle, permanent. The invention of lightweight media and printing made them widespread. The electronic medium made their transmission virtually
instantaneous.

FIGURE 6.18 A Chinese typewriter in Munich University's Institute for Sinology

Source: photo by Dadiolli / Tilman Schalmey, released under the Creative Commons Attribution ShareAlike 3.0 License.

In this section we trace the history of the electronic encoding of text, and discuss some of the technical issues involved in representing language in electrical signals.

6.2.2.1 *Telegraphy* The first electronic code for representing text was invented by Samuel Morse, a professor of arts and design at New York University. Morse Code was invented in the 1830s, concomitant with Morse's demonstration that signals could be transmitted electronically by wire. Morse received US Patent 1,647 on 20 June 1840 for his 'Improvement in the mode of communicating information by signals by the application of electro-magnetism'.

The first public use of Morse Code was on 1 May 1844, to transmit the news that Henry Clay had been nominated by the Whig party's national convention in Baltimore. The news was hand-carried to Annapolis Junction, and then transmitted electronically to Washington over the working portion of the Baltimore/Washington telegraph line, which was still under construction. On May 24, the words 'What hath God wrought' were transmitted by Morse from the old Supreme Court chamber in the US capitol to Baltimore.

Morse's code provided encodings for letters, numbers, and some punctuation in terms of dots and dashes, which were distinguished by the duration of the keypress on the telegraph machine. The encodings for the letters were

TABLE 6.1 Morse code is somewhat frequency-based

Length of code	Letter	Morse code	Frequency in *NYT*	Letter
1	e	.	388,511	e
3	i	. .	183,061	i
3	t	−	299,652	t
5	a	. −	261,160	a
5	n	− .	212,631	n
5	s	. . .	179,480	s
7	d	− . .	149,707	d
7	h	. . . .	267,679	h
7	m	− −	75,696	m
7	r	. − .	160,095	r
7	u	. . −	78,772	u
9	b	− . . .	45,959	b
9	f	. . − .	78,663	f
9	g	− − .	51,982	g
9	k	− . −	21,121	k
9	l	. − . .	122,561	l
9	v	. . . −	28,613	v
9	w	. − −	61,626	w
11	c	− . − .	51,570	c
11	o	− − −	229,419	o
11	p	. − − .	40,792	p
11	x	− . . −	1,390	x
11	z	− − . .	2,893	z
13	j	. − − −	8,396	j
13	q	− − . −	905	q
13	y	− . − −	55,410	y

Note: more frequent letters tend to have shorter codes. The first column is the length of the code: a dot and a space each count as 1, a dash as 3. The fourth column is the frequency of the letter in a sample of the *New York Times*.

roughly frequency-based, in that the commoner letters tended to have shorter codes. This is shown (for international morse code, see below) in Table 6.1, which compares the increasing Morse code length with the (decreasing) frequency as computed from a sample of the *New York Times*. The code length is computed by considering a dot to count as 1, a space (between dots or dashes) also as 1, and a dash as 3. Morse's original code is now termed *American Morse Code*, and it is almost obsolete. International Morse Code, formalized in 1865, has largely replaced it.

Both codes were of course ideally suited to languages with small alphabets. What would one do for Chinese? In 1871, a Danish watchmaker, astronomer, and orientalist, Hans Schjellerup, proposed a system based on four-digit

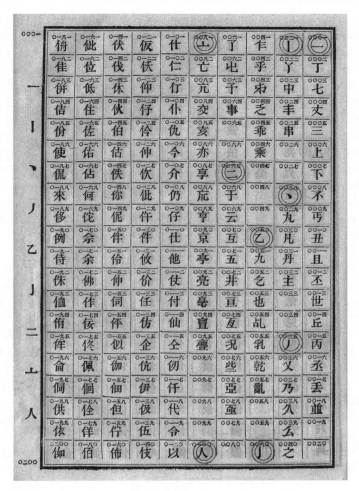

FIGURE 6.19 Chinese telegraph codes from S. A. Viguier, 1872

Note: the code starts at the upper right-hand corner, and proceeds top-to-bottom, right-to-left.

numbers—allowing for up to 10,000 characters—which was introduced into China by the Great Northern Telegraph Company.[29] Septime Auguste Viguier published a version of Schjellerup's code in Shanghai in 1872. A sample of this code can be seen in Figure 6.19. Characters are arranged as in a traditional Chinese dictionary by radicals and number of strokes. In the figure, the code starts at the upper right and proceeds top-to-bottom and right-to-left; above the character is the encoding written in traditional Chinese numerals.

Thus the character — *yī* 'one', has encoding 0001, 丁 *dīng* (the fourth of the ten heavenly stems, used in traditional Chinese enumeration), has encoding 0002, and so forth. The code shown in Figure 6.19 is obsolete, but variants of it are still in use by some ham radio operators; it is also available, though not much used, as a Chinese text input system.[30] But during the age of the telegraph it was heavily used. To be effective, Chinese telegraphers had to memorize the first few thousand codes of characters in common use.

Of course, for all of its widespread use for more than 150 years, telegraphy remained largely the domain of specialists. Very few people learned how to operate telegraphs, or the Morse code needed to send the signals. It was not until the widespread availability of computers that electronic communication of text became available in practice to everyone. The history and some of the design features of computer coding systems for text are the topic of the next section.

6.2.2.2 *EBCDIC and ASCII*   Computers represent text as a sequence of numbers. The numbers represent various things about the text including the characters that make up the text as well as various kinds of *control codes* that serve various special functions. In this discussion we will mostly ignore control codes and concentrate on characters and how they are encoded.

The basic unit of data is the byte or *character*, which consists of eight (binary) bits: thus a byte can represent $2^8 = 256$ distinct numbers. For English, this is far more character positions than are needed. If you look at the keyboard of your computer you should find about 47 keys with symbols on them. Each key has a two characters—a basic character and a shift character (lower and upper case in the case of letters)—and so there are 94 different symbols to encode. Add the space character, a line feed, a tab, and perhaps a couple of others, and you still have less than 100 distinct things that need to be encoded. That means that in fact to encode English you really only need (less than) $2^7 = 128$ positions, which means in turn that English can be encoded using only seven bits of the eight-bit byte. And this is exactly what was done in the first encoding systems.

There were two main systems in common use. One, the Extended Binary Coded Decimal Interchange Code (EBCDIC), was used on IBM mainframes. This standard is effectively dead. The other more widely used system, which is still in use, was the American Standard Code for Information Interchange— ASCII, first published in 1963. Figure 6.20 shows a chart of the standard ASCII character set and the numerical codes assigned to each character.

With the exception of a few archaic spellings that use diacritics—for example *co-operate* spelled as *coöperate*—ASCII is completely adequate for

USASCII code chart

b4 b3 b2 b1	Column/Row	0	1	2	3	4	5	6	7
0 0 0 0	0	NUL	DLE	SP	0	@	P	`	p
0 0 0 1	1	SOH	DC1	!	1	A	Q	a	q
0 0 1 0	2	STX	DC2	"	2	B	R	b	r
0 0 1 1	3	ETX	DC3	#	3	C	S	c	s
0 1 0 0	4	EOT	DC4	$	4	D	T	d	t
0 1 0 1	5	ENQ	NAK	%	5	E	U	e	u
0 1 1 0	6	ACK	SYN	&	6	F	V	f	v
0 1 1 1	7	BEL	ETB	'	7	G	W	g	w
1 0 0 0	8	BS	CAN	(	8	H	X	h	x
1 0 0 1	9	HT	EM	)	9	I	Y	i	y
1 0 1 0	10	LF	SUB	*	:	J	Z	j	z
1 0 1 1	11	VT	ESC	+	;	K	[	k	{
1 1 0 0	12	FF	FS	,	<	L	\	l	|
1 1 0 1	13	CR	GS	−	=	M	]	m	}
1 1 1 0	14	SO	RS	.	>	N	^	n	~
1 1 1 1	15	SI	US	/	?	O	_	o	DEL

FIGURE 6.20 The ASCII character set, as shown in the documentation for a 1972 TermiNet 300 impact type printer/keyboard

Note: the first four columns represent the last four bits associated with the characters in that row. The first header row represents the first three bits *after the first bit, which is always o*. Thus for example 'A' has the binary representation *o1000001*, i.e. 65. The first two columns are mostly control characters, though the linefeed 'LF' is in column 1.

English. But for practically any other language that uses the Latin alphabet, including nearly every major language of Western and Central Europe, the absence of any accented symbols in ASCII is a serious problem. There is simply no way to represent French *étais*, Spanish *cañon*, German *Straße*, or Hungarian *jövő* in ASCII.

And for languages that do not use the Latin alphabet, ASCII is completely irrelevant.

6.2.2.3 *Coding systems for other scripts*   Thus, other coding systems were needed for other languages. Fortunately, since ASCII only uses seven bits— the eighth bit for ASCII characters is always zero—one can double the number of available characters (to 256) by allowing the eighth bit to be set to 1. Then one can have two blocks of characters, one representing the ASCII characters (eighth bit zero) and the other representing another set of characters, such as accented Latin letters for Western European languages, or Cyrillic characters for Russian and other languages. Two such systems from the International Organization for Standardization (ISO)—ISO-8859-1 (1985) for Western European languages and ISO-8859-5 for Cyrillic (1988)—are shown in

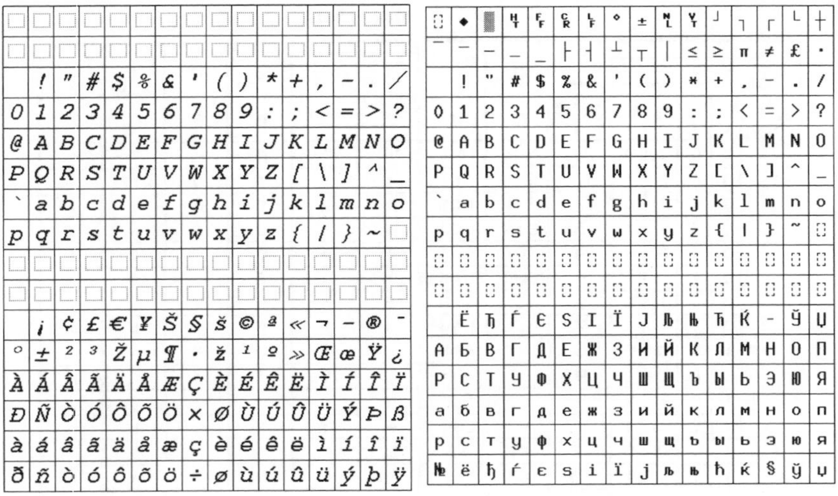

FIGURE 6.21 Two International Organization for Standardization coding schemes, ISO-8859-1 (Western European) and ISO-8859-5 (Cyrillic)

Note: in both cases the coding is divided into two sets. The lower 7-bit set is exactly the same as ASCII. The second, 8-bit set—i.e. with the eighth bit set to 1—contains the extended characters; extended Latin in the case of ISO-8859-1; Cyrillic in the case of ISO-8859-5.

Figure 6.21. Note that in each case, the first half of the page is identical to ASCII, whereas the second half contains the encodings for the additional set of characters. Various encodings of this kind were developed for a variety of scripts under the auspices of the ISO, with parallel developments such as ISCII (Indian Standard Code for Information Exchange) for encoding Indian scripts.

There are two problems with this approach, however. The first problem is that even expanding to 256 characters is not sufficient for some scripts. Clearly for Chinese, for example, there are far more characters than that: there are thousands. So in order to encode Chinese, you simply could not assume a representation where each character is represented by one byte. Various solutions to this problem, usually involving two-byte codes (which in principle allows up to 65,536 characters—more than enough to handle Chinese) were devised. Among the more popular of these were the various *guobiao* ('GB') national standards in Mainland China, aimed initially at encoding simplified characters; and various versions of the Big5 coding system used for traditional characters in Taiwan and Hong Kong.

The second, and more serious problem, was that the various coding systems used the *same* codes to represent different characters, depending upon what standard was being assumed. An 8-bit ISO-8859-1 Latin character will happily display as an 8-bit ISO-8859-5 Cyrillic character, if you happen to be viewing the text in an environment that is set to view Cyrillic text. Anyone who has received garbled-looking text in email, or who has had to fiddle with a browser's character encoding setting to get a page to display correctly, is familiar with this problem. More generally, these schemes for the most part make it impossible, or at least very hard, to mix text from different scripts within the same text document. Clearly a solution was needed where different scripts did not 'invade' each other's space.

6.2.2.4 *Multilingual computing: from Xerox Star to Unicode*   In the late 1970s a team at Xerox's Systems Development Department in El Segundo, California, began work on their vision of the 'office of the future'.[31] Most of the computer tools that we are familiar with today, such as windows, the mouse, clickable icons, 'wysiwyg'[32] interfaces, menus, and the 'desktop' had their origin in the Xerox Star, more formally known as the Xerox 8010. The Star system was released in 1981.

Of interest to us here are the multilingual capabilities of the system, which are described in a *Scientific American* article by Joe Becker, the main designer of that aspect of the Star system.[33] There were a great many innovations in the system. Unlike most systems, which depended on 8-bit character codes of the kind we have already discussed, Star used 16-bit codes, to allow for a much wider range of characters. Input systems had to be designed for all the various languages, as well as fonts to represent the different scripts, and clever rendering algorithms to deal with scripts (such as Arabic, or Devanagari) where putting characters together involves more than just a simple linear arrangement of symbols.

Despite its great ingenuity, Star was not a commercial success. Much of this has been attributed to the fact that Xerox was primarily a manufacturer of photocopiers. The various innovations that came out of the research labs in California—which, by the way, included several fundamental contributions to computational linguistics (the work of Ron Kaplan and colleagues at the Palo Alto Research Center)—were of little interest to the company. But Star was also stymied by issues of computational power: the system was slow to boot, slow to save files, and if the system crashed for any reason, recovery could take hours. The IBM PC, which came out at about the same time, was a less powerful machine running a very primitive operating system (MS-DOS), and had few of the impressive capabilities of the Xerox system. Yet because the software was less demanding on the computing resources of the machine, one could do much of what one wanted to do more efficiently. Thus, with the exception of the relatively few people who absolutely needed full multi-lingual capabilities, the PC was generally a more practical option.

Joe Becker, however, figured prominently in a far more commercially important venture, namely the Unicode Consortium, which he founded in 1987 along with Apple's Mark Davis and Lee Collins. The Consortium was incorporated in 1991. The original conception for Unicode was laid out in a 1988 document by Becker entitled 'Unicode88'.[34] In that document, Becker proposed a 16-bit character encoding scheme, which was quite sufficient to cover the characters in all the scripts in current use; indeed, he explicitly rejected the notion that ancient scripts or rare characters should find a place in the Unicode encoding system.

That is not how things turned out however, and Unicode has evolved significantly in the twenty years it has been in existence. Indeed, one of the most common misconceptions about Unicode is that it is basically a two-byte (sixteen bit) code. It is not.[35] There are two basic reasons for saying that, but first we need to introduce a bit of terminology.

The basic unit in Unicode is the *code point*, which is a particular number assigned to a particular *character* in a script. It is important to realize that a *character* is *not* the same thing as a *glyph*, which is the term used to denote a particular character shape; we will return to this point below. Thus, the Latin capital 'A' is assigned the code point 65. 65 is 41 base 16 (hexadecimal), and the code point for 'A' is conventionally denoted 'U + 0041' in Unicode terminology. Code points are arranged into *blocks* of characters that belong together. Thus there is a block for basic Latin characters, a couple of blocks devoted to various Latin extensions (including various accented characters), a block for Greek (and Coptic), a block for Devanagari, several blocks for Chinese characters, and so forth for a variety of scripts. Finally, blocks are organized into planes, each of which consists of 2^{16} (65,536) code points. All of the characters in common use in modern writing systems are in the lowest *Basic Multilingual Plane*, which ranges from U + 0000 to U + FFFF (= 65,535). Above the Basic Multilingual Plane, there are 16 other planes.

Now, it happens that any number between 0 and 65,536 *can* be represented with two bytes: two bytes have sixteen bits, thus one can represent any number between 0 and $2^{16} - 1$ in two bytes. So code points in the Basic Multilingual Plane could be represented in two bytes: but of course no codepoints in any of the other planes could. So one reason why Unicode is not a two-byte code is the mundane reason that not all the codes would fit in two bytes.

The deeper and more interesting reason is that Unicode is not itself an encoding (like ASCII or ISO-8859-1 or Big5). In Big5, a character with the

	Brahmi	Devanagari	Kannada	Tamil
ka	✚	क	ಕ	க
ki	✦	कि	ಕಿ	கி
kaa	✦	का	ಕಾ	கா
ke	✛	के	ಕೆ	கெ
ko	✚	को	ಕೊ	கொ

FIGURE 6.22 /ka/, /ki/, /kaa/, /ke/, /ko/ in Brahmi and three Brahmi-derived scripts

Note: /ka/ is the basic symbol, with all others involving that symbol plus diacritics. In all of the scripts, /o/ is composed of the diacritics for /aa/ and /e/.

code (hexadecimal) A440 (= 42,048) is represented in a text file by two bytes whose numerical value together is 42,048. The Unicode code point U + A440, in contrast, does *not* specify how that character is represented in a text file. In order to know that, one needs to chose a particular Unicode encoding, of which there are several. The most popular of these is the 8-bit Unicode Transformation Format, more commonly called UTF-8.

As we mentioned above, one of the fundamental philosophies of Unicode is the distinction between characters and glyphs, a concept that goes back to Becker's original description of the Star system.[36] Simply put, characters are abstract objects—one often sees them described as 'Platonic' objects, the 'ideal' 'A'; whereas glyphs are the actual shapes that appear on the screen or on a printed page. More generally, Unicode makes a fundamental distinction between the *logical* representation of a text, and its actual *rendering*, on a screen or a printed page. To see what this means, consider the Brahmi scripts we illustrated in Chapter 3, and in particular in Figure 3.10, repeated here as Figure 6.22. Consider the syllable /ki/, which in Devanagari involves writing the /i/ *before* the /k/, in Kannada, above it, and in Tamil to the right, but in each case ligatured with the /k/. Now, in each case, the *logical order* of the letters is the same: /k/ followed by /i/. And in Unicode, this is the order in which the text is encoded in each of these scripts: the /k/ for that script, followed by the vowel diacritic /i/ for that script. It is up to the rendering phase, as implemented by the display software and the font, to compute how that actually should show up on the page. The particular glyphs chosen will depend on the context. So notice that in Kannada the independent /ka/ has a topstroke that is missing in the /ki/ ligature. It is up to the font to choose the appropriate glyphs for the appropriate context. The logical representation of the text abstracts away from such issues.

But the issue is a bit more subtle than what we have just sketched. In order to understand this, it is necessary to dwell a little bit on the stages of processing that take place between when one types a sequence of characters on the keyboard and what actually shows up on the screen. For this discussion we will be considering only scripts that have a small number of basic symbols, small enough to fit on a standard keyboard. These include any alphabet, any alphasyllabary, as well as Hangul. For scripts such as Chinese, input systems typically have additional layers of processing to what we will describe here to convert from a small character set—say Chinese phonetically transcribed—into the large target character set.

For English there is not a lot to say: you type a character, this results in a character being added to the input buffer of whatever program you are typing in—be it a document editor or email client—and the corresponding character appears on the screen. For a script like Devanagari or Hangul, things are a bit more complicated. Say I am typing Korean and I want to type the syllable *won*. This involves typing four keys in succession corresponding to each of the segmental symbols (*hanja*: ㅇ, ㅜ, ㅓ, and ㄴ). But of course I do not want these to appear linearly on the screen as ㅇ ㅜ ㅓ ㄴ. So what Korean systems will do is actually group the symbols into a well-formed composite syllable after each keystroke: Korean software knows about the legal combinations, and will only group into syllables those sequences of characters that can go together. Thus as I type I will see the following succession:

ㅇ ... 우 ... 워 ... 원

At the end, the screen will display a single glyph 원 (Figure 6.23).

So a sequence of four keystrokes results, in this case, in a single glyph; but we haven't said anything about what gets stored in the text buffer of the program you are typing in—and thus what gets stored when you save the file or send the email message. Is there a representation of each Unicode code-point of character you typed? Or is there just the single Unicode codepoint corresponding to the displayed glyph? In other words, is 원 on my screen represented within the machine by four Unicode codes, or just one? In fact, in the case of Korean, it is the latter that holds. But in principle luther is possible, and in fact both are used in Unicode depending upon what script we are talking about.

To see why both are possible, consider that the process of composing the complex character 원 which I described above did not specify *where* that process occurs. One possibility is to have it occur as part of the text input software for

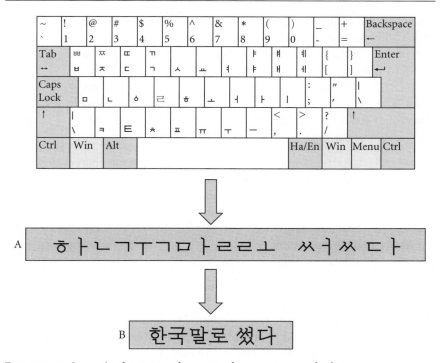

FIGURE 6.23 Stages in the process between what you type and what you see

Note: the Korean sentence is 한국말로 썼다 '(he) wrote in Korean'. From the Korean keyboard, one types a sequence of segments in A. These are converted to a sequence of complex syllable glyphs in B. The issue is *where* this conversion occurs. Is the Korean text encoding represented as in A, with the conversion to B handled by the font? Or is the conversion done as part of the input system, with the text encoding being as in B?

the script in question. Thus, as I type, a process is monitoring my keystrokes and converting sequences of multiple characters into a single Unicode codepoint. The other choice is to have this combination happen as part of the definition of the *font*, that is the code that specifies what glyphs need to be displayed and how they are arranged. The commonly used OpenType font is a fairly complex device, which allows for rules that specify that if a particular combination of characters is to be *rendered* it should be rendered using a particular glyph. To pick an example from Latin script, it is common in many fonts to provide a special ligature for the sequence 'fi', for purely esthetic reasons. In OpenType it is possible in principle to have rules of the form:

ㅇ + ㅜ + ㅓ + ㄴ → 원

Fonts also have the capability of overstriking one glyph with another glyph, which allows one to display, for example, one glyph above another. So fonts provide a couple of options for displaying multiple characters that are arranged non-linearly.

To clarify all of this complexity, it is useful to classify the different ways in which a sequence of typed characters can show up combined in some way other than strict left-to-right (or right-to-left). The possibilities effectively come down to three:

- Typed character sequences correspond to separate characters in the encoding; the font maps multiple characters to single glyphs.
- Typed character sequences correspond to separate characters in the encoding; the font handles the positioning of the glyphs.
- Typed character sequences correspond to *single* characters in the encoding.

By and large the first option is limited to selected groups of characters in particular fonts for particular scripts—for example the 'fi' ligature for Latin script. But the other two options are widely and systematically used. Korean, as we have seen, chooses the third option. The Brahmi-derived alphasyllabaries of India and South-east Asia largely choose the second option. Ethiopic, which is also an alphasyllabary, chooses the third option, like Korean.

The choices here by the Unicode Consortium may seem somewhat arbitrary, but they reflect the realities of working in a domain where standards already exist. In most cases, the decisions were made so as to have minimal impact on existing standards. Thus, while the complexities of layout of Hangul symbols *could* have been implemented in the font, because coding systems already existed for Korean where the composite Hangul syllables had separate code points, that was the avenue chosen.[37]

The persistence of existing standards also affected Unicode's otherwise esthetically pleasing decision to make a distinction between *logical order* and actual order of characters. As we have seen, Brahmi-derived scripts often write vowels before the consonants they logically follow; the short 'i' symbol in Devanagari is an example. In all of the scripts of India, this is treated as a problem of rendering, as we discussed above. Again, the *logical* order for a Devanagari sequence 'ki' is 'k' followed by 'i'. It is up to the font to make sure the 'i' ends up before the 'k'. But the simple beauty of this system was broken by pre-existing coding conventions for Thai and Lao: in these scripts, vowels which show up before consonants they logically follow also show up before the consonants in the encoding. Programs that deal with Thai text (I have written such programs myself) have to take this into account.

Conventions, once set, are often hard to change: like nearly everything else decided by committee, Unicode falls somewhat short of the ideal because, ultimately, compromise was necessary. In some cases, though, Unicode falls short of the ideal for reasons not of compromise, but merely bad judgment. To my mind, the most unfortunate instance of this (as also noted in Chapter 3) is the use of the term 'ideograph' to refer to Chinese characters (the usage goes at least back to Becker's original Unicode88 proposal). Thus one can find many references to 'CJK (Chinese-Japanese-Korean) ideographs' (or '*Han* Ideographs') in the Unicode literature. The ideographic myth surrounding Chinese characters has now, by act of committee, become part of the permanent lexicon of text technology.

But complaints aside, electronic text technology has changed the equation for the mechanical input of text. Gone are the difficulties of designing typewriters for scripts like Hangul or Devanagari, and the virtual impossibility of designing typewriters for Chinese that could be used by non-professional typists. To be sure the solutions are not always pretty. Inputting Chinese is still awkward, as Hannas (2003) rightly observes. Various systems based on the structural properties of the characters have been devised, but these are hard to learn; most users prefer *phonetic* input systems, which usually have dictionaries of tens of thousands of common words and names. But there are many words that sound the same in Chinese yet are written differently ('homophones' in technical parlance). Even with clever disambiguation software, the computer cannot always get it right, so the user must inevitably monitor what is appearing on the screen; for most users of Chinese input systems, touch-typing is not possible. For those willing to forgo keyboards, there are pen-based Chinese input systems that work quite well. But there is no getting around the fact that inputting Chinese text is not as straightforward, and never will be as straightforward as inputting English text. But for all that, the technology works well enough. Among other uses, Chinese input technology is used every day by millions of young Chinese in chatrooms all over the world.

6.3 Braille

The bulk of this chapter has dealt with mechanical and electronic methods for dealing with speech and language that have been developed within the last few centuries. We turn here briefly to one non-mechanical language technology that was also developed within recent times, namely the tactile writing system invented by Louis Braille. The social importance of Braille's invention cannot

	1	2	3	4	5	6
1	a	i	o	u	é	è
2	an	in	on	un	eu	ou
3	b	d	g	j	v	z
4	p	t	q	ch	f	s
5	l	m	n	r	gn	ll
6	oi	oin	ian	ien	ion	ieu

FIGURE 6.24 Barbier's matrix of vowels and consonants

Note: the vowel sequences ending in 'n' represent nasalized vowels.

be overstated: for blind people it allowed access to the written word in a way that had scarcely been possible before.

Braille (1809–52) was a twelve-year-old student at the Institution Royale des Jeunes Aveugles (Royal Institute of Blind Youth) when an artillery officer, Charles Barbier, came to present a system that he called *écriture nocturne*—night writing.[38] The system was based on small cells of raised dots, with six rows, and two columns for each cell. Barbier had originally envisioned his system as a way to transmit messages at night on the battlefield, but the army showed no interest in his invention and he was hunting for other applications. The idea that it might be useful as a reading system for the blind was what sent him to the Institution Royale.

The state of the art in reading systems for the blind was embossed fonts based on standard letters. Such systems had been around for a number of years before Braille first met Barbier's system. One such system had been developed by Wolfgang von Kempelen, the Hungarian scientist whom we have already met as the inventor of the first successful mechanical speech synthesizer.[39] But such systems never really worked. For most users, it was too difficult to train the fingers to feel the differences between letters, as a result of which very few people became successful readers. Louis Braille was one of the few people who did learn to read with embossed letters.

Barbier's system was different: it was much easier for fingers to make out patterns of dots than to trace the curves of embossed letters. But his system was complicated to use. It relied on a matrix of consonants and vowels shown in Figure 6.24. The first column of up to six dots represented a row in the matrix, and the second column represented a column; to interpret the code, one first found the right row, then scanned across to find the right column. For example, "j" would be represented by three dots in the first column and four in the second. Of course, the user had to have the matrix memorized. The second complication of Barbier's system was that it did not rely on standard

French orthography, but rather required the user to encode French quasi-phonetically. For example, Mellor (2006) gives the following example. To encode the sentence

> Une femme était restée veuve avec trois garçons et ne subsistait que de leur travail.
> (A woman had been widowed with three sons and was provided for only by their work)

one might first transform it as follows:

> un fam étè résté veuve avec troi garson é n subsistè q d leur travail

Thus, the spelling 'fam' is intended to reflect the pronunciation of the word *femme*. Similarly, 'garson' reflects the pronunciation of *garçons*.

Braille quickly saw the merits of Barbier's system, and set about during the next three years to deal with the deficiencies. He finalized the system in 1824, when he was fifteen years old. What resulted was a system that was significantly simpler than Barbier's in several respects. The twelve dots had become six, which are far easier to accommodate within the span of a finger. Second, Braille's system was based on standard orthography, so the user was not required to learn a new encoding system. And finally, because of this, Braille symbols represented letters directly, so that the learner merely has to become acquainted with the mapping between the different dot configurations and letters.

The Braille system as it exists today for the basic Latin alphabet, along with standard punctuation, is shown in Figure 6.25. Over time, the system acquired additional symbols; there is a limit of 63 possible configurations, meaning that there are 25 symbols free for other uses beyond the 38 used in Figure 6.25. Given the stringent limitations of how fingertips scan a page as compared to how eyes scan a page, one of the strong forces in Braille design has been ways to speed up the process of reading. Thus modern Braille contains several abbreviatory devices—contractions—that encode common letter sequences or words using a smaller number of symbols than would be needed for a full spell-out. Thus, the common word *but* in English has a single symbol encoding as ∴. While the symbols in Figure 6.25 are universal for languages that use the Latin alphabet, contractions are necessarily language-specific, since they depend upon the statistical properties of the language in question.

Adoption of Braille by the world's blind community was rapid—but by no means completely clear sailing, as documented by Mellor (2006). One of the issues to be overcome was the desire of individual countries to modify the Braille code to suit their language, a practice that was eventually stopped by

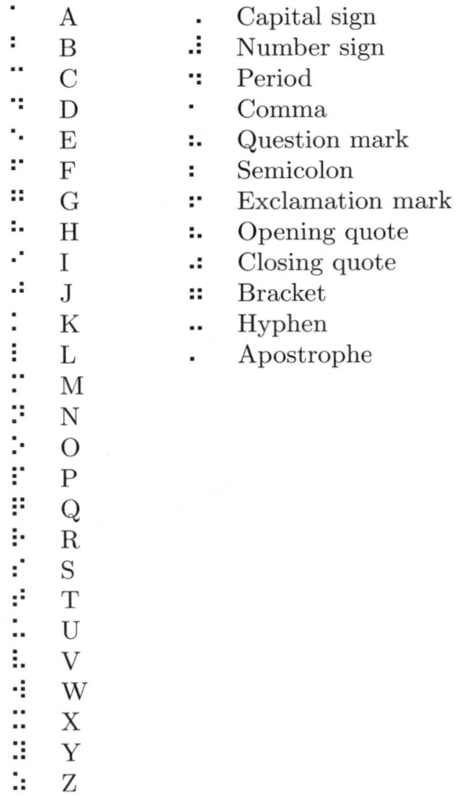

•	A	•	Capital sign
⠒	B	⠼	Number sign
••	C	•:	Period
•:	D	•	Comma
•.	E	:.	Question mark
:•	F	:	Semicolon
::	G	:•	Exclamation mark
:.	H	:.	Opening quote
••	I	.:	Closing quote
•.	J	::	Bracket
:	K	••	Hyphen
:	L	•	Apostrophe
••	M		
:•	N		
:•	O		
:•	P		
::	Q		
:•	R		
:•	S		
:•	T		
•.	U		
:.	V		
•:	W		
::	X		
::	Y		
::	Z		

FIGURE 6.25 Standard Latin Braille

agreement at an international congress in Paris in 1878. Some of the stiffest resistance came in the United States, where standard Braille had to compete with two entrenched systems of embossed type, an alternative code called American Braille, and another dot-based system called New York Point. International Braille eventually became universal in the United States only in 1932.

Systems were of course developed for languages that do not conventionally use the Latin alphabet. For Chinese, a phonetic system is used, with additional symbols to represent tones. For Korean, a system based on the Hangul letters (Section 3.3.1) is used. The Braille used in India—Bharati Braille—is modeled on the Brahmi alphabets we discussed in Section 3.3. Consonants have an inherent vowel, which is 'cancelled' either by a following vowel symbol, or else by an explicit cancellation sign. Bharati Braille is thus a linearized alphasyllabary. For the most part, where possible, Bharati Braille symbols are based on the closest phonetically matching Latin symbols.

In the extent of its penetration into the community it was intended to serve, Braille surely ranks as one of the most successful language technologies ever invented. It is only within the last couple of decades, with the advent of synthetic speech-based document readers of the kind we shall describe in Chapters 7 and 9, that Braille has had any serious competitors.

6.4 Summary

Mechanical devices that deal with language and ultimately with speech have been around for a while. Many of the technologies that we have discussed in this chapter either led directly to, or at least serve as an important component of, the modern speech and language systems we will deal with in the next two chapters. Modern speech synthesis and recognition, which we shall deal with in Chapter 7, evolved rather seamlessly out of the work that started with Kratzenstein and von Kempelen's work in the eighteenth century. The seeds of ideas for the mechanical treatment of language date at least that far back, if Swift's spoof is any guide. And the electronic encodings that evolved in particular during the last half century form the substrate for all of our work on language processing, to which we shall turn in Chapter 8.

7

Modern Speech Technology

We turn now to a discussion of modern language and speech technology, beginning in this chapter with the latter.

When you call up any of a number of telephone-based directory enquiry or other information systems, such as *TellMe* or *Goog411*,[1] you are interacting with a speech recognition system, and you are very likely also interacting with a speech synthesizer. How such systems work is the topic of this chapter.

One of the points that will become clear is that while it is currently possible to do an impressive amount with these systems, there is still a wide gulf between what machines can do and what humans can do. Only part of that can be explained by the facts that humans have a wider range of knowledge and are more flexible than machines. We will end the chapter by talking about some of the areas where a better understanding of what humans do might help improve what machines will be able to do in the future.

7.1 Speech recognition

When you or I understand spoken language, we perform a number of computations that convert a set of sounds into a mental representation of meaning.[2] So, if I say 'John saw the dog', you will interpret what you hear in terms of some kind of mental representation. You might, for example, visualize a male person (perhaps a particular individual you know) viewing a dog (perhaps a particular dog that you know). The auditory system and the brain must do a lot of work to do this. The raw sound, which impacts on the eardrum (tympanum) as a *wave* of alternating high and low pressure, is converted by a device known as the *cochlea* into a set of signals, transmitted by the auditory nerve to the auditory center of the brain. The brain then interprets these signals, mapping them to particular word sequences. These word sequences are further interpreted by other parts of the brain into a representation of meaning, including perhaps a visualization such as the one we just described. So the processing of speech in the human auditory system and brain breaks down into three basic components: the processing of the incoming speech sounds, the conversion of those speech sounds into likely sequence(s) of words, and the interpretation of those words into meanings.

How the brain does this is largely unknown. Even the low-level processing of speech sounds in the auditory system is only beginning to be understood, despite nearly a century of work on this topic, starting with Harvey Fletcher and others at Bell Labs in the 1920s.

Automatic speech recognition (ASR) is the machine equivalent of the human process just described. It should be stressed at the outset that it is highly unlikely that *any* of the processes that modern ASR systems use are in any way analogous to the comparable processes in humans. For example, the *acoustic models* that ASR systems use to process acoustic waves into hypotheses about what speech sounds were said are almost certainly different from how the human cochlea and auditory cortex perform the same computation. Yet the problem to be solved is the same, and it will be useful to break the description of ASR systems down into the same components that we sketched above for human speech recognition. We do need to say something at the outset about what we mean by 'meaning', the end product of the computation. To a large extent this depends upon the task to which a particular ASR system is put. In the case of a system like Goog411, 'meaning' consists of an entry or entries in a database retrieved by the system. If the system asks me to say a city and state (see later in this chapter for a sample dialog with Goog411), it expects me to answer with something that fits that category: 'Chicago, Illinois', 'Palo Alto, California', 'St. Petersburg, Florida' or 'Battle Mountain, Nevada', would all be valid instances. Its notion of 'meaning' in that case is to map what I say to one of the city–state combinations in its database. In that case it is actually unimportant whether it understood the exact sequence of words that I said, so long as it ends up mapping what I say to whatever city–state combination I actually meant. If I say 'Concord, in California' (perhaps because I want to emphasize that I mean the one in California rather than, say, New Hampshire, or Massachusetts), then if the system misses the fact that I said 'in', but still gets the right city and state, the transaction would be counted as a success.

Clearly this would not always be the case however. If my task were rather to transcribe the words that the speaker said, perhaps for an automatic dictation system, then getting the actual words said is much more important, and missing the 'in' in my example above would count as an error. Actually, speech recognition systems are usually evaluated in terms of *word*

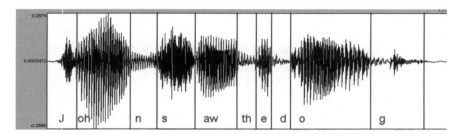

FIGURE 7.1 A waveform of an utterance of *John saw a dog*

Note: here for convenience we represent the sounds of the word using standard English orthography.

error rate—roughly, what percentage of the words they get wrong—and thus are evaluated as if their application task were dictation. This may seem like the wrong thing to do if we are thinking rather of an application like Goog411. But it happens that word error rate correlates well with metrics that one might cook up for other application scenarios, so, despite the obvious inappropriateness for some applications, word error rate turns out not to be such an unreasonable metric.

So how do ASR systems typically work? We have already mentioned *acoustic models*, which convert physical waveforms into hypotheses about which speech sounds—henceforth *phones*, the basic units of speech—were uttered; actually, more accurately, the waves themselves are first converted into a sequence of *acoustic features*, and it is these acoustic feature sequences that the acoustic model converts into phones. From sequences of phones we use a *pronunciation model* to figure out what word sequences might have been said. And finally we use a *language model* to figure out what word sequence was actually most likely, given what the speaker is probably talking about. In what follows, we will sharpen these rather vague notions.

Going back to our example 'John saw the dog', if you hear that uttered by me, your ear will hear a waveform that looks rather like the waveform in Figure 7.1.[3] In this representation one moves through time as one moves from left to right across the waveform; the amplitude of the up and down spikes corresponds to the acoustic amplitude at a particular point in time. The representation is entirely analogous to waves in the sea. As a competent speaker of English, you are not going to have any trouble understanding me when I say this, but in fact there are a number of complexities that your auditory system and brain are dealing with when you do so. First of all, you have likely never heard my voice before, so you will have to do some *adaptation* to my speech. Second, you may be unfamiliar with my dialect, which is likely different from yours: in my case, I speak a mixture of British and American English that reflects my own particular history of a childhood in Britain and adolescence onwards in the USA. My vowels are largely British, so that if you are an American speaker, my pronunciation of *saw* and *dog* will likely differ from yours. Third, it might be noisy: perhaps there are leaves rustling, or a train is passing, or someone else is talking in the background, all of which adds to the auditory stimulus you will be receiving. Fourth, even if you happen to have heard me say this sentence before, it is essentially impossible that I will ever say the sentence again in *exactly* the same way: I may speak faster or slower, or decide to enunciate different vowels slightly differently, or emphasize particular words differently. I might have a cold, or be drunk, or have just bitten my tongue next time you hear me say the sentence, all of which will affect the way it sounds. Yet somehow, as long as the variation in what I say is not too extreme, and as long as my speech is not too extremely different from that of other English speakers you have heard, and as long as the ambient noise is not too overwhelming, you will likely have no problems understanding me.

When speech scientists train acoustic models for ASR systems, they attempt to model the kinds of variation just described. Typically they will train the models on a large number of speakers, include as much variation in the *ways* speakers say things as possible, balance for gender (since the pitch and formants of women's voices are typically higher than those of men), and record in conditions that closely approximate the acoustic conditions that are anticipated when the system is deployed. As an obvious instance of the latter, if you expect the system to be mostly used by people talking over mobile phones, you would be well advised to collect speech over mobile phones, or at least simulate the mobile-phone environment by filtering clean speech so that it sounds as if it was spoken over a mobile phone. ASR systems usually also include algorithms that allow the models to adapt quickly to speech—new speakers, new dialects—that is not well represented in the training data.

To describe the full complexity of acoustic modeling would require too much technical background to include here, so we will limit ourselves in this discussion to a description of how a basic acoustic model works. The acoustic processing of speech in an ASR system starts with the extraction of acoustic features from the waveform—a portion of the processing often termed the *front end* of the system. The waveform is first cut up into a series of short time segments termed *frames*. The length of these frames depends upon the system, but 10 milliseconds (100 frames per second), is a typical length. Within each frame, *acoustic features* are extracted. There are various

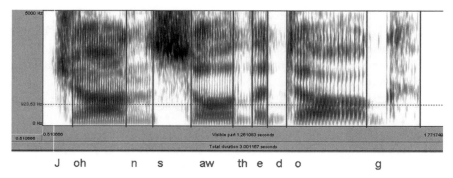

J oh n s aw th e d o g

FIGURE 7.2 A spectrogram of an utterance of *John saw a dog*

types of feature used in current ASR systems, but all of them have in common that they represent information about the amount of energy at different frequencies. To see what is meant by this, consider a different representation of my utterance of 'John saw the dog' than what we saw in Figure 7.1 above, namely the *spectrogram* of the same speech shown in Figure7.2. In this representation the horizontal axis again represents time, but the vertical axis represents frequency starting at zero cycles per second—o *hertz* or *Hz*—at the bottom, and going, in this case, up to 6 kHz (6000 cycles per second) at the top. The shading in the spectrogram itself corresponds to the amount of energy at the particular frequency, with darker bands representing more energy. For example, there is a lot of energy for the vowel 'aw' in *saw* at around 900 Hz. Much of low level speech processing involves tracking the energy at different frequencies, so the spectrogram gives us a lot of information about what was said. Indeed with some training it is possible to learn to read spectrograms.

Rather than spectra, most speech recognition systems rely on *cepstra*, a term coined by John Tukey at Bell Labs based on reversing the first syllable of *spectra*; the cepstrum is derived by computing the spectrum, and then treating the spectrum as if it were a signal and computing the spectrum of that. The cepstrum (like the spectrum, and the original signal) is in principle a continuous function, but in digital signal processing it is represented discretely using a vector of coefficients. Thus, each frame of speech is converted into a set of cepstral coefficients—often there are thirteen of these, representing the original speech waveform in that frame. It was recognized early that this information is not quite enough. Speech is continuously changing, and one of the key types of information that apparently allows humans to understand speech is not just the properties of the speech at a particular point in time, but how those properties relate to previous and subsequent points: the *transitions* between sounds are at least as important as the sounds themselves, as was discovered by Alvin Liberman and colleagues at Haskins Laboratories in the 1950s. To capture change in speech, ASR acoustic models include not only cepstral coefficients, but also changes between frames (so-called *delta* cepstra) and changes in changes (so-called *delta-delta* cepstra). If we started with thirteen cepstral coefficients, for example, we might end up with thirty-nine overall coefficients including these delta and delta-delta coefficients. The speech wave is then represented by a series of vectors, one vector per frame, of these cepstral coefficients.

So far so good, but of course as we noted above there is considerable variation in speech, so that if I say the same sentence twice, one will have two sets of cepstral vector sequences that will surely be similar, but equally surely will not match exactly. How do we deal with this variation?

Consider, if you will, how we might use various features to classify breeds of dog. One might imagine using such traits as hair length (Old English sheepdogs versus Weimaraners versus Mexican Hairless), length/height ratio (bulldogs versus dachshunds), eye color (huskies have blue eyes), and so forth. Within any breed there will be some variation, and if we assume that the variation is roughly normally distributed—that is, follows a 'bell curve' or *Gaussian* curve—we could imagine collecting lots of instances of each breed, and plotting the values for each feature of each breed. For one feature—say length/height ratio—one might imagine a set of data that looked like that shown in Figure 7.3. Suppose then that we come across a dog that we wish to classify into one of the breeds we know about. We compute the values for this dog and we compare the values to the distributions we have seen for the various breeds. Because we assume that each variable is normally distributed, we can compute what probability of any particular values of that variable follows from the supposition that our new dog belongs to a given breed. We then want to pick the breed that maximizes these probabilities over all variables.

The situation for speech is entirely similar. We collect speech from a large number of speakers and compute the distributions for each of the variables for each phone. As we will see shortly, most ASR systems actually consider not phones, but phones in particular contexts, such as an /a/ between a /d/ and a /g/—noted as /$_d$a$_g$/, and they also typically break each context-dependent phone into a beginning, middle, and end part. So rather than models for each phone, we actually have models for each portion of a context-dependent phone. In any event, when we are trying to recognize the speech of a previously unheard speaker, we consider how each frame of speech is best modeled by each phone for which we have trained the system. One wrinkle here is that

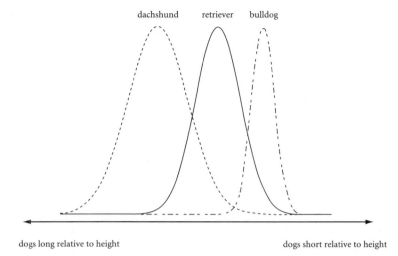

dachshund   retriever   bulldog

dogs long relative to height   dogs short relative to height

FIGURE 7.3 Hypothetical data for length/height ratio for various breeds of dog

Note: for each breed, a normal distribution is shown that represents a range of values for the ratio for that breed.

people usually do not assume a normal distribution for the features, unlike in our dog example. Instead they assume a more complex distribution, one which is generally modeled not by a single Gaussian, but rather by a mixture of Gaussians termed, not surprisingly, a *Gaussian mixture model* (Figure 7.4). These mixture models are then used to predict the probability that the context-dependent segment in question has a particular set of acoustic features.

One thing to bear in mind is that the system will only classify sounds into categories that it knows about, that is categories that it has been trained on. If the system is trained on English, it will not know anything about a sound such as the *velar fricative* of the German pronunciation of the 'ch' in 'Bach' (/x/, in phonetic transcription). So if someone uses that sound, the system will do the best it can and classify it as some other sound. If you are lucky you will get something reasonable such as /h/ or /k/, but if you are unlucky it may be somewhat unpredictable what you will get.

So far we have discussed the acoustic model, but we have said nothing about how we perform the large number of computations involved in deciding the most likely sequence of phones. We turn now to this topic. At the core of most speech recognizers used today is a device called a *Hidden Markov Model* or *HMM*. To explain what HMMs do, let us start with a rather homely example. Suppose that I live in a temperate zone and assume for the sake of this discussion there are only two seasons, which we can call the 'cool' season (autumn/winter)

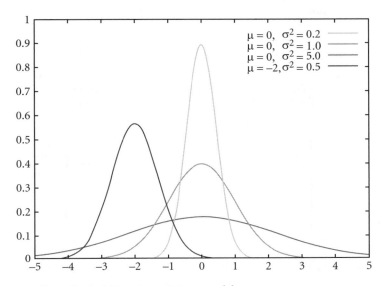

FIGURE 7.4 Hypothetical Gaussian mixture model

Note: this model is a mixture of four models with different means (μ) and variances (σ^2).

Source: from Wikipedia, http://en.wikipedia.org/wiki/File:Normal_distribution_pdf.png, distributed under the GNU Free Documentation License.

and the 'warm' season (spring/summer). Think of a *model* of this situation in which there are two states, one state representing the 'cool' season and the other the 'warm' season. Each of these states generates temperatures for each day. But all we observe are these temperatures, and it is our job to figure out the most likely season to which each day belongs. So, suppose I tell you that the temperature outside is 70° Fahrenheit (21° Celsius) and I ask you what season it is. If you are placing bets on this you would probably say that it's the warm season. But after a moment's reflection you will realize that this is not necessarily the case: after all it can get warm in the winter. Similarly, if I tell you that the temperature is 35° Fahrenheit (1.7° Celsius), you will presumably be most likely to say that it is the cool season, but you will realize that it can also get cold at least in the early part of the warm season. At issue here is the relative *probabilities* of two events, for example the event that it is 70° in spring/summer compared to the event that it is 70° in autumn/winter. The former (the probability that it is 70° given that it is spring/summer) should be much more likely than the latter (the probability that it is 70° given that it is autumn/winter). We can express these relative likelihoods in terms of *conditional probabilities*:

$$P(70°|\text{spring/summer}) > P(70°|\text{autumn/winter})$$

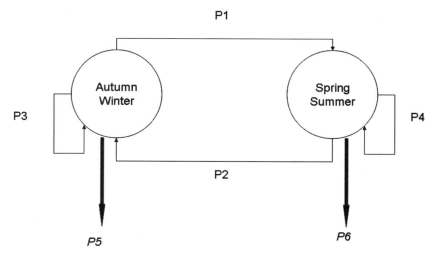

FIGURE 7.5 A simple HMM for seasons

This formula states that the probability of it being 70° given that it's spring/ summer is greater than the probability of it being 70° given that it's autumn/ winter.

Suppose now that I have a sequence of temperatures over successive days: say:

$$\dots 45°, 45°, 46°, 48°, 52°, 54°, 60°, 60°, 65°, 67°, 68°, 70°, 68°, 69°, 72°, 74° \dots$$

I'd like to know, for each day, which season we are in, and this is something that can be done with an HMM. A simple HMM for our little seasonal model is shown in Figure 7.5. There are two *states*, represented by circles, corresponding to the two seasons. Between these states there are *arcs*, marked with P1, P2, P3, and P4. Each of these arcs represents a transition between the two seasons, and the labels P1, etc., denote the probabilities of transitioning between one state and the other. Note in particular the arcs P3 and P4: these correspond to the situation where from one day to the next one stays in the same season. On the contrary, the arcs labeled P1 and P2 correspond to the situation where one changes seasons. Now, presumably P1 and P2 are *much* smaller than P3 and P4: this corresponds to the intuition that one does not change seasons very often, and in nearly all cases (except twice a year) if we are in (say) the warm season one day, we are probably in the warm season the next day.

What we have described so far are the *transition* probabilities of going from one season to the other. There are also the *emission* probabilities indicated with the thick downward arrows P5 and P6, which represent the probabilities of 'emitting' a given temperature given that we are in a particular season— that is the point that we started our discussion with.

In order to recover the sequence of seasons given a set of observed temperatures, we simply need to find the most likely sequence of states that produced the observation. Of course there are many possible sequences of states. Here is one such sequence that could have produced the fragment we saw above (using W for 'warm' and C for 'cool'):

...W W W C C W W W C C C W W C C C...

Here is another:

...C C C C C C W W W W W W W W W W...

Intuitively the second seems as if it should be more likely than the first since it corresponds to the situation where we are moving from the cool season into the warm season, which is what the sequence of temperatures given above appears to suggest. Of course, whether this is indeed the sequence of states that will score the best depends upon how we set up the probabilities P1...P6. But in any case we can compute the probability of seeing a particular sequence of observations given a particular sequence of states by simply multiplying the probabilities of moving between the states (the *transition* probabilities) and the probabilities of seeing a certain temperature given each state (the *emission* probabilities).

If we really have to enumerate all the possible sequences of states for a given set of observations, we are in poor shape. This is because the number of possible state sequences is *exponential* in the length of the number of observations. For this machine, for a sequence of N observations, there are 2^N possible state sequences. If we have 100 days' worth of temperatures, this is intractable. However, it turns out that there are efficient ways of computing the best sequence that do not involve enumerating all the possible sequences; the algorithm in question is the *Viterbi algorithm*, named after its inventor Andrew Viterbi, an electrical engineer formerly at UCLA and UCSD, and co-founder of Qualcomm.

All well and good, but how does this apply to speech? Consider that instead of seasons we have *phones*, which we already introduced, and consider that instead of temperatures we have the vectors of acoustic features that we discussed above. Then the problem to be solved is how to go from a sequence of these acoustic vectors into a sequence of phones. Rather than modeling the transitions between seasons, the transition probabilities of an ASR HMM will model the probabilities of transitions between phones. And rather than predicting temperatures, each HMM state will assign a probability to each of the values associated with the acoustic vectors. The HMM involved is naturally a lot more complicated than the seasonal HMM we have been discussing, but the idea is entirely the same. Actually, as we already noted, it is even more complicated than what this sketch suggests, since a typical HMM used in speech recognition will have states corresponding not to single phones but rather phones in a given context. Thus we would have a state not for the phone /t/, but the phone /t/ between, say, an /a/ and an /ɪ/. In addition there are typically multiple states per phone corresponding to the start, middle, and end of a phone. It is not unusual for an HMM in a speech recognizer to have thousands of states.

The acoustic model of an ASR system does not actually output a single hypothesis of the phone sequence, but rather a large number of hypotheses (typically many thousands). These hypotheses are then further combined with the *language model*, the other main component of a speech recognition system, to which we turn directly. As the name suggests, a language model is simply a model of the kinds of things a person might say to the system. Speech recognition researchers often cast the problem as one of assigning a probability to a particular sequence of words.

Two things may puzzle the reader at this point. First, what sense does it even make to talk about the probability of a sentence? Second, did we not just finish talking about acoustic modeling where we predict sequences of phones from the acoustics; why not just read off the words from the output of the acoustic model?

It does indeed seem odd to ask about the probability of a sentence: what is the probability that the next sentence I will say is *The aardvark won at roulette in Monte Carlo*? But it might begin to make more sense if I tell you the general type of stuff I am talking about. If I am talking about financial news, then surely that sentence is much less likely than the following sentence from the April 17, 2007, *New York Times* business section:

Stocks rose yesterday as better-than-expected profits at Citigroup and a healthy increase in consumer spending renewed the optimism of investors about the economy.

On the other hand, if I have been telling a children's story about an adventuresome aardvark, my silly sentence would all of a sudden seem a lot more likely than the markets-related one I just quoted. So one of the first rules in language modeling is to have a good model of the kind of stuff you expect people to talk about, and this is typically achieved by modeling examples from the domain of interest.

With respect to the second question, we now have to make an admission of a point that likely would not have been clear before: acoustic models, left to their own devices, actually do very poorly at transcribing what was said. So if you rely solely upon the acoustic model to give you a sequence of sounds that was uttered, the resulting transcription will contain a lot of garbage. On the other hand, if you allow the acoustic model to give not just its best guess, but N best guesses (for a reasonably large N), then one can pass all of those guesses to the language model and allow it to sift through the alternatives for ones that it likes. We will be more precise about how this is done later on.

The domain to be modeled depends, of course, on the application, and even within a given application, there may be many subdomains. To see this, consider the following interaction with Goog411 (in the United States, 1-800-GOOG411):[4]

Goog411	What city and state?
User	Urbana, Illinois
Goog411	Urbana, Illinois. What business name or category?
User	Bike shops
Goog411	Bike shops. If this is incorrect say 'go back'
	Top eight matches:
	Number 1: Durst Cycle Co, on University
	To listen to number 1, say 'number 1'
	Number 2: Bike Works, on W Main St
	⋮

If you follow this dialog, you will see that the set of things that the system is expecting from the user is different in each case. The first question asks for a city and state. A reasonable language model for this situation is simply a list of city–state combinations. If the user says something else—'banana plantations', for example—the system will have to compute whether it thinks that utterance is close enough to something it knows as a city and state. If it does, then the user will be offered whatever matches and the opportunity to say 'go back' if this is not correct. If the match is too weak—the system really does not think that any city–state combination could be pronounced to sound like that—then the user will be asked to try again. (Tweaking *rejection models* to make this decision is one of the black arts of ASR.)

Once the system has recognized the city–state combination, it is ready to recognize business names and categories. For this the language model would consist of a list of business names known to be associated with the location, plus a list of general categories from the Yellow Pages. The user's request for 'bike shops' narrows the field considerably: the user is then offered up to eight alternatives, at which point he or she can say basically only 'number 1' through 'number 8', or 'go back'.

At each stage of the interaction only a few kinds of things are relevant, so the system will take advantage of that fact by using a language model that is specific to what is relevant at the particular point in the dialog. Standard technologies such as VoiceXML are useful for building systems that structure a dialog in this way, loading in specific language models as needed.

These kinds of simple language models are sufficient for many current applications of ASR technology, but they are of course not enough for handling more complex domains, such as newsreading or conversational speech. For that a wider coverage *statistical* language model is needed. Here we return to the question of probabilities and we take up again the point that what we are interested in is an estimate of the probability of a sentence, in a particular domain. Expressed formally, what is:

P(the aardvark won at roulette in Monte Carlo)

A basic rule of probability, the *chain rule*, tells us that we can express this equivalently as:

$$P(the) \times$$
$$P(aardvark|the) \times$$
$$P(won|the\ aardvark) \times$$

$$\cdots$$

$$P(Carlo|the\ aardvark\ won\ at\ roulette\ in\ Monte)$$

Read this as follows: the probability of the whole sentence, is equal to the probability of the first word, times the probability of the second word given the first, times the probabilty of the third word given the first and second, and so forth up to the probability of the final word given all the preceding words (in the order they occur).

At this point it is necessary to say something about the basic method by which probabilities are computed, namely counting occurrences in a corpus of sentences that is representative of the domain to be modeled: if you want a system that will work well on financial news, a large corpus (tens or hundreds of millions of words) of the *Wall Street Journal* or similar material would be a good start. For a conditional probability such as P(won|the aardvark), I want to know two things; how many times does *the aardvark* occur, and how many times does *the aardvark won* occur? Dividing the former by the latter (C(the aardvark won)/C(the aardvark)—where 'C(X)' is the *count* of X in the corpus) will give us an estimate of the probability of seeing *won* given that the last two words were *the aardvark*. Thus all the probabilities needed could in theory be computed, but in practice there is a serious problem: most of the sequences of words that we need will never have been seen, and many will have only been seen a few times, not enough times to give us a reliable probability estimate. (If I tell you an event X occurred twice, and that one of those times an event Y also occurred, do you really believe that P(Y|X) is 0.5? Most likely you would say that we don't have enough data to be sure.) We are up against the most serious problem in language modeling, namely *data sparsity*. We cannot eliminate the problem of sparsity, but we can make it less of a problem by making a simplifying assumption. In our formula for the probability of a sentence we assumed that each word was dependent on all the words that had preceded it. What if we assume instead that each word is dependent only on the k previous words, for some small k. This is the *Markov assumption*: we assume that only a bounded amount of history is needed in order to be able to guess the behavior at a given point. (Indeed the Markov models that we introduced in our previous discussion are also Markovian in this sense, in that the machine has no memory beyond the current state that it is in.) Suppose we set k to be 1, so that we only care about the previous word. In this case we would have a *bigram* language model, so-called because we just care at any point about two words, namely the present word and the previous word. Then our formula from above would be rewritten:

$$P(\text{the aardvark won at roulette in Monte Carlo}) \approx \qquad (7.1)$$
$$P(\text{the}| <s>) \times$$
$$P(\text{aardvark}|\text{the}) \times$$
$$P(\text{won}|\text{aardvark}) \times$$
$$P(\text{at}|\text{won}) \times$$
$$P(\text{roulette}|\text{at}) \times$$
$$P(\text{in}|\text{roulette}) \times$$
$$P(\text{Monte}|\text{in}) \times$$
$$P(\text{Carlo}|\text{Monte})$$

Here we have done one additional thing, namely *padded* the beginning of the sentence with a special tag <s>, so that we can write that the first word is conditioned on being at the beginning of the sentence—that is it's not just the probability of *the*, but the probability of *the* starting a sentence.

We could of course condition on more than just the previous word: conditioning on the previous *two* words, for example, gives us a *trigram* model. But any way you look at it, this is a ludicrous assumption. It is obvious that words can depend upon other words that are very far away. A simple example will illustrate this. Consider the following sentence and before going on, ask yourself which word is most likely to fill in the blank:

Which ice cream did you tell Mary that John ate for _____ yesterday?

If you said *dessert*, you are like many others, and even if you did not, chances are you would agree that *dessert* is far more likely than *lunch*, for the obvious reason that we are talking about icecream and not, say, spaghetti. Yet a trigram language model would entirely lose the connection between the much earlier *icecream* and the position we are looking at, because the only evidence it would have would be that the previous two words were *ate for*. To capture that dependency requires a window of nine previous words, or in other words a *decagram* model, something far bigger than ASR systems normally use.

Yet for all of the ludicrousness of the assumption, it is surprisingly hard to do much better than an n-gram language model, and this is not for want of some very serious efforts by highly competent researchers. People have shown that one can get some improvements in ASR by using more sophisticated sentence analysis, which would take into account non-local effects such as the one we just considered. But for the most part the improvements have been marginal, and do not offset the added cost of computation—a significant factor in a real-time ASR system. Why should this be? The reason has to do with a general property of language: while it is perfectly straightforward to come up with examples that will break simple assumptions, such examples do not come up often enough in actual use to be a major source of errors. To see why this might be so one only has to look at the example sentence above and consider that most of the words are largely dependent on their local context. So one is not too surprised if a word like *did* follows a question phrase like *which ice cream*; a name such as *Mary* is not unexpected after *you tell*; a verb such as *ate* would not be surprising after *that John*. Given that many words seem to depend most upon their immediate neighbors, it is perhaps not so mysterious that n-gram models work as well as they do. In addition, it is worth noting that n-gram models implicitly incorporate three sources of information that are certainly important for determining likelihoods of word sequences. First, they incorporate syntactic dependencies: a language model trained on sufficient amounts of text will learn that *this dog* is a much more likely sequence than *this dogs* because of the singular–plural agreement

```
AAA    T R IH2 P AHO L EY1
AABERG    AA1 B ERO G
AACHEN    AA1 K AHO N
AAKER    AA1 K ERO
AALSETH    AA1 L S EHO TH
AAMODT    AA1 M AHO T
AANCOR    AA1 N K AO2 R
AARDEMA    AAO R D EH1 M AHO
AARDVARK    AA1 R D V AA2 R K
AARON    EH1 R AHO N
AARON'S    EH1 R AHO N Z
AARONS    EH1 R AHO N Z
AARONSON    EH1 R AHO N S AHO N
AARONSON'S    EH1 R AHO N S AHO N Z
AARONSON'S(2)    AA1 R AHO N S AHO N Z
AARONSON(2)    AA1 R AHO N S AHO N
AARTI    AA1 R T IY2
AASE    AA1 S
```

FIGURE 7.6 A fragment of the CMU lexicon, version 0.6

Note: The transcription system is ARPABet, a phonetic transcription system for American English that is popular in the ASR community. Numbers in parentheses denote alternative pronunciations.

requirement for demonstrative determiners like *this*. Second, they incorporate semantic dependencies: *eat a meal* is far more likely than *eat a dissertation*, because of what *eat* means. Finally, they incorporate some knowledge about the world: *flightless birds* is more likely than *flightless amphibians* simply because most birds fly and *flightless* is therefore a notable characteristic of those that do not.

To recap: acoustic models give us hypotheses about what phonemes might have been uttered by the speaker. Language models give us hypotheses about plausible sequences of words. What remains is to connect these together. Obviously one additional piece that is missing is a model of the pronunciation of words. For most ASR applications this is accomplished straightforwardly by having a pronunciation lexicon, simply a list of words with one or more pronunciations for each. This is a practical solution in ASR—though not, as we shall see, in speech synthesis—since ASR language models always assume a finite (if large) number of words. A fragment of the widely used Carnegie Mellon University (CMU) lexicon is given in Figure 7.6.[5]

A lexicon, combined with the language and acoustic models, gives one the basic information needed for decoding an utterance into words, but there is also the important issue of how to do this efficiently. Notionally what happens is as follows: the acoustic model enumerates a large number of scored sequences of phones corresponding to what the talker said. Then each of these sequences is converted to one or more possible sequences of words using the pronunciation dictionary (mapping from sequences of phones into words). Finally each of the word sequences is scored with the language model. For a medium length sentence (say twenty words), a typical speech recognizer may consider thousands or tens of thousands of possible word sequences, each of these word sequences being a hypothesis of what the talker said. A moment's reflection will assure you that the notional 'algorithm' I just sketched would be computationally infeasible: it would simply take too long for the system to weed through all of the possible sequences. Once again, though, there are efficient algorithms that help speed the process by several orders of magnitude. We have already mentioned one of these, the Viterbi algorithm, which can be used in situations where we only have to consider a bounded amount of past information in order to figure out the best move in a given situation. Other techniques used in ASR include *beam search*, which removes ('prunes') hypotheses that are worse than the best current hypothesis by more than a fixed amount or 'beam'. For example if the utterance was 'She had your dark suit in greasy wash water all year', other candidates might be 'She had your dark soup in Greece watched all year' or 'Gee, Haj, your tar souk increased what's Walter's oily ear' (ASR hypotheses frequently don't make much semantic sense). Analyzing left to right, when the system gets to the point in the utterance corresponding to 'suit', it may be the case that the alternative 'Gee, Haj, your tar souk ...' scores sufficiently badly that we can drop it. This is not guaranteed to be a good decision—something later in the utterance might have swung the evidence back in favor of that sentence—but provided we set the beam large enough, it will be reasonable most of the time.

What is the current performance of ASR systems? As you can appreciate, this depends very much upon the particular application domain, as well as the acoustic conditions of the speech (is it noisy? how much distortion is there from the microphone?), as well as how performance is measured. But to give a sense of the range of performance, consider the following. For clean read speech from English newspaper text such as the *Wall Street Journal* with a vocabulary of perhaps 100,000 words, word error rates in the range of about 5 per cent are not uncommon; note that an error rate of 5 per cent means that on average one in every twenty words is mistranscribed. English broadcast news, consisting mostly of speech from trained newsreaders, performs slightly worse than this (5–10 per cent word error rate). Conversational speech between strangers (who can be expected not to slip into overly casual modes of speech) over the telephone, but otherwise reasonably noise-free, has error rates in the range of about 30 per cent. But for conversational speech in noisy environments, error rates of 50 per cent or more can be expected. This is for English: for other languages, the error rates are generally higher across the board. This is not necessarily because languages besides English are intrinsically harder, but is often rather because there are fewer resources (training databases of text and speech) and because less attention has been paid to them. And indeed, as the amount of work and resources on languages like Mandarin Chinese and Standard Arabic has increased, so have the error rates begun to approach those we have for English.[6]

7.2 Speech synthesis

Speech recognition mimics, at some level, the process of understanding speech. Speech synthesis is the opposite of that, modeling (again at some level) the process of producing speech from linguistic input. Properly speaking, the term 'speech synthesis' denotes the technology for getting computers to talk from any kind of input. However, people quite often use 'speech synthesis' to refer to 'text-to-speech synthesis', where the input is text, typically written in the standard orthography of some language, where the goal is to mimic a native speaker of the language in question.

To clarify the distinction, consider that when you read a page of text aloud, you go through a number of processes. First you process the text visually (or, if you are blind and are reading Braille, through tactile sensations), and you form a mental model of what the text is saying. This will include information on what words there are, in what order they are spoken, how each word is pronounced, how much emphasis to give to each word, and higher-level issues such as whether the particular sentence should be read as a statement, a question, with an intonation conveying incredulity, and so forth. You then use this linguistic information to utter the text. The main alternative is the situation when we are engaged in conversation, or a monologue, where we are not (typically) reading, but instead are speaking in order to convey a message. In this case, the linguistic information that we utter is not the result of reading, but is instead the result of a mental process of language generation.

In this discussion we will focus largely on text-to-speech synthesis. Systems that produce speech by first generating language from information in a database do exist: they are often called 'concept-to-speech systems'. But text-to-speech is generally regarded as the harder problem and so a discussion of that will help the reader better understand the full complexity of the technology.

On the analog of our sketch of the mental process of reading aloud that we presented above, it is useful to think of text-to-speech synthesis (TTS) as breaking down into two components. The first starts with input text, the kind you are reading now, and computes a linguistic analysis of that text. The linguistic analysis is an attempt to model exactly the same knowledge that you have when you read a text aloud. Again, this includes the pronunciations of words, how much emphasis to assign to each word, what intonation pattern to apply to the sentence and so forth. The second component then takes this linguistic analysis and produces speech corresponding to the linguistic analysis.

For many years, up to the late 1990s, speech synthesis was the poor man of speech technology: far more resources were being poured into speech recognition than into speech synthesis. There were probably a number of reasons for this asymmetry, but an important issue was the perception that speech synthesis was essentially easier than speech recognition, and was basically solved. Another issue was the belief that speech synthesis did not have serious applications that did not merely piggyback off ASR—for example telephony-based information systems such as Goog411. Yet for many of those applications the quality of current TTS was not deemed good enough, and many developers ended up using canned prompts, despite the obvious costs of recording that this entailed. Thus a curious kind of Orwellian doublethink obtained for TTS: the problem was 'solved', yet the technology was not 'good enough'. Work over the past decade has improved the situation immensely: TTS is still not a solved problem, but it is at least good enough that people will tolerate it.

To explicate the various components of a text-to-speech system, it is useful to work with a concrete example, and step through the stages of analysis that anyone, human or machine, must go through in order to read the text aloud. To that end, consider the following first two paragraphs from an article from the business section of the *New York Times* for Tuesday, 24 April 2007, entitled 'AT&T's First-Quarter Profit Doubles to $2.8 Billion':

Telecommunications heavyweight AT&T Inc. said Tuesday its profit doubled to $2.85 billion in the first three months of the year, its first full quarter since completing its acquisition of BellSouth.

The earnings, which reflected growth in the company's wireless unit and regional business services, amounted to 45 cents per share for the period ended March 31. That was up from $1.45 billion, or 37 cents per share, earned by AT&T in the first quarter of 2006, when it had not yet acquired BellSouth.

Consider first the problem of linguistically analyzing this text so that we can identify the pronunciation of the words, and other linguistic information that we discussed. One of the first things that needs to be done is to break the text up into meaningful chunks. If you read the text aloud to yourself you will probably find that you break at sentence boundaries and elsewhere too. These breaks are not usually motivated by the need to breathe: rather they are done on purpose in order to convey meaningful information about the structure of the message. Normal punctuation helps, but it can be misleading and is often not sufficient. For example consider that the first full stop in the quote does not mark a sentence boundary at all, but rather marks the abbrevation *Inc.* Indeed the next full stop is also not marking the end of a sentence—it marks the decimal point in *$2.85*. So determining whether a full-stop-like mark actually marks the end of a sentence requires some analysis of the *context* in which it occurs. This theme, the need for an analysis of the context, will recur again and again in this discussion.

Of the two instances of full stops we have considered, the case of *$2.85* is the simpler: since there are no spaces on either side and it is surrounded by digits, this is pretty strong evidence that it is a decimal point. The case with *Inc.* is more subtle. TTS systems include lists of abbreviations and their expansions, so that we would know that *Inc.* is to be read as *Incorporated*, so here we could look up the abbreviation and then deduce that the stop marks an abbreviation. Unfortunately, this does not fully decide the matter. Consider the following made-up example:

> Things no longer look quite so good for AT&T Inc. The telecommunications giant announced Thursday...

Here the period in *Inc.* is being used to mark the abbreviation, but notice here that it is clearly at the end of a sentence. In fact it has a *dual role*, marking both the abbreviation and the end of sentence. This is a convention of English spelling: you do not double periods. Indeed, the following looks quite odd:

> Things no longer look quite so good for AT&T Inc.. The telecommunications giant announced Thursday...

In this case, the clue is the capitalized word *The* following *Inc.* (Of course this clue would fail in case someone simply omitted the use of uppercase letters, as people frequently do in email.) But capitalization clues are not always enough. Consider the following two cases:

> I live on Smith Dr. Jones, on the other hand lives on Park Ave.
> I live with Dr. Jones, who lives on Park Ave.

In the first case, *Dr.* (*Drive*) is at the end of the sentence, and our clue that the following word is capitalized would help us. But in the following similar example, this feature fails to give us the right answer, since in this case *Dr.* (*Doctor*) is a title that goes with the following name *Jones*.

We saw for speech recognition that it is generally sufficient to have a fixed dictionary with one or more pronunciations for each word; in principle, such a dictionary can be created by hand. This is possible for the simple reason that ASR systems have fixed wordlists. Obviously such a restriction can never work for TTS, because TTS systems must have ways to deal with any text that is thrown at them, and this includes words that are not likely to be in the system's fixed dictionary, or indeed in any dictionary. For example take a word like *Groke.* It turns out that there is a surname *Groke,* and there are also other uses that one can find via an online search. Yet the word does not occur in the CMU Lexicon of 100,000 words, nor does it occur in a lexicon of 50,000 names that was developed as part of the Bell Labs TTS system. Yet despite these omissions, the word should really not cause any problems, since it is obvious how to pronounce it, with the *oke* rhyming with *oak* and the *gr* pronounced as in *grin.*

In TTS systems word pronunciation is typically handled by a variety of methods, which depend to some extent upon the language being synthesized. Literate speakers of English are used to complex letter–sound correspondences: sets of words such as *though, through, bough, rough, cough,* and *hiccough,* which share letter sequences but have radically different pronunciations, are fairly common. In such cases one can do little besides listing the words in a dictionary with their pronunciation. But for words that are not in the dictionary one must have algorithms to predict the pronunciation. A number of different approaches have been taken to this problem. The earliest methods involved writing rules specifying how letters or sequences of letters are pronounced. To take our example *Groke* again, one might write rules that say that by default 'g' is pronounced as /g/, 'r' as /r/, 'k' defaults to /k/, 'e' at the end of a word after a consonant is typically silent, and 'o' before a stop consonant such as /k/ followed by a silent 'e' is pronounced as /o/. The set of such rules for English can become quite intricate, and while it is certainly possible to make rule-sets that have good coverage and are highly accurate, the development of such rule-sets is a non-trivial undertaking.

As a result many researchers, starting in the mid 1980s, have applied *machine learning* methods to automatically learn letter–sound correspondences from training data. In such approaches, one starts with a dictionary, typically several tens of thousands of words with their pronunciations. One then trains one's machine learning method on the training data, and the result of this training is a model that, given a written string, will predict one or more pronunciations for that string. Such systems are evaluated on *held-out* data consisting of words that the system did not see during the training phase. Recall the discussion of held-out data in Chapter 4 in the context of decipherment. The best current systems for English are able to get over 95 per cent of the phonemes right, on average. Note though that since there are typically several phonemes in a word, there are therefore several opportunities in any given word to get something wrong, the result being that a 95 per cent accuracy in phoneme prediction may only correspond to a 70 per cent accuracy when one considers how many words are completely correct.

Various machine-learning methods have been applied to this problem: *neural networks, decision trees, perceptrons, analogical reasoning,* and varieties of related approaches. One of the very first such systems was the *NETtalk* system due to Terence Sejnowski and Charles Rosenberg. In the mid 1980s, Sejnowski and Rosenberg trained a simple artificial neural net to transduce letters to phonemes based upon the context in which the letters occurred. For example, in the word *octahedron*, the middle 'e' is pronounced as /i/. Let us say that we only consider a window of letters around this 'e' three letters on the left and three on the right: so the left context is *tah* and the right context is *dro*. So, if this word occurred in the training data the system would be taught that a possible rendition of 'e' in that context is as /i/. These sorts of contextual features are simple, but reasonably effective, and much work subsequent to Sejnowski and Rosenberg has used these kinds of features.

Sejnowski and Rosenberg's work received a lot of attention when it was first published, in part because it was one of the first applications of the new *connectionist* approaches to language processing, and in part because Sejnowski and Rosenberg were very clever in their publicity. One of the things they did was run the output of the system through the DECtalk TTS system using a child's voice. Connectionist models are trained by exposing the system to the training data multiple times; one of Sejnowski and Rosenberg's experiments used at least fifty such *epochs* in the training. As the system was trained, it gradually got closer and closer to a correct solution. When the output was fed through the TTS system with the child's voice, it made for a very convincing emulation of a human child going through the typical babbling phase where it produces sounds seemingly at random, followed by phases where the system settled down into something that more and more approximated English phonology. In fact, NETtalk did not work very well: it only got 95 per cent of the *phonemes* right on the *training data*—that is on words that it had already seen (multiple times). That number has to be compared with the performance of modern systems which get over 95 per cent on data the system has *not* seen; Sejnowski and Rosenberg report 78 per cent phoneme accuracy on held-out data.

We turn next to the actual production of speech sounds from the linguistic representation. This is the aspect of speech synthesis that has changed the most from the inception of work on synthesis in the 1950s to the present. The original people who worked on digital synthesis—engineers like Gunnar Fant at KTH in Stockholm, or Dennis Klatt at MIT—were interested in understanding human speech, by simulating the acoustics of speech production. Such work involved building a digital analog of the various states of the human vocal tract. The approach is very challenging, and while Dennis Klatt's work eventually led to the commercial DECtalk system of the early 1980s—one of the best systems of its time—such *formant synthesizers*, as they are are usually termed, never sounded very natural.

Starting in the 1960s with work by Dixon and Maxey, an alternative approach of using segments of real speech was proposed. The idea here is to record a sequence of utterances from a speaker that would cover all of the sounds and sound combinations in the language, and then cut those utterances up into small chunks corresponding to *transitions* between sounds. Those transitions would then be spliced back together at synthesis time.

Why transitions as opposed to phones? As we noted above, early work on the perception of speech sounds done at Haskins Laboratories demonstrated that transitions between sounds are key to identifying the sounds. To convince yourself of why this might be so, consider the sound 't' in English, and consider in particular the sound that is produced for the 't' itself, when the tongue tip is touching the alveolar ridge, the vocal chords are not vibrating (because the sound is voiceless) and there is essentially no air flowing out of the mouth. In such a configuration, the vocal tract is producing *silence*. Indeed, it is common in phonetics and speech technology to refer to the silence of stops such as English 'p', 't', or 'k'. Obviously not much can be identified from silence, other than that the phone is likely to be a stop. However there turns out to be a lot of information in the transition between the 't' and the preceding and following sounds, especially if these are vowels. This shows up in, among other things, the *formant transitions* between the sounds (Figure 7.7).

The simplest concatenative speech synthesis system is a *diphone* synthesizer, where the speech database consists of transitions between phones; for any language we only have to consider the phones that can occur adjacent to each other. To explain by way of example, suppose we have in our database the phrases:

The cat is on the table
I went to the lab.

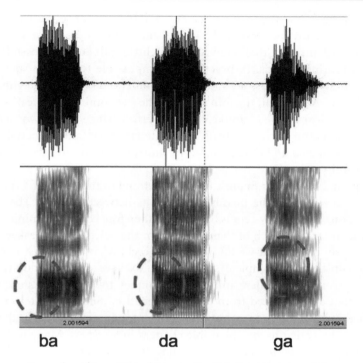

ba   **da**   **ga**

FIGURE 7.7 Examples of transitions between English /b/, /d/, /g/, and the vowel /a/ in English

Note: the circles indicate salient features for each. In the case of /b/ the first two formants (counting from the bottom upwards) have a slight upward motion coming out of the /b/. In the case of /d/ the first formant moves up whereas the second moves down. The same is true in the case of /g/, but in addition there is a noticeable "pinch" in the second and third formants, with the third formant moving away from the second formant coming out of the /g/.

From these phrases we can synthesize the phrase 'the cab' as follows. In order to synthesize this, in principle we need transitions between adjacent sounds as follows. Here we use '*' to represent silence at the beginning and ends of phrases, and IPA symbols for other segments:

   -ð   ð-ə   ə-k   k-æ   æ-b   b-

The first four units can be derived from the transitions between segments in the first utterance above, up to the /æ/ of 'cat'. The last two units can be found from the /æ/ of 'lab' onwards in the second utterance.

   The exact position of the beginning and end of the units is a bit of a black art. For the /æ-b/ unit, for example, one would not generally cut from the exact middle of the /æ/, but rather one would look for a place where the formant structure is reasonably stable and thus 'representative' of the formant structure for that sound, with as little influence as possible from the neighboring sounds. In practice it is impossible to achieve such complete stability of sounds; all sounds are influenced by their neighbors to some degree. As a result, the join between the /æ/ coming from 'cat' and the /æ/ coming from 'lab' is unlikely to be perfect, since these two /æ/ have differing left and right contexts. Concatenative systems generally have techniques to *smooth* between adjacent units, to try to hide these kinds of discontinuity.

A diphone system for English needs something in the order of a thousand units, to cover all of the possible transitions between sounds. The speech database on which the system is based must therefore cover, at a minimum, at least one instance of each of these units from the voice of the speaker.

Obviously given what we know about speech, what I have just described cannot constitute a complete system. Sounds have different durations in different contexts, so there must be techniques to stretch or shorten the sounds that are produced from the concatenation. Similarly, pitch must be modified appropriately to convey different intonation patterns, and amplitude must be varied to give plausible changes in loudness. Many techniques have been developed to handle these kinds of manipulations.

In practice few purely diphonic systems have been built in recent years, and most systems include at least some longer units. Sounds are often strongly colored by neighboring sounds, as well as sounds that are relatively far away. As an example, in most American pronunciations of the word 'rural', the two 'r's and the 'l' have a strong influence on the quality of the two vowels in the word. As a result, trying to synthesize 'rural' from, for example, the 'ru' of 'Rubik' and the 'ural' of 'Ural', would produce a very unnatural sounding result. Instead, one might simply 'cheat' a little and have this whole word as a unit in the database (something that was in fact done in one version of the Bell Labs text-to-speech system dating from the mid 1990s). The natural endpoint of this progression is to have a system that has no intrinsic limits on the size of the units, one that will find the longest units it can in the database. These are so-called *Unit Selection* synthesis systems, a concept that started with the CHATR system from Advanced Telecommunications Research labs in Japan in the early 1990s, and which now forms the dominant methodology used in current commercial systems. Since the units can be of arbitrary length, it would be impractical to pre-cut the units as is done in a traditional diphone synthesizer. Rather the units are selected at run-time from the whole speech database—hence the term 'unit selection'. Since the databases of modern systems often involve several hours' worth of speech, one can imagine that part of the issue in designing such a system is efficient algorithms for finding matching units. Indeed, a major component of such systems involves creating an index that can be efficiently searched at run-time.[7]

The search is accomplished by first indexing the database with features and associated time information. The minimal features that are used are the phonetic segments, as in a diphone system. But in principle any features can be used, so it is common also to index the database with features for duration, pitch, and so forth. Indeed, one of the properties of most unit selection systems is that they try to minimize the amount of processing of the speech, so that they prefer to use natural durations and natural pitch contours rather than, as must be done in diphone synthesizers, generating these and superimposing them at run-time.

Say I want to synthesize the phrase 'the cab' with a particular duration for the /æ/ in 'cab' and a particular pitch contour: I can go to the database and look up those features—the particular segments and duration and pitch information. If I am (very) lucky I will find exactly what I want, and I will just use that; for instance, I might want the system to say 'Hello' with a 'question intonation'; with any luck, the designer of the database actually had the speaker say exactly that phrase with exactly that intonation, in which case I can just use that. More often though, I will not find an exact match for what I want, and I shall have to find something that is approximately what I want, While in principle one could balance this decision any way one wants, systems will typically aim to get *exactly* the required segment sequence, and will make do with less good results for the intonation, duration, and other 'secondary' features. Even if one just considers the segment sequence, it is unlikely that one will find exactly the sequence that one wants for a given utterance. If my desired sentence is "Pucca zapped Garu when he was holding a kendo stick", it is rather unlikely that the speaker would have actually uttered that sentence in any form. So, as with diphone systems, we will need to splice it together from smaller pieces, hoping that we will also be able to get reasonable intonation contours at the end. Since we need to splice in many cases, there are actually two costs associated with synthesis in these systems. One cost measures how well a given unit matches what we want, and the second measures how well two adjacent units join. A significant portion of the work that has gone into unit selection systems has focused on good designs for these costs.

In practice the quality of unit selection systems ranges from highly 'natural' to very weird. On the whole, most such systems tend to produce good quality speech in most cases, though it has been frequently claimed (with some justification) that while unit selection systems are often more 'natural' and pleasanter to listen to than diphone systems, they are sometimes less intelligible than earlier systems. One point that is not so often noted is that precisely because unit selection systems try to minimize the modification of the speech, they are in some ways less flexible than earlier systems. Thus, you tend to get a fairly good quality voice, with a given pitch range and so forth; but unit selection systems usually do not offer one the opportunity to change parameters of that voice to produce, say, a voice with a different pitch range, or different overall voice quality. This becomes an issue in applications of TTS systems to aids for the visually impaired, a topic we will return to in a later chapter.

As noted, unit selection synthesis is now the dominant paradigm. Some well-known systems include the AT&T 'Natural Voices' system, voices produced by Cepstral, LLC, and various systems marketed by Nuance. A version of the AT&T System, via SpeechWorks (now Nuance) is used by the US National Oceanic and Atmospheric Administration (NOAA) weather radio: in that system, regional weather reports, including special warnings (e.g. tornado or hurricane warnings, as well as missing child alerts), are read, 24 hours a day, using a unit-selection speech synthesizer.

7.3 Putting things together. Issues for the future

We have talked about two principal components of a *dialog system* such as Goog411, namely the speech recognition and speech synthesis components. There is much more to such systems than just these two components, of course. One major component we have not discussed is the *dialog manager*, the piece that manages how the interaction with the user proceeds. This is typically handled by a *state machine*, where each state represents a point in the dialog and transitions between states are given that represent how one can move from one state in the dialog to another. For example, one state might represent the case where the user is being asked to specify a city and state. After the user gives an answer (e.g. 'Palo Alto, California'), the system then transitions to a state where it asks for a business name or category. From that state, depending upon the user's input, it will transition directly to a state that lists a particular business, or a state that lists a set of businesses in the category.

Beyond this, and the basic technology that we have already discussed, there is a large amount of engineering that must go into making something that actually works in practice. Just as there is a huge gulf between the basic workings of an internal combustion engine, whose principles are easy to explain, and a modern fuel-efficient gasoline-powered vehicle, much tuning goes into the building of a working dialog system. Here we get out of the area of basic technology and into the area of craft, something that goes well beyond the scope of this discussion.

In the technology itself some impressive advances have been made over the last few decades, yet there is much more that needs to be done. Even a casual interaction with a voice interface will likely convince you that automatic speech recognition is not nearly as robust as human speech recognition, and that in no sense can current speech synthesizers be called 'natural'. How do we progress from here?

There is a growing view in the field that the standard techniques that we have focused on in this chapter have more or less run their course. It is always possible to improve things by getting more data—more training data for acoustic models for ASR, larger databases for unit selection for TTS. But such improvements will be marginal, and the more data we use the more we shall face a problem of diminishing returns. Clearly new techniques are needed. For ASR, much of the focus in recent years has been on approaches to acoustic modeling that more closely resemble the way the human auditory system works, going back to the work of Fletcher and others mentioned above. So far this work is in its early phases, and nobody has yet demonstrated consistent improvements by including this kind of information in acoustic models. At the language modeling end, researchers have for some years now tried to improve over the current state of the art—n-gram models—by including more sophisticated linguistic analysis. Again though, most of this work has afforded relatively little overall improvement.

For TTS the issue is more subtle. For the voice itself, one of the challenges is to provide more flexibility and control over the speech output, in particular in the area of intonation. On the one hand, unit-selection systems can sound quite unnatural in some cases due to odd intonation produced by less than fully appropriate units, suggesting that one would like to be able to do things like superimpose an intonation contour on the output speech to 'smooth things up'. On the other hand, we do not understand enough about how to generate plausible intonation contours in all cases, and the signal processing techniques needed to take speech and resynthesize it with a different intonation contour often have audible side effects, which can reduce quality. For text processing, we have also probably gone about as far as we can with current techniques, and my own skeptical prediction is that only marginal incremental progress can be made until we achieve more complete natural language understanding—a goal that has been bort one of the earliest goals of artificial intelligence, and one of the most elusive.

8

Language Processing and Translation

Aficionados of the first *Star Trek* series from the 1960s will remember the 'universal language translator', a small hand-held tube-shaped device that was brought out whenever the crew of the Enterprise needed to communicate with an alien who did not already speak flawless English. Set in the twenty-third century, the series was full of technological wonders including faster-than-light travel, teleportation, and brain transplants. In contrast to these other marvels the universal translator may well have seemed quite tame. Mechanical translation devices permeate science fiction. In Larry Niven's *Ringworld* (1970), set in the distant future of the twenty-ninth century, Louis Wu and his companions are equipped with communicator disks linked to their ship's autopilot, which 'should be able to translate any new language'. Unlike the universal language translator, Niven gives us a hint as to how this device works: the autopilot requires data for training, and in their first encounter with the Ringworlders, this data is provided in the form of an impromptu welcoming speech delivered by a native spokesman.

Of all of the hopes and dreams that have been bestowed upon technology, one of the deepest and most persistent is the goal of automated translation. Throughout history barriers have been created by the fact that humans speak upwards of 5,000 distinct languages. Such barriers are so significant to us that myths have been constructed to explain the diversity of languages. In the most famous of these, the Biblical myth of the Tower of Babel, God bestowed multilinguality on us as punishment for trying to build a tower to reach heaven (Genesis 11). Thus, our inability to communicate with one another is a curse.

With the advent of the twentieth century and the development of computers, people started to see the possibility of applying mechanical methods to what had always been the domain of trained human translators. Indeed the first patents on the concept of mechanical translation date from the 1930s, before the invention of modern computers. Two inventors, Georges Artsrouni from France and Petr Troyanskii from the Soviet Union applied (separately) for patents on translating machines.

Troyanskii's invention is described in a fascinating paper by Hutchins and Lovtskii (2000). The invention itself was essentially a mechanized multilingual dictionary. It consisted of a sloping desk, upon which a 'belt', which was proposed to be about 2 by 4 meters in size, could move. Upon this belt were imprinted lines that contained head words and their translations into one or more languages. The machine was operated by moving the belt so that the desired word to be translated was aligned with a slit that was placed in front of the sloping desk on a horizontal surface. In front of this slit was a photographic camera which would snap a picture of the set of translated words onto a strip of film. Affixed or otherwise synchronized with this film was a strip of paper fed through a special typewriter, upon which the operator of the device would type various annotations of the word being translated. The annotations would include various kinds of grammatical information, as well as requests for clarification about the word which were, for some reason, to be posed in Esperanto. (When, in the late 1930s, Esperantists came under suspicion by Stalin of being foreign collaborationists, Troyanskii dropped the requirement of using Esperanto.)

Troyanskii envisioned the use of the system as follows. A speaker of the *source language* (the language from which the translation was being made) would first annotate the source text with various kinds of grammatical information, and would identify roots of words. Then, the device just described would be employed to find equivalent roots in the *target language(s)* (the language into which the translation was being performed). Simultaneously, the operator would type the linguistic annotations added in the original analysis of the source text. The paired target roots and grammatical information would then be passed to a 'reviser', who would assemble the two columns (the roots and their annotations) into a single stream of text in the target language. A 'literary editor' would then go over the translation and would make various changes to make it more idiomatic and so forth. The system is what we would today call a *machine aided translation* system.

It is not known where Troyanskii got his idea for this device, but Hutchins and Lovtskii speculate that his original inspiration may have been Swift's description of the 'literary engine' of the Academy of Lagado, which we discussed already in Chapter 6. As Hutchins and Lovtskii point out, *Gulliver's Travels* was popular in the Soviet Union at the time, and during the 1930s a film version was made.

Whatever the source of Troyanskii's inspiration, his idea and others like them were to a large extent inevitable. As we noted in the introduction to this book, it was inevitable that technology and language should conjoin in the first place, as they did millennia ago in Mesopotamia. It was similarly inevitable that one of the products of the Enlightenment should have been an interest in speaking machines, as we saw in Chapter 6. And it was inevitable that, with the seeds of computing devices in the late nineteenth and early twentieth century, people would turn their attention to mechanical translation.

We will describe Machine Translation (MT) systems in this chapter and give some idea of how they work. In many ways MT is the most overarching of all natural language technologies. Parsers (syntactic analyzers), semantic analysis, morphological (word structure) analyzers, generators (systems that produce sentences), and systems that align streams of text in multiple languages are used in other applications; but only MT combines them all. For that reason MT makes for a wonderful introduction to all of language processing technology—an ironic situation given that, as we shall see in Section 8.2 below, there was a long period when MT was the pariah of the field.

8.1 Early MT

Work on MT started in earnest after the Second World War, and was inspired in large measure by two factors. One was the perceived threat of the Soviet Union in the realm of science, technology, and weapons research. Since few Western scientists knew Russian, and since the cost of human translation was deemed to be high, a solution was sought that would reduce, or eliminate, the human labor involved.

The second factor was the advances in codebreaking during the War, the most famous of these being the British work on the Enigma project, which included one of the founders of computer science, Alan Turing. The advances in codebreaking were concomitant with and depended upon advances in information theory: Claude Shannon, the father of information theory, started his work on the theory at Bell Laboratories during the war, with the initial applications being to military intelligence. After the war, many mathematicians and information theorists were anxious to apply their techniques to a wider range of problems than military codes and ciphers. Researchers started to think of translation as an instance of decoding.[1]

The person most often credited with the idea of applying a computational codebreaking approach to translation is Warren Weaver, who wrote to the mathematician Norbert Wiener on March 4, 1947:

Recognizing fully, even though necessarily vaguely, the semantic difficulties because of multiple meanings, etc., I have wondered if it were unthinkable to design a computer which would translate. Even if it would translate only scientific material (where the semantic difficulties are very notably less), and even if it did produce an inelegant (but intelligible) result, it would seem to me worth while. Also knowing nothing official about, but having guessed and inferred considerable about, powerful new mechanized methods in cryptography—methods which I believe succeed even when one does not know what language has been coded—one naturally wonders if the problem of translation could conceivably be treated as a problem in cryptography. When I look at an article in Russian, I say 'This is really written in English, but it has been coded in some strange symbols. I will now proceed to decode.'[2]

Wiener was fairly dismissive of the idea, citing the great vagueness and ambiguity of natural language. But others had had similar ideas, among them Alan Turing.

Weaver was not daunted by Wiener's negative response, and in 1949 he circulated a memorandum entitled 'Translation' among about thirty colleagues. The memorandum laid out the goals of his envisioned research program in the first two paragraphs, wherein Weaver simultaneously displays both his ambition and his modesty:[3]

There is no need to do more than mention the obvious fact that a multiplicity of languages impedes cultural interchange between the peoples of the earth, and is a serious deterrent to international understanding. The present memorandum, assuming the validity and importance of this fact, contains some comments and suggestions bearing on the possibility of contributing at least something to the solution of the world-wide translation problem through the use of electronic computers of great capacity, flexibility, and speed.

The suggestions of this memorandum will surely be incomplete and naïve, and may well be patently silly to an expert in the field for the author is certainly not such.

Weaver recognized that one of the most significant problems facing mechanical translation is ambiguity. How do I know if I should translate English *drugs* as French *médicaments* or *drogues*? The latter would be appropriate if I am talking about illicit drugs, the former if I am talking about medicine.

His answer to this problem is worth quoting at length since it is quite prescient:

First, let us think of a way in which the problem of multiple meaning can, in principle at least, be solved. If one examines the words in a book, one at a time as through an opaque mask with a hole in it one word wide, then it is obviously impossible to determine, one at a time, the meaning of the words. 'Fast' may mean 'rapid'; or it may mean 'motionless'; and there is no way of telling which.

But, if one lengthens the slit in the opaque mask, until one can see not only the central word in question but also say N words on either side, then, if N is large enough one can unambiguously decide the meaning of the central word. The formal truth of this statement becomes clear when one mentions that the middle word of a whole article or a whole book is unambiguous if one has read the whole article or book, providing of course that the article or book is sufficiently well written to communicate at all.

The practical question is: 'What minimum value of N will, at least in a tolerable fraction of cases, lead to the correct choice of meaning for the central word?'

This is a question concerning the statistical semantic character of language which could certainly be answered, at least in some interesting and perhaps in a useful way. Clearly N varies with the type of writing in question. It may be zero for an article known to be about a specific mathematical subject. It may be very low for chemistry, physics, engineering, etc. If N were equal to 5, and the article or book in question were on some sociological subject, would there be a probability of 0.95 that the choice of meaning would be correct 98% of the time? Doubtless not: but a statement of this sort could be made, and values of N could be determined that would meet given demands.

Ambiguity, moreover, attaches primarily to nouns, verbs, and adjectives; and actually (at least so I suppose) to relatively few nouns, verbs, and adjectives. Here again is a good subject for study concerning the statistical semantic character of languages. But one can imagine using a value of N that varies from word to word, is zero for he, the, etc., and needs to be large only rather occasionally. Or would it determine unique meaning in a satisfactory fraction of cases, to examine not the 2N adjacent words, but perhaps the 2N adjacent nouns? What choice of adjacent words maximizes the probability of correct choice of meaning, and at the same time leads to a small value of N?

What Weaver describes here is a methodology for *sense disambiguation* which is remarkably similar to modern statistical approaches to this problem, which predict the senses of words—for example the *drugs* example above—based on co-occurrences with other words in the context. But Weaver was wrong in the supposition expressed in the last paragraph: ambiguity is not just a property of a few nouns, verbs, and adjectives. It is rampant.

Weaver's proposal was not sketched in great detail, but he did make it clear that he viewed it as critical that one pursue 'an approach that goes so deeply into the structure of languages as to come down to the level where they exhibit common traits'. This notion, which has permeated linguistic and computational-linguistic thinking for the last half century, is related to the notion of 'Universal Grammar' in linguistics, and to 'interlingua' approaches to MT, which we will have more to say about below.

Weaver's memorandum stimulated a lot of interest. One result was that the Massachusetts Institute of Technology hired Yehoshua Bar-Hillel as a researcher tasked specifically with working on computer applications to natural language, including MT. In 1952 he organized a conference at MIT and published a survey of the issues in MT as he understood them. He spoke of the need for MT, stressing 'the urgency of having foreign language publications, mainly in the fields of science, finance and diplomacy, translated with high accuracy and reasonable speed.' Bar-Hillel recognized that completely automatic translation would always be inaccurate, but that one could trade off accuracy with effort; the effort that would improve the result was in the form of *pre-editing* the source text and *post-editing* the target text. These techniques have been used at various times in the history of Machine Translation.[4]

The first public demonstration of a machine translation system was the Georgetown–IBM system, in 1954. Perhaps predictably, this was a Russian–English system. It was a small experiment, involving just six grammar rules and 250 words.[5] The words were selected to cover precisely the set of sentences that were to be covered in the demo. The six rules involved lexical-choice decisions and syntactic rearrangements of words based upon specially coded features of words in the lexicon.

Reporters from various publications were present at the demonstration, and they were clearly overwhelmed by what they considered the success that the researchers had achieved. It was expected that within a few years the problem would be largely solved. The following was typical of the reports:

It is expected by IBM and Georgetown University, which collaborated on this project, that within a few years there will be a number of 'brains' translating all languages with equal aplomb and dispatch.   (Harry Kenny, *Christian Science Monitor*, 11 January 1954)

In fact the main problem that concerned the observers was the time bottleneck of inputting the sentences onto punched cards and feeding these into the computer.

So, despite misgivings expressed in some quarters (e.g. by Wiener), the early days of machine translation were characterized by unbridled confidence that the basic problem would be solved within a matter of a few years' time. The following excerpt from an interview with J. McDaniel, a British MT researcher, from some time during the mid 1960s, is typical of the enthusiasm prevalent at the time:

Interviewer: At present of course, you're just in the experimental stage. When you go in for full-scale production, what will the capacity be?

McDaniel: We should be able to do about—with a modern commercial computer—about one to two million words an hour, and this will be quite an adequate speed to cope with the whole output of the Soviet Union in just a few hours' computer time a week.

Interviewer: When do you hope to be able to achieve this speed?

McDaniel: If our experiments go well, then perhaps within about five years or so.
Interviewer: And finally Mr. McDaniel, does this mean the end of human translators?
McDaniel: I'd say 'yes' for translators of scientific and technical material. But as regards poetry and novels, no I don't think we'll ever replace the translators of that type of material.

8.2 The ALPAC report

However in 1966 a damper was to be placed on this enthusiasm, at least in the United States. That damper was the *ALPAC Report*, one of the most famous and at the same time infamous events in the early history of machine translation. The Automatic Language Processing Advisory Committee (ALPAC) was formed under the auspices of the National Academy of Sciences and the National Research Council. It was headed by John Pierce—Vice-President for Research at Bell Laboratories, and supervisor of the Bell Labs team that invented the transistor[6]—and included a multidisciplinary panel of experts including the linguists Charles Hockett and Eric Hamp. The Committee was tasked with assessing the state of the art in machine translation and reporting on whether it was worth funding further work in this area. The committee published its Report as Pierce et al. (1966).

In the report, the committee questioned the need for Machine Translation research at a couple of levels. First, in the 1960s the main focus of translation work was the translation of Russian technical documents into English. According to the Report, there was no shortage of human translators to do the job, and in fact it was likely that too much material was being translated. It is worth stressing that this was a direct contradiction of Bar-Hillel's argument for the need for MT, quoted above.

Second, MT just did not work well enough. The technology of the early 1960s was sufficiently limited that much of what was produced automatically was effectively useless and required much too much post-editing to be usable. As an example of the quality of MT available at the time of the *ALPAC Report*, consider the following sample of a Russian–English translation, from Pierce et al. (1966: 21):

The biological experiments that were carried out on different cosmic flying apparatus, ASTROFIZICESKIE the research of cosmic PROSTRANSTVA and the flights of Soviet and American KOSMONAVTOV with sufficient UBEDITEL6NOST6H showed, that the short-time orbital flights below of the radiational belts of earth in the absence that was raised by the SOLNECNOI one of activity in a radiational attitude are BEZO-PASNYMI. Dose of radiation at the expense of primary cosmic radiation and the radiation of an exterior radiational belt the obtained by KOSMONAVTAMI are so little, that aren't able to render a harmful influence to the organism of man.

The capitalized words are words that were left untranslated from Russian, presumably because the system did not have those words in its dictionary; surprisingly, the common word *cosmonaut* (*KOSMONAVTOV, KOSMONAV-TAMI*) was left untranslated. While it is clearly possible to get a sense of roughly what this text was about, it is also very hard to glean much actual information from this translation.

One might have thought that at least MT could be useful in that it would do part of the job, leaving it to a competent translator to finish the work. But in fact, post-editing a badly translated document can end up being more expensive than simply having a human translator do the whole job.

The main point of the Report was not to argue that MT should never be done, but rather that at that point in time it was premature. Too little was known about basic issues in linguistics and computational linguistics. So rather than fund work on developing MT systems—for ten years prior to the time of publication of the report, the government had spent $20 million on MT research and development—the government would be advised instead to invest in basic research in linguistics and computational linguistics, as well as to conduct *experimental* work on MT. The Committee suggested earmarking $2.5–3 million per annum for this purpose ($16–19 million in 2007 dollars, using the Consumer Price Index).

As one might expect, the government found compelling the Committee's suggestion to suspend funding for further work on developing MT systems, but neglected to follow up on the suggestion to increase funding for more basic research in linguistics and computational linguistics.[5] The upshot of this was that sponsored work on MT virtually ceased in the United States, and MT became a pariah of the field: in 1968 the *Association for Machine Translation and Computational Linguistics* changed its name to the *Association for Computational Linguistics*, the name that it has retained to this day.

For these reasons, the *ALPAC Report* has a bad name in Computational Linguistics—undeservedly so, in my view. It is hard, if one reads the *Report* dispassionately, not to agree with their basic conclusions. MT had been seriously hyped. There was little practical need for it at the time, and the quality of the translations that were possible fell far short of both expectations and the bare minimum of quality needed to make the systems usable. The Committee recognized that MT work had been useful in one sense: by trying to build systems that worked, it was quickly discovered just how complicated natural language is. Disambiguating words, and converting complex constructions from one language into another, are things that may seem tractable when one thinks about them in the abstract, but immediately become difficult when one tries to build a computational model to handle them. In light of that, the Committee's recommendation that we should step away from MT and concentrate rather on more basic work in linguistics was very level-headed. Ploughing ahead on full-scale production of MT systems, which would result in automatically translated documents that nobody could read, would have made little sense.

8.3 The middle years

While government-sponsored MT research in the United States effectively stopped as a result of the ALPAC report, work continued elsewhere, including in Canada and Europe, and at private companies in the USA. One of these companies, Systran, actually grew out of the original Georgetown work, and the company still exists to this day: when Google started offering automatic translation of web pages in about 2003, they initially used Systran systems, though they have now replaced these with in-house statistical MT systems, which we shall discuss below.

One further point to bear in mind about ALPAC is that its comments were directed against machine translation of *unrestricted* text. Clearly, if one could find an application domain where the text is so restricted that one could write rules that would cover most of the cases one is ever likely to see, then the problem becomes significantly easier. The problem is that there are not very many application domains that are both simple enough in this sense, and at the same time are important enough to make it worth developing an automated translation system.

Nonetheless, at least one such domain was found early on.

8.3.1 *TAUM-Météo*

In 1965, a year before the ALPAC committee published its Report, the Canadian government started funding for the Traduction Automatique à l'Université de Montréal (Automatic Translation at the University of Montreal) group. According to Slocum (1985: 5), a 'chance remark by a bored translator in the Canadian Meteorological Center (CMC)' was the original motivation for the TAUM group to develop a system for translating weather forecasts from English into French, required by the Canadian mandate that all official documents be in both languages. Weather forecasts are so rigid in their style and limited in scope that the task of translating them was monotonous in the extreme, so much so that on average translators would only last about six months in the job before finding something more challenging to do. In 1975 the Canadian government commissioned TAUM to produce a working English–French system; a prototype was demonstrated in 1976 and TAUM-Météo was deployed in 1977.[8] As of 1984, according to Isabelle and Bourbeau (1985), TAUM-Météo was translating 8.5 million words per year. The system accepted 90–95 per cent of the text input to it,[9] and handled these texts *without any human intervention*. TAUM-Météo was the first, and in fact the *only*, MT system to be deployed in a task where perfect translation was expected, and no post-editing was possible.[10] TAUM-Météo was used by Environment Canada up until about 2003, when it was replaced by another system.[11]

8.3.2 *Interlingual versus transfer approaches*

In early MT work, one of the main ideological differences was between those who favored an *interlingua* approach, with those who favored a more language-pair-specific approach, termed *transfer*.

In an interlingua approach, the text in the source language is mapped to a representation of the meaning which is intended to be language-independent. From this language-independent *interlingual* representation, text in the target language was to be generated.

A transfer approach is geared to a specific language pair. Text in the source language is analyzed into a representation of the meaning that is geared to that source language, and then rules transfer the resulting structure into a form from which sentences in the target language can be generated. TAUM-Météo was an example of a *transfer* system.

To illustrate the difference between the two approaches, consider a simple sentence *I see a brown dog* and its translation into Spanish *Veo un perro moreno*. Under a transfer system, one might analyze the English sentence into some sort of phrase-structure analysis, such as:

[I [see [a [brown dog]]]]

This structure reflects the fact that *brown* is closely associated with the word *dog*, that *a* is associated with the phrase *brown dog*, that the action being described is one of *see(ing) a brown dog* and that *I* am the one performing the action. In order to perform this kind of analysis, one would use a *parser*, and possibly other kinds of common natural-language analysis tools, such as a *part-of-speech tagger* (which assigns tags such as *noun*, *verb*, or *adjective* to words).

A set of *transfer rules* would then transform this structure into something appropriate for Spanish. For one thing, in Spanish most adjectives come after the nouns they modify, so one thing the transfer grammar would need to do is flip the order of *dog* and *brown* (Figure 8.1). Additional Spanish-specific rules would be needed to guarantee that the article *un* 'a', the adjective *moreno* 'brown' and the noun *perro* 'dog' all agree in gender: *perro* is masculine, and so the modifying article and adjective have to be masculine too. Another Spanish-specific rule would make sure that the verb form for 'see' is marked with the appropriate person and number marking: *veo*, on its own, means 'I see', and usually one does not express the 'I' with a separate word, since the verb already marks that information.

The system we have just sketched is geared to English and Spanish: one produces an analysis of the English source, and one manipulates that analysis to produce a Spanish output. In an interlingual approach, the English source would be mapped to a more abstract representation, one that represents the concept of me seeing a brown dog in a way that is not particular to the source language: if I had said the same sentence in Chinese or Korean, then the same representation would be used. Given that representation, one then generates a sentence in the target language.

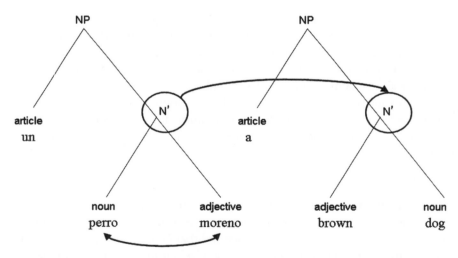

FIGURE 8.1 Tree transformation for the Spanish/English pair *un perro moreno/a brown dog*

Note: the adjective/noun reordering can be modeled as a "flipping" of the order of the words under the N' node.

The advantage of the interlingual approach (if one could actually do it) becomes apparent when one considers building systems that can translate between a variety of languages—for example all of the official languages of the European Union. In a transfer approach, for five languages one would need $5 \times 4 = 20$ systems, since for each language pair (L_1, L_2), one needs to build a system that transfers from an analysis of sentences in L_1 into sentences of L_2. In an interlingual approach, one only needs analyzers for five languages, which map sentences in those languages into the interlingua; and generators for five languages from the interlingual representation. If one is dealing with ten languages, then the difference is even greater: ninety systems for the transfer approach, versus twenty components for the interlingual approach.

But interlingual approaches are much harder to design than transfer approaches. In practice, all interlingual MT systems have been toys, working only on a small set of data, and never scaling to deal with arbitrary source texts. One reason for this is that the whole notion of an interlingual representation is suspect. Languages differ widely in what kind of information they choose to encode. In English, for example, definiteness and number are generally obligatorily marked, so that there is a difference in interpretation between *my brother saw a dog, my brother saw the dog*, and *my brother saw dogs*. On the other hand it does not matter how old my brother is relative to me: I still use the same word *brother* to refer to him. Mandarin is exactly the opposite: there are separate words for older and younger brother, but there is no way to mark definiteness or (on most nouns) number: *wǒ dìdì kàndàole gǒu* could mean 'my (younger) brother saw a dog', 'my (younger) brother saw the dog', or 'my (younger) brother saw dogs'. One can only know from context what the intended reading is. Russian is somewhere in between: there is no separate word for younger or older brother, and like English, Russian marks number. But it does not mark definiteness. So *moj brat videl sobaku* could mean 'my brother saw a dog' or 'my brother saw the dog'. In Korean, a new dimension is brought in with an elaborate system of verb markers to indicate levels of politeness or formality. Thus *dongsaeng-i gaereul bwasseoyo* means '(my) younger brother saw a dog' in a simple polite form. If one were saying this sentence to a small child one might simply omit the *-yo* ending to give a less polite more intimate reading: *dongsaeng-i gaereul bwasseo*. If one were reporting the action in a formal setting one could use the form *dongsaeng-i gaereul bwasssubnida*. In a newspaper style it would be simply *dongsaeng-i gaereul bwassda*. There is no direct way to encode any of these distinctions in English.

The question then becomes: does it make sense to believe that there is some Platonic language-independent representation that includes exactly the set of information that might be encoded in *some* language? As a point of fact, in general one's brother must be either younger or older than oneself (even, technically, for identical twins). English speakers are obviously aware therefore that the named brother in *my brother saw a dog* must have the property of being younger or older than the speaker. But it would be odd to think of this as part of the *meaning* of this sentence, since English does not encode this distinction. Needless to say, such issues are problematic for transfer systems as well: translating between two languages that encode such different kinds of information as English and Chinese, or English and Korean, is hard no matter what you do. But the interlingua approach adds a layer of complexity in that it commits one to the design and implementation of a language-independent representation of meaning, something that has eluded linguists and philosophers for centuries.

8.3.3 *Knowledge-based machine translation*

As if this were not hard enough, some researchers (perhaps most notably Jaime Carbonell of Carnegie Mellon University) have proposed what is often termed *knowledge-based machine translation*. The basic idea is that in addition to linguistic knowledge about the source and target languages and the relationships between the two, one also brings world knowledge to bear on the task. A standard example is the following. Suppose you have to translate the following text from English into Spanish:

John was driving to LA. He took a curve a bit too fast and hit a tree.

How should the verb *hit* be translated? In Spanish there are three verbs that might reasonably correspond to English *hit*: *pegar, golpear,* and *chocar. Pegar* and *golpear* denote hitting with one's hand; the correct translation of *hit* in this example is *chocar.* In order to get this right, one has to realize that it is actually John's car that is hitting the tree rather than, for example, John hitting the tree with his hand (in which case *golpear* would be a more appropriate translation). But nowhere is this explicitly stated in the text fragment that we just saw: rather this must be inferred on the basis of our knowledge of what the text is about. Clearly, if one could implement this kind of real-world knowledge in a system, it could help one pick contextually appropriate translations. This is the basic idea behind knowledge-based MT.

The problem with this approach is that outside a toy domain, it is impossible to implement this kind of real-world knowledge. This is not for want of trying. Perhaps the most famous attempt to model such 'common-sense' real world knowledge is the Cyc project that was founded in 1984 by Douglas Lenat. The purpose of this was to provide en*cyc*lopedic knowledge that could be applied in various areas, including natural language processing. The knowledge was to be arranged in a network, along with a deductive logic mechanism that would allow one to make inferences from fragments of knowledge to others. In theory if I have a text that mentions that John is in his kitchen, I should be able to infer (if we are talking about a typical Western-style kitchen) that there is probably a stove, a sink, a counter, and a refrigerator. This is what Cyc was intended to provide. Unfortunately, despite many person-decades of work on the project, it has fallen substantially short of this goal. There is a huge amount of knowledge built into the system, yet one cannot in general hope to make even the most common-sense inferences using the system. Rather, Cyc has evolved into a platform for building 'expert systems' that are specialized for particular technical domains. The goals of providing general common-sense knowledge of the kind that one would need for a wide-coverage knowledge-based MT system have been largely abandoned.

8.3.4 *EUROTRA and VerbMobil*

Throughout the 1970s, 1980s, and into the 1990s, researchers continued to work on largely hand-constructed MT systems. Some of the more noteworthy research systems included EUROTRA, and VerbMobil. The initial motivation for EUROTRA was rather like that of TAUM-Météo in that it was sponsored by a government agency that felt it had a problem in dealing with multiple languages. In this case the government was the European Union, and the problem was the need to translate documents of the Union into the various official languages. VerbMobil was one of the first attempts at machine translation of speech, where the goal was to construct a portable device that would perform speech recognition and real-time translation between a pair of languages; many of the demos involved German and Japanese.

Both EUROTRA and VerbMobil were multi-site and indeed multi-country efforts, with research groups at different locations working on different parts of the problem. The projects allowed for the development of many component technologies, and many research papers were published under their auspices. But neither project resulted in an end-product that was a practical working MT system.

8.4 Statistical MT

Translation is a process. In the case of human translators, the process obviously involves understanding the source language, understanding the correspondences between words and phrases of the source language and those of the target language, and knowing how to render the message being conveyed in the target language. But what do we really mean by *understanding*? Depending upon the type of translation—scientific, or literary—*deep* understanding of the source material may not be required. A technical translator faced with the following text in mycology, may not need to know what terms such as *ascus*, *operculate*, *prototunicate*, and so forth, actually denote, so long as they know the appropriate translation into the target language:

The major ascus types include operculate, inoperculate, prototunicate, unitunicate and bitunicate, which are based primarily on the number and thickness of functional ascus walls and mechanisms of dehiscence.[12]

Machine translation is an attempt to model the process that the human translator performs. Up until the early 1990s, the modeling was done with intensive manual labor, building dictionaries and writing parsers and generators. Around 1990, with the work of researchers at IBM and others, people began to look for less labor-intensive ways, harnessing the computing power of machines to *learn* the models from data. How such systems work is the topic we now turn to.

We need to understand at the outset that machines do not actually learn models. Rather, they learn the parameters of models that have been given to them. In the case of the language models we saw in Chapter 7, the models are typically stated in terms of predicting the probability of a word given the last n words—$P(w_i|w_{i-n}w_{i-n+1} \ldots w_{i-1})$. Then, in training an instance of the model, one needs to come up with estimates of that probability given particular word assignments for all the $w_{i-n}w_{i-n+1} \ldots w_{i-1}$.

In machine translation the problem is similar, just more complicated. Before we define what the models for statistical machine translation look like, we need to explain how the problem of translation is viewed by such approaches. Recall automatic speech recognition. The problem there is to uncover a 'hidden' underlying utterance, say a sentence of English, from an observed acoustic signal. As we saw in the last chapter, this is typically broken down into a number of subproblems, including modeling the underlying language, modeling the mapping between words and pronunciations, and modeling the mapping between pronunciations and actual sounds. The problem of translation is rather similar to this. Recall again Weaver's famous statement: 'When I look at an article in Russian, I say "This is really written in English, but it has been coded in some strange symbols." ' This is exactly the view that statistical machine translation takes. The observed data is the source language, the language you are translating out of. The underlying 'hidden' data is a sequence of words in the target language. As with speech recognition, one has a language model for the target language. One also needs a mapping between the target language and the source language, something that explains how a given word or words in the source language could have been 'generated' from a given word in the target language. At the end of the day, what one wants is a model that allows us to answer the question: what is the probability of observing the French sentence *je suis aussi le cauchemar des romains* given that the English sentence (the one we want to translate into) was *I am also the Romans' nightmare*. Given that the IBM researchers who developed the first statistical MT system had previously worked on speech recognition, none of this is perhaps surprising.

In order to see how this all works in more detail, it will be worth stepping through a small example. Consider the opening passage of Lewis Carroll's *Alice's Adventures in Wonderland* and a German translation, given below:

Alice was beginning to get very tired of sitting by her sister on the bank, and of having nothing to do: once or twice she had peeped into the book her sister was reading, but it had no pictures or conversations in it, 'and what is the use of a book,' thought Alice 'without pictures or conversation?'

So she was considering in her own mind (as well as she could, for the hot day made her feel very sleepy and stupid), whether the pleasure of making a daisy-chain would be worth the trouble of getting up and picking the daisies, when suddenly a White Rabbit with pink eyes ran close by her.

Alice hatte allmählich keine Lust mehr, neben ihrer Schwester an dem kleinen Fluß zu sitzen, denn sie hatte überhaupt nichts zu tun. Ein- oder zweimal hatte sie einen Blick in das Buch geworfen, das ihre Schwester las, aber es enthielt weder Bilder noch irgendwelche Gespräche. „Und was nützt ein Buch", dachte Alice, wenn es keine Bilder und Gespräche darin gibt?"

Sie überlegte daher (so gut es ging, denn die Hitze machte sie schläfrig und ganz dumpf im Kopf), ob es sich lohnen würde, aufzustehen und Gänseblümchen zu pflücken, um eine Kette daraus zu machen, als plötzlich direkt vor ihr ein weißes Kaninchen mit rosa Augen vorbeilief.[13]

The first task that must be accomplished in training a model from such data is to align the sentences. Translations do not generally come with information on which translated sentence corresponds to which original sentence, and it is also not always the case that a single sentence in the source language corresponds to a single sentence in the target language. For example, the first paragraph of Lewis Carroll's original contains just one long sentence, or perhaps two if you count the colon as a sentence boundary. The German translation of the first paragraph has three sentences. So in general one has to allow that one sentence in the source language may show up as more than one sentence in the target language, or contrariwise, that a single sentence in the target language might have come from multiple sentences in the source language; one must also consider the possibility that a pair of sentences in the source language corresponds to a pair in the target language, but that the decision on where to place the sentence boundary is different in each case.

Sentence aligment methods use a variety of features to determine the most likely sentence-to-sentence correspondences between languages. One difference between languages is how much information can be encoded in a given space. For example, written Chinese tends to require less space to convey a message compared to the equivalent message in English. This is in part because Chinese lacks very many grammatical morphemes, in part because the writing system packs more information into each character (as we have seen), and in part for other reasons. So a reasonable measure to use to determine sentence correspondences would be the ratio in length between two sentences, taking into account the expected difference in length given the differences between the two languages. A sentence in the target language that is significantly longer than this ratio, vis-à-vis a given source-language sentence, is unlikely to be a translation of that source-language sentence alone.

Obviously length is a weak feature, though, so sentence-alignment methods also use lexical features, in that they look for sentences that share a lot of terms in common. Numbers are particularly useful in this context since they often appear in the identical form—for example as dates—in the two languages, but names are also good. If the languages are written in the same script, then names often appear in identical form in both languages; if they are written in different scripts, then a model of name transliteration between the two scripts can be useful. If the languages are related, or there has been a lot of borrowing between the languages, cognates or borrowed words can be helpful: even without a bilingual dictionary for, say, English and Spanish, one can guess based on letter correspondences that *conserve* and *conservar* might be related. If one does have a bilingual dictionary, then word pairs from the dictionary can also be clues to correspondences. Of course, any of these features by themselves might lead one astray: as any student of French can tell you, *il ignore* in French does not mean *he ignores*. But as with anything in statistical language processing, it is the mass of such features that is the key to success, and in general one can get very good sentence alignments by considering features such as length and lexical correspondences.

One does need to constrain the search to a set of reasonable things. If you have a document in two languages, one model of alignment would say that the first sentence in the source language is the source of *all* the sentences in the target language, and the rest of the sentences in the source language have been left untranslated. That would be a very silly model. Generally, sentence alignment methods limit the search to reasonable possibilities: one-to-one, one-to-two, two-to-one, two-to-two (with a different placement of the boundary), and so forth.

Once sentences are aligned, the next task is to align words. Word correspondences have already played a role in sentence alignment, but here we are interested in a much finer-grained analysis. To determine if two sentences are likely to be translations of each other given that we know that the texts are parallel, it is often sufficient to pick out a few words in each sentence. For example, the presence of *Hitze* 'heat', *Gänseblümchen* 'daisies', and *Kaninchen* 'rabbit' in the last sentence of the German translation of *Alice* above is enough to confirm that this sentence aligns with the final sentence of the English fragment. But now we need to know more than this. For the sentence in question we would like to be able to compute a table of correpondences such as that in Table 8.1.

The translation that we are looking at here is a pretty close one, but even here there are cases where the English and German texts diverge. In Table 8.1, words or word sequences that are more or less exact translations of each other are shown in regular font. Words that correspond in the sense that they are clearly motivated in the German translation on the basis of the corresponding English word(s), but are not really exact translations, are shown in italics. So, for example *Kette* corresponds to English *daisy-chain* but really just means *chain*. The German translation literally reads, "... whether it would be worth the trouble to get up and pick daisies, in order to make a chain out of them." In some cases there is no direct English correspondence for the German word.

If one has a bilingual dictionary for the language pair in question, some of the correspondences can be found by looking up the words. Any German–English dictionary will tell you that *Kaninchen* is *rabbit*, *rosa* is *pink*, and *pflücken* is 'pick'. But dictionaries, even if we have them for the languages in question are not enough on their own. First of all, there will almost certainly be words that are not found in the dictionary, resulting in an *out-of-vocabulary* (OOV) problem. Second, the dictionary may list the word *Auge* 'eye', but it may well not list the plural form *Augen*; it may list *vorbeilaufen* 'to run past', but likely will not list the actual form used here *vorbeilief* 'ran past'. The latter problem can be addressed if one has morphological analysis tools—tools that handle variations in word forms—for the languages in question, but even with these, there will still be forms that will not be recognized.

One can augment whatever lexical resources one has by computing statistics on the cooccurrence of words across the two languages. Obviously the fragment of *Alice* we gave above would not be enough to derive significant

TABLE 8.1 English/German correspondences from the fragment of *Alice*

German	English
sie	she
überlegte	was considering
daher	so
so gut	as well as
es ging	*she could*
denn	for
die	the
Hitze	*hot day*
machte	made
sie	her
schläfrig	sleepy
und	and
ganz dumpf im Kopf	stupid
ob	whether
es	it
sich lohnen	be worth the trouble
würde	would
aufzustehen	getting up
und	and
Gänseblümchen	daisies
zu	to
pflücken	pick
um	
eine	a
Kette	*daisy-chain*
daraus	
zu machen	making
als	when
plötzlich	suddenly
direkt vor	close
ihr	her
ein	a
weißes	white
Kaninchen	rabbit
mit	with
rosa	pink
Augen	eyes
vorbeilief	ran by

statistics, and even the entire text of Carroll's two *Alice* books would scarcely suffice. But if one has millions of words of parallel text, one can infer that a pair of words—or a pair of word sequences—are probably related because when you see the one in a sentence in the first language, you tend to see the other in a sentence in the second; and when you fail to see the other in the second language you tend not to see the one in the first language. There are a number of statistical measures of association that have been developed that can indicate the strength of the association and whether it is significant.

Of course, as with sentences, and as we saw in the small example above, a single word in one language may correspond to more than one word, or no words in the other; and a sequence of words may have to be translated as a whole into another sequence of words in the other language. We return again to our generative metaphor that says that translating German into English is really just uncovering the model whereby an original English text generated the German text we are now faced with. In that model, we can think of English words (or word sequences) as generating German words (or word sequences). In statistical MT, a word's ability to 'spawn' words in the other language is termed its *fertility*. Let's say we are translating from French into English and we come across the sentence *Jean ne ressemble pas à Jacques* ('Jean does not resemble Jacques'); recall that in the metaphor for translation we have been adopting, we are looking for the sentence in English that was most likely to have generated the observed French sentence. At the level of the individual French words we want to ask a similar question: what English word(s) could have been the source of those French words? For some of the French words, the answer seems to be straightforward. The names *Jean* and *Jacques* have straightforward sources as the same names in English. But what about the other words *ne, pas, ressemble*, and *à*? On initial inspection, *ressemble* would appear to correspond one-for-one with the English word *resemble*, with which it is obviously related. But looking more closely, we can see there is a difference. In English, *resemble* is followed by a noun phrase with no preposition: *resemble Jacques, resemble a purple pineapple*. In French, on the other hand, the verb *ressembler*, needs a preposition—*à*, usually translated as 'to': thus *ressemble à Jacques* (literally, 'resemble to Jacques'). Thus one word in English in effect maps to two in French. In a similar way, the word *not* in English corresponds to the two French words *ne* and *pas*, which surround *ressemble*. On the other hand, the auxiliary verb *does* seems to correspond to no word in French. Thus we would say that *does* has fertility zero, whereas *not* and *resemble* each have fertility two, and *Jean* and *Jacques* have fertility one.

More modern approaches to statistical MT make use of phrase-based rather than just word-based translation. Rather than learn the mappings between single words and their (possibly multiword) translations, instead collocations of words in one language are learned that have statistically reliable translations into collocations of words in the other language. Such systems tend to work better than fertility-based models, and it is not hard to see why. Suppose we are translating between Korean and English and we are dealing with the Korean expressions *yindiana daehaggyo* and *yillinoyi daehaggyo*. *Daehaggyo* is 'university' and the other two words are placenames—'Indiana' and 'Illinois'. In both cases the state name occurs before the word for 'university'. Now it happens that the conventional way to refer to these institutions in English is *Indiana University* (not *University of Indiana*), and *University of Illinois* (not *Illinois University*). A fertility-based model would learn the relation between *daehaggyo* and the state names and their English counterparts, but it would rely on the reordering and language models (below), to get the words in the right order in each case. In a phrase-based model the system just learns that *yindiana daehaggyo* should be translated as *Indiana University* and that *yillinoyi daehaggyo* should be *University of Illinois*, which is more direct, hence more robust.

So, given a sentence in the source language, we now have the data to predict plausible words, or phrases, in the target language, corresponding to the words, or phrases, in the source language. But of course we need to do more than just predict words: we also need them in the right order.

There are two components to doing this. One is a model of the transformations that take place between words and phrases in the language pair in question. So as we saw above, when translating between English and Spanish, we need in general to swap the order of the adjective and the noun: *brown dog* becomes *perro moreno* (dog brown). These transformations can also be learned from parallel data. Of course, as with sentence alignment and word fertility, one has to limit the space of possibilities. Much work in statistical MT has been done on this topic. Recent work (the work of Dekai Wu at Hong Kong University of Science and Technology is particularly notable here) has focused on structural methods that make use of one or another kind of tree structure. The basic idea is that if one can assign a reasonable tree structure over the sentences being translated, one can learn the transformations that need to be applied, and furthermore these transformations will be constrained since they will involve manipulations of the tree. If we take as our example the sentence *I see a brown dog*, then the transformation that derives the adjective–noun order in Spanish would apply at the level of the node labeled N′ in Figure 8.1: the words under that node would flip their order. Note that in this representation, it would be much more complicated to do a reordering where, say, *brown* shows up at the beginning of the sentence before *see*. In general this is a welcome result, since such reorderings are more unusual than the 'local' ones that one sees in this example. Again, though, the model is a generative one. So in training a model to translate from Spanish to English we are asking: what English sentence is the likely source of the observed Spanish sentence? In the training process this is modeled by building a tree over the English source, and then learning the transformations on that structure needed to produce the observed Spanish sentence.

The second component required for getting the words in the right order is a *language model* of the target language. Again, we have already seen language models in the context of speech recognition in Chapter 7. In the context of MT, language models are used to rank competing hypotheses for an appropriate translation. Thus, to take an example we have seen in a different context, if I want to translate *He hit a tree*, possible translations include *Ha golpeado un árbol* and *Ha chocado contra un árbol*, the second one being the correct one for describing a traffic accident. It also turns out that the phrase *chocado contra un árbol* is far more common than *golpeado un árbol*, presumably reflecting the fact that one more often talks about hitting a tree in the context of a traffic accident, than thumping one with one's hand. So the language model will prefer the hypothesis involving *chocar* to the one involving *golpear*. Since language models are trained from monolingual data, they are a lot easier to train than translation models; for one thing, there is vastly more monolingual data than bilingual data available. And language models help. The main reason that the Google MT team won the National Institute of Standards and Technology (NIST)-sponsored 2006 MT competition was because it was able to build an English language model over more data than anyone else.

A word needs to be said about how MT systems are evaluated. Obviously the ideal case would be to have expert human translators go over the output and grade it. Equally obviously this would be prohibitively expensive for anything but small amounts of text. So agencies such as NIST, who host MT competitive, have had to rely on automatic methods. But with MT, automatic evaluation is a tricky business. In the case of speech recognition, we know what the speaker said, and there is usually a single correct transcription (putting aside issues such as alternative spellings for words). In the case of translation, there is rarely a single correct translation, and in most cases there would be many possible translations. So while, for any MT evaluation, there is an actual human translation against which to compare the output of the MT system, one cannot simply do a string comparison. Instead a compromise has been proposed, one that a lot of researchers are unhappy with, but which has the advantage of being relatively easy to implement. This is the so-called

BLEU score (pronounced as *blue*). The basic idea behind the BLEU score is simple. Let's say the source language is English, and the target language is German, and we are faced with the sentence:

> Alice was beginning to get very tired of sitting by her sister on the bank, and of having nothing to do.

The reference translation is:

> Alice hatte allmählich keine Lust mehr, neben ihrer Schwester an dem kleinen Fluß zu sitzen, denn sie hatte überhaupt nichts zu tun.

It is unreasonable to expect that any MT system will produce exactly this translation, since it is not the only reasonable translation. But it is not unreasonable that there should at least be fragments in common. In particular, one could look at how many *n-grams*—single words, pairs of words, triples of words—and so forth are shared between the reference translation and the translation produced by the system. The system with the highest score wins.

It is debatable how well the BLEU score correlates with what a human judge would assign to a translation. Critics claim that the correlation is weak, though the original paper that proposed the measure[14] argued that there is a correlation. Often in such cases the argument of simplicity wins—that is, until someone can propose an automatic technique that performs substantially better.

NIST evaluations aside, the real test of an MT system for you, the typical user, is whether it works on *your* text. Some sense of the current state of the technology (current at the time of writing in Autumn 2008) can be had by considering the output of the Google English–German MT system on the same paragraph of *Alice* as we started our discussion with:

Alice war zu Beginn sehr müde der Sitzung von ihrer Schwester auf der Bank, und der mit nichts zu tun: ein-oder zweimal hatte sie guckte in das Buch ihrer Schwester war Lesung, aber es hatte keine Bilder oder Gespräche in sie, "und was ist die Verwendung eines Buches," dachte Alice "ohne Bilder oder Konversation?"

So war sie erwägt in ihrem eigenen Geist (ebenso wie sie konnte, für die heißen Tag machten sie fühlen sich sehr schläfrig und dumm), unabhängig davon, ob das Vergnügen, eine Daisy-Chain wäre die Mühe wert, von dem Aufstehen und Kommissionierung der Gänseblümchen, als plötzlich ein Weißes Kaninchen mit rosa Augen lief der Nähe von ihr.

For those who do not read German, I attempt to give a flavor of the quality of the translation with a fairly literal translation back into English:

Alice was at the beginning very tired of sitting of her sister on the bank, and that with nothing to do: once or twice she peeked in the book of her sister was the reading, but it had no pictures or dialog in it, "and what is the use of a book," thought Alice "without pictures or conversation?"

Thus was she pondered in her own heart (as well as she could for the hot day made her feel sleepy and stupid), independently of that, whether the pleasure, a daisy-chain would be worth the effort, of getting up and the (order)-picking of the daisies, when suddenly a white rabbit with pink eyes ran of the nearby of her.

This back-translation does not fully capture the infelicities of the German text, since German makes grammatical distinctions that are lacking in English, and where there is no way to express the equivalent error in English. For example, the phrase *die heißen Tag machten*, intended as a translation for *the hot day made* is wrong at a couple of levels. The article *die* 'the' and the adjective form *heißen* 'hot' are appropriate if the following word were plural; similarly the verb form *machten* is a plural past-tense verb. Yet the word for *day* here is *Tag*, which is a singular form. One could make the fragment grammatical by pluralizing the word for *day*: *die heißen Täge machten* 'the hot days made'—but of course that would not be a particularly good translation of the English original.

It is important to bear in mind that the Google MT system was not trained on this kind of text, or at least that the majority of the bilingual text upon which it would have been trained is not literary text. The bias of the training data can be seen in the choice of word *Kommissionierung*, as a translate of 'pick': this is *pick* in the sense of *order picking*, the logistics of filling orders from a warehouse.

One point that shows up nicely in this example is the lack of any global control over the output. In the original text, the word *conversation* is used twice in the same sentence:

...but it had no pictures or **conversations** in it, 'and what is the use of a book,' thought Alice 'without pictures or **conversation?**'

This is natural: while it would have been possible for Lewis Carroll to use a synonym for 'conversation', say in the second mention of the concept, stylistically the repetition of the word makes much more sense. The automatic translation lacks this higher-level notion of stylistics. Two different translations of *conversation(s)* are used, *Gespräche* and *Konversation*, because the system is evaluating the goodness of one translation separately from the goodness of the other.

All in all though, the translation is not after all that bad. It is at least comprehensible, which is more than could be said for many of the translations from the early Georgetown MT system illustrated above. The system will not win any prizes for literary quality: McDaniel's forty-year-old expectation, quoted above, that 'as regards poetry and novels, [we will never] replace the translators of that type of material', has yet to be proven wrong. But perhaps this is as it should be. As we shall argue in the final chapter, language technology has been, and always will be, a way to augment our creative abilities. It is not likely to replace them. So it seems perfectly reasonable that MT should evolve into a tool that helps with the drudge-work of translating technical documents that have no aspirations to literary value; whereas the artistic component of a literary translation will forever remain the domain of humans.

Some of these problems will be solved in time with more data, and better ways of inferring good models from data. I have no doubt that given time and effort, it will be possible to implement a document-level stylistic model that ensures that the same word is translated the same way within a document (provided it really *does* mean the same thing). Whether there will ever be enough data to solve all of the problems, though, is a topic of much debate within the field of computational linguistics. There are some who have argued that all we need is ever more data, better machine-learning techniques, and a minimum of linguistic insight. Others have argued that we never will have enough data, and that we will not be able to solve a problem like machine translation solely by so-called 'data-driven' methods. Though it is hackneyed to say so, time will tell.

8.5 Synopsis

One thing that is certain is that not only has the technology of MT improved manyfold since the days of the *ALPAC Report*, but the economics has also changed substantially since 1966. For one thing machines are simply faster. One year previous to the publication of the ALPAC report, in 1965, Intel cofounder Gordon Moore published his prediction—now known as 'Moore's law'—that the number of transistors one could pack into a given area of an integrated circuit would double roughly every two years. This means that computers of today are about two million times more powerful than the machines available to the first MT researchers in the early 1960s. Second, there is now a huge amount text available in many languages, and a not inconsiderable amount of translated text, as well as resources such as bilingual dictionaries, language analysis tools (parsers, part-of-speech taggers), and so forth. Third, we have a much greater understanding of how to use those resources to build models of language, if not wholly automatically, at least with a minimum of human intervention: no company that wants to field a new MT product today would build it in the way that early MT companies such as Systran did.

Finally, the wealth of material on the Web in multiple languages has created a niche for MT. Machine translation is still a long way from the goal of producing text that is the equivalent of what a human translator could produce. I could not, for example, produce a German translation of this book using Google's MT technology, unless I was prepared to do a lot of post-editing. Yet at the same time it is clear that the state of the art has improved dramatically in the past five decades. As a quick-and-dirty way to get information from text in a language that one does not speak, current MT technology is pretty useful. And precisely because so much text is out there and available immediately, there is now a need for MT that simply did not exist in the 1960s. When it was published, the *ALPAC Report* was correct in its assessment and in its recommendations. Now, over forty years later, the gap in quality between machine translation and human translation has narrowed. But equally importantly, the information needs of the world have changed.

9

The Future

Humans throughout history have invented many ways of communicating, but language remains central for reasons that we laid out when we started this discussion: it is the only form of communication that is effectively unlimited in what it can convey.

Language technology—whether it be writing on clay tablets, or a speech recognition system that allows one to search the Internet over the phone, or a speech synthesizer that allows a mute person to talk—is an augmentative device. Just as automobiles or airplanes allow us to travel in ways and at speeds that would not be possible given our biological capacities, so language technology helps us use language in a way that would not otherwise be possible.

This chapter asks the question: where do we go from here? There are several facets to this question: How does language technology augment our abilities and how will it continue to do so? How will the technology itself improve? How will continued improvements affect society for good or ill?

9.1 Language technology augments our abilities

The technologies that we have examined in this book fall into two basic categories: passive and active. Writing, printing presses, typewriters, and telegraphs are passive tools, helpers in encoding language but not actively involved in the process. Computers are different: modern dialog systems or translation systems use algorithms to make active choices in how to interpret the speech or text input of one user, and how to output speech or text to another (or the same) user. Currently, computers are obviously far inferior to humans in their ability to deal with language and speech. But even now there are some things that computers can do that humans cannot.

A trivial but at the same time rather telling example is the pronunciation of personal names. Everyone has had the experience of encountering names that they have no idea how to pronounce, or are simply wrong about. My own name is a good case in point. Many people pronounce it as if it were spelled

Sprout: I am willing to wager that at least some of you reading this book thought that this is how it is pronounced. But if you think about it, that pronunciation is impossible: there is no English word ending in -*oat* that has a pronunciation that rhymes with *out*. Any native word so spelled—*oat, groat, boat, shoat, moat*...—rhymes with *note*. Indeed the only common exception to this is the word *Croat* (rhyming with *throw at*), which is of course not a native word to begin with. One can speculate as to why people get my name wrong: the most obvious explanation is that there *is* a word *sprout*, which differs in only one letter, and which is surely more common in the language than *Sproat*. Presumably people are analogizing from that. No halfway decent text-to-speech system would make this mistake, and it is not hard to understand why. As we saw in Chapter 7, TTS systems derive their pronunciations from a combination of dictionary lookup and either hand-crafted or, more commonly, learned rules. One assumes that dictionaries will have correct pronunciations for the words listed there; obviously one does encounter mistakes, but these will be corrected by the system developers. As for pronunciation rules, these will only allow correspondences between letters and sounds for which they have seen evidence, and there is ample evidence for -*oat* being pronounced to rhyme with *note*. It is possible a system could incorrectly generalize *Croat* so that my name would rhyme with that. But there would be no reason for it to pronounce it as *sprout*.

In fact, TTS systems are generally *better* than most humans are at pronouncing personal names—one of the very few areas in speech and language technology where machines outperform humans. This is not to say they always get them right: a *possible* pronunciation for a name may not correspond to an actual one. But people are notoriously bad at this task, so the competition is relatively easy.

So this is one thing that computers can do in the realm of speech and language that is better than what humans are able to achieve. Let us turn to a much more interesting one.

Take the case of T. V. Raman, a blind computer scientist who, as of the time of writing, works at Google. Like many blind computer users, Raman has used screen-readers, which as the name implies read to the user what is on the screen. A screen reader is simply a program that does some analysis of the text that appears on a screen, or in a window, and passes it to a text-to-speech synthesizer. Most screen readers are phenomenally unintelligent about their analysis of what is on the screen. Commonly, for example, they will read a text line-by-line, without any consideration of what *kind* of text it is and therefore whether it is appropriate to read it in that fashion—for example, in the case of poetry or a list of short bullet items; or if it is ordinary prose text, such as what you are reading now, where line breaks serve no function other than to fit text on the page.

Doing marginally better than this—at least detecting whether or not to treat line breaks as marking boundaries that should be paid attention to when reading—is doable, though not always entirely trivial. This alone, though, significantly improves the intelligibility of the read speech. But Raman was interested in going far further than that. How, for example, should a complex mathematical formula be read to a blind user? Mathematicians obviously can read formulae aloud if they need to and have them understood by their colleagues, but this is not something that is typically done. And what about tables and matrices, which are hardly ever read aloud? *Reading for the Blind*, a Princeton, New Jersey-based company that produces audio texts using (human) readers, publishes a set of guidelines for how to read such material aloud. It includes specifications such as one requiring readers to repeat the column headings of tables every few rows, something that requires the reader to analyze the structure of the table, and decide what the relevant headings (and subheadings) are that need to be repeated.

The analysis of arbitrary tables is mostly beyond the capabilities of current technology, and Raman was in any case more interested in his dissertation work on the problem of treating mathematical expressions, which are more formally constrained and hence more algorithmic. But he also realized that computer speech has an advantage over human speech in that one can control many parameters of the voice much more than most people are capable of. For example, suppose one wants to indicate superscripting, as with exponentiation in an expression like:

$$x^{(y+2)^3}$$

In Raman's system the $y+2$ superscript and the 3 superscript on that are read with successively higher frequencies. In a matrix such as the following:

$$\begin{vmatrix} a_{11} & a_{12} & \cdots & a_{1n} \\ a_{21} & a_{22} & \cdots & a_{2n} \\ \vdots & \vdots & \ddots & \vdots \\ a_{mn} & a_{m2} & \cdots & a_{mn} \end{vmatrix}$$

various cues are given such as reading *and so on, and so on* in an ever fading voice, to indicate the ellipses (. . .). Using these techniques, Raman was able to effectively encode in audio some very complicated formulae. The interested reader can still find his material online at `http://www.cs.cornell.edu/home/raman/aster/aster-toplevel.html`. A system such as Raman's does imply that

```
 _____ _____ ___    ':'...''.  ___
|                   |                            |       '::.''''':;:
||Michael  Farber | |mfarber@lucent.com |        '::;         ;;:
| ------------------  ---------------------        :::,,         :;;
| Lucent Technologies |                           ;:;'         ;::;
| 1432 Pine St., 3D-403 |   _____  ;;:          .;:
| Liberty Corner       |  | Lucent Technologies |  ;;:         ,:;:
| New Jersey, 07934    |  |Bell Labs Innovations|  :;:,      ,:;:
|_phone: 908-712-9993 __|_____ '::;;:;:'
                         ____fax: 908-712-9980_ |
```

FIGURE 9.1 A 'signature block'

one needs fairly fine control over pitch: the more 'natural' sounding unit-selection systems we discussed in Chapter 7 are thus rather ill-suited to this kind of application.

Since his thesis work, Raman has expanded the coverage of his system significantly. Since he is a software engineer, one of his focuses has been on reading computer code in languages such as C++ or Java. Like matrices, this is something that people rarely read aloud, yet it is critical for blind programmers who need a means of 'seeing' complex code.

There are other domains where this kind of *audio rendering* is useful. Some years ago, back in the late 1990s, when I was working at Bell Labs, I developed a reader for email, which I affectionately called *Emu*. Inspired by Raman's work, I set out to try to do an intelligent job of analyzing the content of what was in the message, and deciding how to render each part into audio. Reading email is a very difficult task, because email can in principle contain almost anything. Some things are easier to deal with than others: email headers (the *From:*, *To:*, and *Subject:* fields, etc.) are easy in that they consist of pre-defined fields, often with a limited range of values. Many of these fields are of interest only to mail software and can safely be skipped when rendering the message into speech.

Similarly, included graphics can be identified and ignored.

But what do you do when you have to deal with tables written in plain text? Or someone's attempt to draw a map, using plain text, of how to get to a particular building? Or an elaborate 'signature block' as in Figure 9.1? In cases like this one has to do some analysis of the *layout* of the text.[1] Notice that the text is organized into more or less coherent blocks. So there is a block containing the address, another block containing a slogan ('Lucent Technologies, Bell Labs Innovations'), a line/block containing the phone and fax numbers, and separate single-line-segment blocks for the name and the email address—in addition to an attempt to render the company's logo in ASCII symbols. Communicating all this information effectively requires more

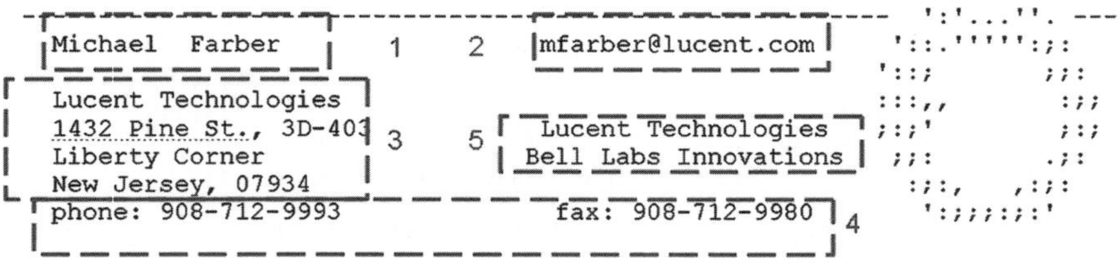

```
 ┌─ ── ── ── ── ┐ ┌─ ── ── ── ── ── ── ── ── ┐   ';'...''. ───
 │Michael  Farber │  1   2  │mfarber@lucent.com│   ':: .''''':;:
 └─ ── ── ── ── ┘         └─ ── ── ── ── ── ┘   '::;           ;;;
┌─ ── ── ── ── ── ── ┐                              :::,,         :;;
│  Lucent Technologies │                            :::,,         :;;
│  1432 Pine St., 3D-40│ 3   5  ┌─ Lucent Technologies ┐ ;:;'        ;::;
│  Liberty Corner       │       │  Bell Labs Innovations │ ;;:        .;:
│  New Jersey, 07934    │       └─ ── ── ── ── ── ── ┘ :;:,     ,:;:
└─ ── ── ── ── ── ── ┘                              ':;;;:;:'
  │  phone: 908-712-9993 │ ── ──     fax: 908-712-9980 │ 4
  └─ ── ── ── ── ── ── ── ── ── ── ── ── ── ── ┘
```

FIGURE 9.2 The signature block segmented and labelled for name (1), email (2), address (3), phone/fax (4) and slogan (5)

than a simple line-by-line read of the text. It requires that one segment and classify the different regions that are contained in the block (Figure 9.2). Techniques from automatic image analysis can be used to identify regions of text that are connected together and thus form blocks. Classifying the blocks can be achieved by text-classification techniques, the same kind of techniques that can be used to determine if a news story is likely to be about sports or finance. Furthermore, classification of the text regions can further subdivide the blocks that were computed on purely structural grounds: note that the phone number in the example we have been considering is joined to the address block, but should really be considered part of a separate block.

In work such as Raman's, or our own work on email reading, computers can sometimes do a better job than (most) humans would be capable of doing. Few humans, when reading an email message aloud to someone, would bother to switch voices to indicate quotation. Even fewer would, or could, indicate the two-dimensional layout of a page by changing the direction from which their voice appears to come (thus mimicking spatial layout) or by changing the pitch of the voice to indicate superscripts or subscripts.

One area where we can expect language and speech technology to play an increasing role is in the area of *Augmentative and Alternative Communication.* We have already seen a reference to this area in our discussion of Blissymbolics in Chapter 2, where it was noted that Charles Bliss's invention is now exclusively used as an alternative communication medium for people with severe mental impairment or communications disorders. In fact it is one of several such schemes. Communications problems can come about for a variety of reasons, and the full range of causes and effects is only just beginning to be understood. One syndrome that has only recently come to be recognized is *Primary Progressive Aphasia* (PPA).[2] PPA is like more well-known aphasias in that it involves the loss of one or more language-related abilities, usually with no concomitant lost of other cognitive functions. The difference is that, as the name implies, the condition is gradual. A patient with PPA can expect to gradually lose his or her ability to retrieve words, to name objects, and to comprehend spoken words. Generally, this loss takes place over a two-year period. Since non-linguistic cognitive function is mostly unaffected, the patients are generally fully aware of what is happening—which is, needless to say, highly distressing to them. Patients do seem to be able to recognize words if they see them written, and so this has led to the development of techniques involving notebooks filled with words arranged by topic, which they can then use as an aid to memory during conversation. Fried-Oken (2008) notes that in some cases, 'speech generating devices'—in other words, speech synthesizers—hooked up to an electronic version of these notebooks may be useful. This in turn suggests a whole range of possible ways in which speech and language technology might be useful: devices that talk in the patient's own voice, have statistical tables of their normal vocabulary use, have speech recognition systems that can monitor the ambient conversation topic and suggest words that are relevant to that topic. None of these areas has been adequately explored.

9.2 Language and speech technology: the future

Any discussion of the future of language and speech technology would do well to remember one fundamental point, and that is that, as with any technology, it requires investment: somebody has to pay for the development of the technology, whether it be a government funding agency in the form of research grants, or a private company with its eye on what it hopes will be a lucrative market. No matter how 'cool' a technology is, it will not be developed if nobody is willing to pay for it. And companies generally will not invest in something unless they believe there is strong market potential. Of course, it is not always so easy to evaluate market potential, and speech technology has had no shortage of unrealized expectations in this regard.

Companies that develop applications often depend upon predictions from market analysts in order to justify their investment in a particular technology development effort, whether it be text-to-speech synthesis, speech recognition, or machine translation. Such market predictions are notoriously difficult to evaluate, and frequently turn out to be wildly inaccurate. For example, in the late 1990s analysts predicted that the speech-technology business would be worth $8 billion worldwide by 2003 (compared to about half a billion in 1997). The website that quotes this figure (http://home.att.net/~thehessians/ StockMarketPredictions.html) does not cite its source, but it seems credible that such a claim was in fact made: I remember hearing such numbers when I was working at Bell Labs in the late 1990s.

The truth is rather less rosy. To be sure there are areas where speech technology seems to be doing very well as a business: one such area is health care, where there has for many years now been demand from practitioners for devices that can save labor in filing reports. Doctors would often rather speak their reports about a patient and have them transcribed, than type them. Prior to the advent of working speech recognition, the only choice for doctors not wishing to type was to record the report and have it sent to human transcribers. This provided a natural niche for ASR, and it had the added benefit that it increased the privacy of patient records, since a human transcriber would no longer be needed. So as a result, ASR in health care is doing well, and as recently as 30 June 2008 an article in *Healthcare IT News* was predicting a $340 million market by 2013.

But the broader picture is that outside particular niche applications such as health care it is pretty hard to make much money selling speech or language technology. In large part this is because speech technology has become commoditized. End users do not want to buy a speech recognition system or a speech synthesis system or even a machine translation system: they may want to buy a dictation engine, or an automated call-center application, or a game that includes synthetic speech, or they may be happy to use a web-based service that allows them to translate documents from one language into another, but they have little interest in the underlying technology as long as it works. Speech and language technology has become raw material out of which other technologies are built. Oddly, while this seems somewhat obvious now, this was a point that seemed to be little understood during the early years of the Internet boom. As a result, of the many companies that attempted to enter the business starting from about 1995 onwards (with some companies dating back far earlier than that), there are really only a handful of companies left whose main or sole business is selling speech technology. Apart from the few remaining small speech technology companies, the main industrial players that are left are large companies, like AT&T, for which speech technology is not their, main business, but who presumably do not mind making a little extra money; and companies like Google where the whole business model is based on giving people high quality access to information in as wide a variety of media as possible, and access via voice (and delivery of information via synthetic speech) is, in business parlance, 'value added'. The same point applies to Machine Translation in the context of information access.

So the conclusion is that speech and language technology is unlikely to be a serious money-maker in its own right, but in support of other information-access technologies it is surely here to stay. And to the extent that improvements in the technology lead to increases in people's willingness to use the system, this will in turn lead to a desire on the part of companies (and, one hopes, governments) to invest in further research and development.

Indeed, there are areas where speech and language technologies will eventually become indispensable. Most of these exist already today in one form or another. People will more and more come to take them for granted, just as we have already come to take computers and the Internet for granted:

- Information access ('search'). Voice search of text data, and voice or text search of audio and video data on sites like YouTube (often called 'audio indexing').
- More specialized information access, e.g. driving directions, business information over the phone (such as the Goog411 application discussed in Chapter 7).
- Text input ('dictation machines'), both in specialized areas (e.g. health care) where people prefer not to type, and for people with disabilities (e.g. repetitive stress injuries) who cannot type.
- Further and more sophisticated interfaces for people with disabilities.
- Voice control of simple devices, such as switches or microwaves.
- Automated testing of writing and speech—e.g. essays or the speech of second language learners. Such technology already exists,[3] but we can expect it to become far more common.
- Interactive games, in particular Role Playing Games (RPGs). Synthetic voices, and the ability to understand language or speech input by bots in games, will become commonplace.

The list could go on...

People will continue to experiment with applications. Some will fade away, much like the 'talking cars' which made a brief appearance during the 1980s when the first digital signal processing chips became available. But others will be adopted generally, and over time will come to seem as indispensable as mobile phones now seem to be. Certainly there are no shortage of predictions about how indispensable speech interfaces will become. In a recent survey report on future trends in how people will connect to the Internet, Anderson and Rainie (2008) argue that mobile devices will be the *primary* interface to the Internet for most people by the year 2020. Text input on small mobile devices is notoriously tricky, and input via speech is the most obvious alternative. Indeed, one prediction, with which 64 per cent of expert respondents agreed, is that

In 2020, the most commonly used communications appliances prominently feature built-in voice recognition. People have adjusted to hearing individuals dictating information in public to their computing devices.[4]

It is important not to overstate this point: there are certainly some tasks that today are done with keyboards which almost certainly will continue to be done with keyboards by most people. For example, while I might like to get the weather for Portland, Oregon, by saying something like 'Weather, Portland, Oregon' to my mobile phone, I would not like to write Java code by talking to my computer. The interface must be suited to the particular application. But there are surely enough applications where speech interfaces *do* make sense for Anderson and Rainie's prediction to seem plausible.

9.3 Social implications

And all of this will continue to have social implications. We have already seen how language technology, from the earliest times, has had profound influences on society. The most notable of these was the prized position that literacy held in most societies throughout most of human history. The ability to read and write was guarded jealously by the literate elite in many societies. In many cases—in Egypt, in Mesopotamia, in China, Japan, and Korea—a complex and inefficient writing system was kept for many centuries in part because there was a social advantage (to some) in making the technology difficult to learn. Technological complexity served the needs of a hierarchical society. In some cases, as we saw with Japanese writing, this led to even more complexity being added to the system.

Limited access to literacy was in part motivated by simple economics. When written documents had to be produced by hand, they were expensive and it was simply not possible to produce them in large numbers. Printing changed that, and led slowly but inexorably to the democratization of writing. This too was partly a matter of economics. Printing makes little economic sense if it is not done in bulk, but there is little point in printing in bulk if the majority of potential customers cannot read. Other ways of disseminating the written word, such as the typewriter and the telegraph, furthered the need for wider literacy.

This is all viewed as progress, and rightly so, yet it is as well to remember that technology is a tool, and as such can be used for ill or good. One should always bear this point in mind when considering the social implications of a technology.

A good starting place for prognostication is to have a look at how language and speech technology has appeared in works of political fiction. In Francis Bacon's utopian vision in *New Atlantis* (1626), the enlightened Bensalemians inform the narrator that:

We have also sound-houses, where we practise and demonstrate all sounds and their generation. We have harmony which you have not, of quarter-sounds and lesser slides of sounds. Divers instruments of music likewise to you unknown, some sweeter than any you have; with bells and rings that are dainty and sweet. We represent small sounds as great and deep, likewise great sounds extenuate and sharp; we make divers tremblings and warblings of sounds, which in their original are entire. We represent and imitate all articulate sounds and letters, and the voices and notes of beasts and birds. We have certain helps which, set to the ear, do further the hearing greatly; we have also divers strange and artificial echoes, reflecting the voice many times, and, as it were, tossing it; and some that give back the voice louder than it came, some shriller and some deeper; yea, some rendering the voice, differing in the letters or articulate sound from that they receive. We have all means to convey sounds in trunks and pipes, in strange lines and distances.

One can see in this description hints at early conceptions of speech synthesis, speech modification, and telecommunications. Bacon does not make clear the purposes of these contrivances: perhaps they were purely for scientific curiosity or amusement. Yet the fact that such technology is associated with a Utopia is consistent with other philosophical views in the seventeenth century that linked technology in general with the betterment of humanity.[5] Of course, this view did have its detractors, most notably Jonathan Swift, whose views on technology in general we discussed in Chapter 6. But Swift did not necessarily believe that technology was evil: he was just reacting to the overzealous technophilia that the 'Age of Reason' engendered. He would have been a useful counterbalance to the similar zeal of the late 1990s.

A wholly different view of the role of speech and language technology is offered by Orwell's dystopic vision in *Nineteen Eighty-Four*. The novel introduces two technologies that would appear to depend upon language or speech technology. The first is the *speakwrite*, essentially a dictation machine used by Ministry workers such as Winston Smith to compose text. The second are the novel-writing machines and their kin the song-writing machine or 'versificator', which produce entertainment for consumption by the underclass of proles.

The speakwrite is for all intents and purposes identical to a modern dictation system, such as *Dragon NaturallySpeaking*. Such technology is clearly within the bounds of what is possible today, even if it would not have been possible in a 1984 that had been for decades under the yoke of a scientifically backward totalitarian regime. Dictation machines are usually trained for a particular talker, something that would have also been practical for the speakwrite, and as such, they have a fairly low word error rate. The performance would be enhanced further by the fact that the language used by Ministry workers for official communication is very limited, the 'hybrid jargon of the Ministries' being a cross between normal English and the much more limited *Newspeak*.

The novel-writing machines are more problematic.[6] Programs that compose prose in a particular style do exist. A famous example is the *Chomskybot* (http://rubberducky.org/cgi-bin/chomsky.pl) which generates texts in the style of Noam Chomsky. For example:

> Presumably, the systematic use of complex symbols is not quite equivalent to a parasitic gap construction. On our assumptions, the descriptive power of the base component is, apparently, determined by the system of base rules exclusive of the lexicon. Comparing these examples with their parasitic gap counterparts in (96) and (97), we see that most of the methodological work in modern linguistics is to be regarded as a general convention regarding the forms of the grammar.

The system works, as the author notes, by the 'American Chinese Menu' principle: one from column A, one from column B. More specifically, sentences are composed of four phrases—initiating, subject, verbal, and terminating phrases—and a new sentence is generated by randomly selecting from a large pre-stored list of each type of phrase. The program can generate something on the order of 2.2×10^{25} distinct paragraphs (each paragraph consisting of five sentences). But while the system can produce prose that is amusingly similar to Chomsky's own frequently impenetrable style, it becomes clear after a very short time that the text is globally incoherent. The production of coherent stories—a minimal prerequisite for the novel-writing machine—has been a research area in Artificial Intelligence for many decades, but we are nowhere near being able to create stories that could pass even as pulp fiction.

But for the current purposes the feasibility or infeasibility of Orwell's technological creations is of less interest than the social use they serve. Clearly in the case of both the speakwrite and the novel-writing machines, they serve the interests of the State, but they do so in rather different ways. Consider the purpose of each in turn. The speakwrite is a labor-saving device: the implicit assumption is that it is easier to speak than to write and one can therefore can get one's job done more efficiently by having a machine that allows one to dictate one's messages rather than type them or write them by hand. The job of Winston Smith's department at the Ministry of Truth is to alter the past by constantly updating the archival texts to reflect the Party's current needs. Presumably the speakwrite helps that process of rectification of the past by speeding it up. The speakwrite is a mere tool.

The novel-writing machines, on the other hand, are a much more socially active device, since they represent a form of social control, a dystopic version of Juvenal's *panem et circenses*. The proles, who form 85 per cent of the population, but are considered by the Party members to be not fully human, need to be controlled by giving them material that will occupy their limited mental capacities. The entertainment and 'literature' produced by machines serves this purpose, and presumably does it more efficiently (by producing more material faster) than could be done by human writers. Indeed, Orwell makes it clear that this is indeed the intention behind having books written by machinery:

In Oceania at the present day, Science, in the old sense, has almost ceased to exist. In Newspeak there is no word for 'Science'. The empirical method of thought, on which all the scientific achievements of the past were founded, is opposed to the most fundamental principles of Ingsoc. And even technological progress only happens when its products can in some way be used for the diminution of human liberty. In all the useful arts the world is either standing still or going backwards. The fields are cultivated with horse-ploughs while books are written by machinery.   (Part 2, Chapter 9).

By having the entertainment of the majority of the population produced by machines, Orwell was clearly also implying a large amount of cynical disrespect for the underclass by the Party's inner circles:

It was only an 'opeless fancy.
It passed like an Ipril dye,
But a look an' a word an' the dreams they stirred!
They 'ave stolen my 'eart awye!

The tune had been haunting London for weeks past. It was one of countless similar songs published for the benefit of the proles by a sub-section of the Music Department. The words of these songs were composed without any human intervention whatever on an instrument known as a versificator. But the woman sang so tunefully as to turn the dreadful rubbish into an almost pleasant sound.
(George Orwell, *Nineteen Eighty-Four*, Part 2, Chapter 4.)

The possible sinister applications of speech and language technology are not limited to the writings of political thinkers like Orwell. When I was a graduate student at MIT in the early 1980s one of my classmates in the linguistics department openly expressed concern about the purpose of developing computers with speech and language capabilities. His worry, which he was apparently quite serious about, was that this would lead to the development of bombs that could understand and respond in speech, ones that could presumably obey a direct spoken order from a general. Such fears seem at best fanciful: speech is probably not the most efficient way of communicating with a Tomahawk missile. Nonetheless, speech and language technology, like any technology, can surely be put to malignant as well as benign uses.

This point must also be borne in mind when evaluating the oft-heard claims about how mass communication systems and information technology are bringing us all closer together. The catch-phrase 'Global Village', ascribed to the Canadian philosopher Marshall McLuhan, conjures up in the mind of many people a quaint English village on a worldwide scale. This is a calming image to be sure, but it is also a highly misleading one. Certainly, technologies *are* bringing us closer together, and in that sense we are becoming more like a village. But the metaphor, or perhaps more accurately most people's image of what the metaphor means, is misleading. For one thing, villages need not be harmonious places.

More to the point, however, is that what seems to be happening instead is that differences between people are being accentuated. Certainly scholars are beginning to question the idea that the official media are being globalized, and if anything the opposite is happening.[7] More generally, it is now much easier for fringe groups, some with hateful messages, to gain critical mass and flourish. The 'Londonistan' phenomenon—the fact that Islamist groups have flourished in places, like London, where fifty years previously they would have been too isolated—is certainly in part due to the fact that communication is now so much simpler. To see how mass communication can have this effect, let us conduct a little thought experiment. Imagine for a moment that you hold a peculiar view that only one in a million people hold. That means that there are 6,000 other people on earth just like you. A hundred years ago, it would have been highly unlikely you would meet even a single one of them. You could write a letter, but to whom would you send it? Perhaps you could post an advertisement in major cities, or in newspapers. You might get a few responses if people happened to run across your ad. Today of course, you merely need to put up a web page stating your views on any reasonably accessible site, and you can be sure that eventually search engines will pick it up, and people will run across it. Within a few weeks or months you could have an international club of a few thousand people who think exactly the same way you do.

None of this is to say that dystopic visions of abuse of technology will come to pass; or that we need collapse in upon ourselves because radical groups abuse the rapid spread of information to further their odious causes on a global scale. But it does mean that we need to be careful. With the spread of awareness of global warming, we have reluctantly come to the realization that two hundred years of industrialization are altering our planet in disastrous ways. In a similar vein we are perhaps beginning to realize that ready access to information—much of it involving the language technologies we have been discussing—can have a dark side. Language and technology are, more than anything else, what makes us human. But language can be abused, and so can the technology that supports it. We would do well to remember this: that what we term 'history'—the recorded events of human activity—started with the invention of writing. We will need another human faculty, wisdom, to ensure that writing, in the form of intolerant messages of hate, recorded electronically, and perhaps translated at the touch of a button into a hundred other languages, does not endanger the future of history itself.

10

Further Reading

Clearly there is a lot more to most of the issues that have been discussed in this book than we had space for here, and it is my hope that the reader will have found one or more of the issues discussed here sufficiently interesting that they would like to follow them up. This brief chapter gives some suggestions for sources of more information on various topics, some of which have been mentioned before, others not.

The best single source for the prehistory of writing in Mesopotamia discussed in Chapter 1 is Denise Schmandt-Besserat's *How Writing Came About* (1996).

Fortunately there are a number of good books for a general audience that deal with writing systems and decipherment (Chapters 3 and 4). The most prolific writer of such books is Andrew Robinson. His *Story of Writing* (2006*b*) is a general introduction to writing systems that also deals with the esthetic properties of scripts. His three books that deal with decipherment are all highly recommended: *The Man who Deciphered Linear B* (2002) on Michael Ventris, *The Last Man who Knew Everything* (2006*a*) on Thomas Young, and *Lost Languages* (2009), which discusses undeciphered scripts. Richard Parkinson's book *Cracking Codes* (1999) gives a detailed history of the decipherment of Egyptian, and Maurice Pope's *The Story of Decipherment* (1999) is a good general introduction to the topic. A recent book by Amalia Gnanadesikan, *The Writing Revolution* (2008), gives a nice review of how writing works, along with some interesting interpretations of a number of milestones in the history of writing, such as the development of the Greek alphabet from Phoenician, and Sequoyah's invention of Cherokee script. The best textbook on writing systems is Henry Rogers's *Writing Systems: A Linguistic Approach* (2005).

For some of the issues discussed in Chapter 5 see: John DeFrancis's *The Chinese Language: Fact and Fantasy* (1984), which has a good discussion of the attempts at Chinese writing reform; William Harris's *Ancient Literacy* (1989), which gives a sober account of the real state of literacy in Ancient Greece and Rome; and Jack Goody's classic *The Domestication of the Savage*

Mind (1977), which documents the differences between oral and literate cultures.

Early work on speech synthesis (Chapter 6) is discussed in the *Journal of the Acoustical Society* paper by Homer Dudley and T. H. Tarnoczy (1950). *JASA* can be found in many university libraries; alternatively one can buy a copy of the Dudley–Tarnoczy paper online (e.g. http://scitation.aip.org/jasa). Darren Wershler-Henry's book *The Iron Whim* (2005) contains a reasonable account of the early development of the typewriter; Richard Current's book *The Typewriter and the Men who Made it* (1954) is unfortunately out of print, as is Michael Adler's *The Writing Machine* (1973). Darryl Rehr's website at http://home.earthlink.net/~dcrehr/ is also a good source of information on the QWERTY keyboard. Joe Becker's *Scientific American* article on 'Multilingual Word Processing' (1984) discusses the Xerox Star system, and in so doing lays out nicely the most important issues in multilingual computing. In my view, the best starting point for a discussion of how Unicode works can be found at http://www.joelonsoftware.com/articles/Unicode.html. C. Michael Mellor's book *Louis Braille: A Touch of Genius* (2006) is a brief account of the life of the inventor of the most widely used reading system for the blind.

It is somewhat more of a challenge to find introductions to modern speech and language technology (Chapters 7 and 8) aimed at a general audience. A few of the chapters in David Stork's *Hal's Legacy: 2001's Computer as Dream and Reality* (1997) deal with some of the issues: Joseph Olive's chapter on speech synthesis, Raymond Kurzweil's chapter on speech recognition, and Roger Schank's chapter on natural language understanding make for easy reading. The authors are all very senior researchers in their fields—and Raymond Kurzweil is in addition well known as a 'visionary'. The downside of that arrangement is that the technologies that the authors discuss were not necessarily particularly up-to-date, even when the book was published. For an account of speech and language processing that is very up-to-date, the textbook by Dan Jurafsky and James Martin, *Speech and Language Processing: An Introduction to Natural Language Processing, Computational Linguistics, and Speech Recognition* (2008), is highly recommended.

Glossary

The following are definitions of some terms that may be unfamiliar to the reader. At the end of this section I also list some possibly unfamiliar phonetic symbols (from the International Phonetic Alphabet) that are used in the text.

Terminology

Alveolar (consonant). A consonant, such as /t/, /d/, or /n/ in English, which is produced by contact between the tip of the tongue and the alveolar ridge right behind the teeth.

Dental (consonant). A consonant, such as /t/, /d/, or /n/ in Spanish, which is produced by contact between the tip of the tongue and the teeth.

Formant (resonance). Natural frequencies at which an acoustic tube resonates. If a source sound such as that of the vibrating vocal chords in the larynx is passed through the vocal tract (the pharynx and mouth), the vocal tract will *filter* the sound by enhancing the energy of the sound at frequencies corresponding to the formants, and damping the energy at other frequencies. The formants depend upon the shape of the vocal tract, which is controlled by movements of the jaw, tongue, lips, and velum.

Front rounded vowels. Vowels like the 'u' in French *du*, the 'ü' in German *über*, or the 'u' in Mandarin 去 *qù*, where the tongue is forward as for vowels like 'i' in *machine*, but where the lips are also rounded as for 'u' in *loot*.

Front vowels. Vowels like 'i' in *machine* or *ai* in *bait*, where the tongue is relatively forward in the mouth.

(Grammatical) gender. A system whereby each noun must fall into one of a predetermined set of classes, where the classes are identified conventionally with terms that relate to natural gender—masculine, feminine, or neuter. Languages that have grammatical gender also exhibit grammatical agreement whereby, for instance, adjectives, articles, and sometimes verbs must agree with nouns in gender. French and other Romance languages, for instance, have two genders—masculine and feminine: in French, *le pain* 'the bread' is masculine, whereas *la rose* 'the rose' is feminine. German has three genders: masculine (*der Hund* 'the dog'); feminine (*die Schnecke* 'the snail'); and neuter (*das Pferd* 'the horse'). When a term denotes an object with natural gender—a human, or male or female animal—the grammatical gender usually, but not always, coincides with the natural gender.

Glide. A consonant that is vowel-like in that it is produced without a full closure of the vocal tract. Examples in English are /w/ as in *want* or /j/ as in *you*.

Glottal Stop. A stop consonant formed by closing off then releasing the glottis by closing the vocal chords. Glottal stops are not phonemes in English, but they are commonly found at the beginnings of words that start with vowels. Thus if you say *apple*, chances are that you produce it by first closing then releasing the vocal chords before setting them to vibrate for the production of the first vowel.

Glyph. A basic shape that forms part of a writing system. In English any of the letters of the alphabet would constitute glyphs; lower and upper case letters constitute different glyphs so that 'A' is a distinct glyph from 'a'. In Chinese, each character constitutes a glyph.

Inflection. A change in the form of a word to mark a difference in grammatical function. Common instances of inflection are person/number marking on verbs (e.g. English *am* versus *are*), or number marking on nouns (*dog* versus *dogs*).

Intonation. When people speak (in any language) they naturally vary the pitch of the voice: usually, speaking a sentence in a complete monotone is quite unnatural. The pitch varies in part to convey information: to emphasize or de-emphasize certain words, to indicate the ends of important phrases, to indicate that a phrase is a question or a statement, to convey emotion or rhetorical style. This set of phenomena comprises intonation. Unfortunately, in common parlance the term *inflection* is often used to refer to this phenomenon.

Labial. A sound produced by closing or constricting the lips. In English, labial sounds include /m/ and /p/.

Logogram. A written symbol that represents a word or morpheme.

Morpheme. A basic component of words, usually defined as the basic unit of meaning in a language. The word *cabbage* has one morpheme, but the word *cabbages* has two, one being the noun *cabbage* denoting the plant *Brassica oleracea*, the other *s*, marking the plural.

Morphology. The study of the structure of words.

Nasal. A sound that is produced with the velum lowered so that the nasal tract is open. In English, nasal sounds include /n/ and /m/. Some languages, such as French, have distinctive nasal vowels.

Onset. The initial consonant(s) of a syllable up to (but obviously not including) the vowel.

Parser. A computational device that computes the structure of a sentence.

Person/number marking. A morphological marking system, typically on verbs, that indicates the person (first, second, third) and number (singular, plural) of the subject of the verb (in some languages also the object.)

Pharyngeal. A consonant sound produced by constricting the pharynx (back of the throat) with the root of the tongue. Pharyngeal sounds are not common, but occur in several Semitic languages, notably Arabic.

Phone. Not a technical term in linguistics, but used in the speech technology community to refer to a basic sound of a language. Note that this does *not* necessarily correspond directly to a phoneme.

Phoneme. The basic *distinctive* unit of sound in a language. 'Distinctive' here means that a phonemic difference will typically correspond to a difference in meaning. Thus *cat* and *cad* are different words in English, reflecting the fact that /t/ and /d/ are different phonemes. On the other hand, the /t/ in *take* is pronounced differently from the /t/ in *stake*; the first is pronounced with aspiration—a puff of air—the second not. But these are not distinctive differences in English since one does not find pairs of words that differ only in having aspirated versus unaspirated /t/.

Phonogram. A written symbol that represents a sound.

Phonology. The study of the sound structure of a language.

Pitch. In music, or in speech, the perceived frequency of a sound. In speech, the intonation of a sentence can be described in terms of variation in pitch. For instance, in a typical yes/no question in English (*Do you like mangosteens?*), the pitch will often rise at the end of the sentence.

Prosodic Foot. A combination of a stressed and zero or more unstressed syllables. The word *cantaloupe*, for instance has two feet. The main stress is on the first syllable *cán* and there is a secondary stress on the final syllable *lòupe*. The first foot is *canta*—a stressed followed by an unstressed syllable (thus a trochaic foot)—and the second foot consists of the single syllable *loupe*. So, the word can be parsed into feet thus: *[(cán) (ta)] [(lòupe)]*

Root-and-pattern Morphology. A type of word formation that involves skeletal roots, and patterns that flesh out the roots into words. Canonical instances of root-and-pattern morphology are found in Semitic languages such as Arabic and Hebrew. Thus the root *ktb* 'write' in Arabic can appear in the shape *CaCaC* in *katab* 'wrote', *CuCiC* in *kutib* 'was written', *ma + CCaC* in *maktab* 'office' (a place where writing is done), *CiCaaC* in *kitaab* 'book', and so forth. In each case the pattern imposes a shape on the three-consonant root *ktb*.

Rounded (Vowels). Vowel sounds that are produced with lip rounding: examples in English are 'u' as in 'loot' or 'o' as in 'mote'.

Semasiogram. A written symbol that represents a meaning (idea, or concept.)

Stop. A consonant that is produced by closing off the vocal tract with the lips, tongue or vocal chords. In English examples are /p/, /t/, /k/, /m/, /n/.

Syllabogram. A written symbol that represents a syllable.

Syntax. The study of how words are combined into sentences.

Unvoiced. A sound that is produced without vibration of the vocal chords.

Uvular. A consonant sound produced with contact between the tongue back and the uvula.

Velar. A consonant sound produced by bringing the tongue body in contact with the soft palate (velum). Examples in English are /k/ and /g/.

Voiced (sound). A sound that is produced with the vibration of the vocal chords.

Phonetic Symbols

a   as in "banana"

æ   as in "ash"

aɪ   as in "my"

ð   as in "that"

ə   as in "banana"

ɪ   as in "hit"

kʰ   aspirated /k/, as in English 'kick'

ɔ   as in the British pronunciation of 'dog'

pʰ   aspirated /p/, as in English 'pick'

q   a uvular consonant (see above)

x   as in Scottish 'loch'

ʒ   as in 'pleasure'

ʔ   a glottal stop (see glossary)

ʕ   a voiced pharyngeal (see glossary)

Notes

Chapter 1

1. Griesser (2008).
2. Sinha (2003).
3. Hauser *et al.* (2002).
4. Sanz *et al.* (2009).
5. Oppenheim (1959); Schmandt-Besserat (1996).
6. Ibid., pp 102–3.

Chapter 2

1. http://voyager.jpl.nasa.gov/spacecraft/goldenrec.html
2. A short biography of Bliss can be found at http://www.blissymbolics.us/biography/
3. The discussion here is based on Bliss (1965).
4. Blissymbolics symbols in this chapter were created using the freeware Blisstool http://membres.lycos.fr/jfbouzereau/BLISS/blisso.html
5. Note that '!' may be used iteratively: '!!' is more intense than '!'.
6. See DeFrancis (1989: 132).
7. Though Bliss would surely not have appreciated the comparison, Orwell's *Newspeak* in *1984* is another instance of a minimal language; Orwell was inspired in part by Basic English, of which he was initially a fan, but then became critical. In the case of Newspeak the goal was to eliminate as many words as possible, not for the purposes of promoting communication but stifling it, and in particular stifling heretical ideas. The premise was that ideas cannot arise if there are no words to express them.
8. When I first taught writing systems in a class at the University of Illinois in 2004, I discussed Blissymbolics, but there were at that time, to my knowledge, no standard textbooks on writing systems that even mentioned it. Since that date, the excellent textbook by Henry Rogers (2005) has rectified that situation, but I still believe that most specialists in writing systems are not aware of Bliss's work.
9. There has even been work on converting between Blissymbolic sentences and sentences in natural language. For example Netzer (2006) presents such a system for generating English and Hebrew sentences from Blissymbolic input. Earlier work by speech researcher Sharon Hunnicutt (1986) presented a system for converting from Blissymbols to speech.
10. From Clammer (1976: 67).
11. As of 2009, plans to develop the Yucca Mountain site have been abandoned.

12. Trauth *et al.* (1993).

13. According to the Information Center at WIPP, as of the time of writing, plans for what they now term 'Passive Institutional Controls' have not been finalized. The document on their website that discusses this—*Permanent Markers Monument Survey*, a contractor report prepared by John Hart and Associates, dated 31 August 2000—deals entirely with the question of preservation of markers, mostly by considering how Native American petroglyphs in the region have fared over the centuries. Nothing is said about what kind of message the markers should contain.

Chapter 3

1. Robinson (2006*b*).
2. Gnanadesikan (2008).
3. Morais *et al.* (1986).
4. For reasons that would take us far too far afield, this simple statement is not as uncontroversial as you might think, since many linguists disagree on what constitutes a valid definition for a morpheme.
5. Sampson (1985).
6. Developed at the Language Technologies Institute, Carnegie Mellon University.
7. Technically this means "word writing", but the more apt term *morphemographic* has never taken root.
8. Or possibly another writing system of Mesoamerica, such as Zapotec, which may have been the precursor to Mayan.
9. DeFrancis (1984: 134).
10. DeFrancis (1984), DeFrancis (1989).
11. I use the standard Pinyin transcription system, which is based on Mandarin pronunciation, throughout.
12. So as not to help propagate another myth about Chinese, I want to stress that the Kangxi dictionary was intended to be a compendium of all the characters that had been used up to that time. The implication was not that anyone actually *knew* all 48,641 characters, nor was there any need that they know them, because most were rarely attested. To put this in perspective, most literate Chinese today probably know on the order of 7,000 characters. A Chinese scholar might know a few thousand more than this.
13. Appendix to Lehman and Faust (1951).
14. See Sampson (1985) for a fuller discussion of these points.
15. Hannas (2003).
16. McLuhan and Logan (1977). We will return briefly to Hannas's argument in Chapter 5.
17. For a detailed discussion of the history of Sequoyah's achievement see Gnanadesikan (2008).
18. Smith (1996).

19. Another contender was cuneiform Hittite, from Anatolia of the second millennium BC. As with Japanese, Hittite was a borrowed writing system. The Hittites adopted their cuneiform system from the Akkadians, who in turn had learned to write from the Sumerians.
20. Shi (1996).
21. One could do the same thing for Chinese—i.e. represent each syllable with just *one* of the characters that are used to write it in standard orthography. But with about 1,300 distinct syllables (including tone) in Mandarin, that would not afford much of a savings over the roughly 5,000-odd characters in common use in the standard orthography. See also DeFrancis (1984).
22. Strictly speaking, Arabic does not really mark tense, but rather *aspect*.
23. I say 'more or less' here because it is frequently the case that a language will have a sound that is close to, but not identical to a sound in another language. English and Dutch both have /p/, /t/, and /k/, but unlike the English sounds which are aspirated (the puff of air we described earlier in this chapter), Dutch /p/, /t/, and /k/ are unaspirated.
24. Haile (1996).
25. Etruscan, however, when not written boustrophedon, was usually written right to left.
26. de Kerckhove and Lumsden (1988).
27. King (1996).
28. Pratt (2006: 105).
29. King (1996).
30. During the early twentieth century, partly because of the difficulties of typing Hangul, there was an attempt to linearize the script, but this never took hold; see King (1996).
31. Korean personal names are Chinese names, and everyone learns the characters for their name. The Chinese rendition of personal names is official on identity cards.

Chapter 4

1. Pernier (1908); Godart (1995).
2. Eisenberg (2008).
3. Aleff (1982).
4. None of these are foolproof however: if the artisan who created the text was illiterate and was merely copying symbols drawn for him by a scribe, then he need not have followed the correct reading direction when he created the final document.
5. This principle is used to transcribe Linear A texts, though there is a certain circularity here: we do not know the language that the Cretan inventors of Linear A spoke, and so we have no way to check that the assigned values really reflect the original pronunciation.
6. Fischer (1997*b*).

7. Massey and Massey (2000).
8. Allen (2000).
9. Chadwick (1987).
10. Fischer (1997*a*).
11. "'Five Elamit [sic] professional linguists from different countries have studied the brick inscription discovered in Jiroft. According to the studies, they have concluded that this discovered inscription is 300 years older than that found in Susa; and most probably the written language went to Susa from this region. However, more studies are still needed to give a final approval to this thesis,' said Yousof Majid Zadeh, head of archeological excavation team in Jiroft. 'This inscription was discovered in a palace. Although it is not yet known which Elamit king this inscription belongs to, it is definitely an Elamit inscription. More studies are needed to determine the exact time in which it was inscribed, but most probably it is the most ancient written language. Further excavations are being carried out to find the rest of the inscription. However, what is obvious about this discovered inscription is that it is older than the Elamit inscription of Susa,' explained Majidzadeh." Cultural Heritage News Agency, http://www.chnpress.com/news/?section=28rid=6096.
12. Ramsey (1989).
13. Elfenbein (1998).
14. The discussion here follows closely the account given in Robinson (2006*b*). According to the *Encyclopaedia Britannica* (eleventh edition) article on Grotefend, his achievement resulted from a bet that he made with friends at a bar that he could crack cuneiform. Grotefend's first reports on his work appeared in 1800.
15. Ventris (1988).
16. Chadwick (1958: 70).
17. Ventris and Chadwick (1956).
18. Couture (1984).
19. Robinson (2006*b*); Parkinson (1999).
20. Farmer *et al.* (2004).
21. Mahadevan (2003).
22. Parpola *et al.* (1969); Parpola (1970).
23. Readers may have seen the paper by Rao and colleagues that appeared in *Science* in April 2009 (Rao *et al.* 2009), or run across some of the numerous press reports. This paper claimed to have provided refutation of the Farmer *et al.* hypothesis by showing that the Indus symbol corpus looks more like a linguistic system than a non-linguistic system, using a statistical measure, conditional entropy. A detailed discussion of why Rao *et al.*'s argument is fallacious would take us too far afield. Our own counterargument can be found at http://www.safarmer.com/Refutation3.pdf, but the most eloquent and simple explanation of the fallacy is probably that of the computational linguist Fernando Pereira, which can be found at http://earningmyturns.blogspot.com/2009/04/falling-for-magic-formula.html.

Chapter 5

1. United Nations Development Programme, *Human Development Reports*, http://hdrstats.undp.org/indicators/272.html and http://hdrstats.undp.org/indicators/273.html.
2. This glosses over the fact that there is often a differential ability between reading and writing. Quite often, people's reading abilities are ahead of their writing abilities, especially if the writing system in question is a complicated one that needs constant practice to maintain: for instance, I can read many more Chinese characters than I can remember how to write, and this is something that many expatriate native speakers of Chinese also find as they gradually forget how to write characters that they have not used for a long while.
3. In China, where Classical Chinese served as the literary language right up to the early twentieth century, the situation was much the same as in Korea: when you went to school to learn to read and write you had to learn to read and write in a language that was as different from your own as Latin would be to a speaker of modern French.
4. Anna Maria Escobar, p.c., July 2008. One of the complicating factors with Quechua is that it is spoken in several countries—Ecuador, Bolivia, and Peru—and in each country there are proposals for a Quechua orthography: Peru has at least two such competing proposals. To some extent these differences in orthography reflect differences in dialect.
5. Keightley (1978); Chang (1980).
6. Farmer (1998); Farmer *et al.* (2002).
7. Goody (1977).
8. As we will see in a later chapter, rendering tables in speech (as in reading for the blind) requires very careful techniques for presenting the material in a comprehensible way.
9. Moorhouse (1953).
10. Hannas (2003).
11. Hannas's investigation is not a controlled study. He argues that Japan, China, and Korea have, over the past several decades, engaged in various methods for acquiring scientific knowledge from the West, ranging from sending graduate students abroad to train and then enticing them home, to outright industrial espionage. The problem is that while this may all be true, one would like to know that what Hannas claims of East Asia is not also true of countries that use segmental systems of writing, such as France, or Israel.
12. Sproat (2004).
13. Farmer (1998).
14. Shu and Anderson (1997).
15. Farmer *et al.* (2002).
16. Ehrmann (2003).

17. Rabiner and Schafer (1978): 63, Eqn. 3.4.
18. As we will see in Chapter 6, this relationship between the acoustical and electrical domains was extremely useful in the development of early electronic speech synthesizers.
19. Routledge (1919).
20. Guy (1990).
21. Zhao and Baldauf (2008).
22. Ibid.
23. However, as Zhao and Baldauf (2008) note, the effective limitation of electronic encoding still does not force people to forgo characters in non-electronic contexts, and this continues to lead to problems, especially in the area of personal names.
24. DeFrancis (1984).
25. *CIA World Factbook*, 2003, https://www.cia.gov/library/publications/the-world-factbook/print/tw.html.
26. Sproat (2008).
27. Harris (1989: 25–6).
28. United Nations Development Programme, 2007, *Measuring Human Development: A Primer*. Available at http://hdr.undp.org/en/reports/publications/title,4182,en.html.
29. Ibid., p. 36.
30. Note that for the Arabic-derived scripts, the set of symbols is relatively large because most letters have different initial, final, medial, and independent forms.
31. Or if not the true past, then at least some version of the past that is not created to serve current political needs.
32. Pinker (2002).

Chapter 6

1. Shufelt (2005).
2. Formants are the natural frequencies at which the vocal tract resonates—i.e. the frequencies which will show the highest energy when sound from a source such as vibrating vocal chords is passed through it. These resonant frequencies change as we move our tongue and jaw, or open and close the velum, thus opening or closing the nasal tract.
3. Dudley and Tarnoczy (1950). Note that this is the same Homer Dudley that we will meet later in this chapter as the inventor of the Voder.
4. Some sample speech from a variety of speech synthesizers, dating back to the Voder, can be found on the Helsinki University of Technology website at http://www.acoustics.hut.fi/publications/files/theses/lemmetty_mst/appa.html.
5. Pratt (2006: 74).
6. Ibid., p. 111.
7. Wershler-Henry (2005: 66).
8. Weller (1918). Since it is out of copyright, Weller's book can be found in its entirety on Google Books.
9. Wershler-Henry (2005).

10. Ibid.
11. I am indebted to Martin Howard, an expert and collector of antique typewriters, for explaining the layout of the typebars on the earliest Remington models. See Martin's website at www.antiquetypewriters.com.
12. An early engraving that purports to be of a pre-Remington version of the Sholes machine shows the 'r' and '.' keys swapped. This would do much to reduce the potential of clash for 'r' and 'e'. However, there were other differences from QWERTY in that keyboard: 'x' and 'c' were swapped, as were 'i' and 'u'.
13. Current (1954).
14. To obtain the score, what I did for the top ten most frequent letter pairs in the *King James Bible* was multiply the typebar distance by the frequency of the letter pair, normalized (divided by) the sum of the frequencies for the top ten.
15. Liebowitz and Margolis (1990).
16. Ibid.
17. Dvorak *et al.* (1936).
18. Wershler-Henry (2005).
19. Dial-up in the sense that you actually dialed up using a normal phone, and then cradled the handset on a pair of receivers on the modem: data was transmitted via audio.
20. Christensen (1997).
21. Kipling (1913).
22. Keep (1997: 402).
23. Wershler-Henry (2005).
24. Keep (1997: 412).
25. Ibid.
26. Pyung Woo Kong, US Patent 2,625,251, 13 January 1953.
27. It is not clear from Kong's description if the ordering of ㅏ and ㅗ is critical: this is the opposite order to the 'logical' order of the corresponding sounds, and is also the opposite order to what one would type on a modern Korean keyboard.
28. King (1996).
29. Jacobsen (1997).
30. Jim Reeds has a good discussion of the Chinese code at http://www.njstar.com/tools/telecode/jim-reeds-ctc.htm.
31. The Wikipedia article on the Xerox Star system at http://en.wikipedia.org/wiki/Xerox_Star gives a good history of the main points.
32. What you see is what you get.
33. Becker (1984).
34. Available at http://www.unicode.org/history/unicode88.pdf
35. A good discussion of this and many other issues can be found at http://www.joelonsoftware.com/articles/Unicode.html.
36. Becker (1984).
37. Note also that to implement Hangul combination in the font would have required a font with a rather unwieldly number of ligature rules in the font's *glyph metamorphosis table*.

38. Braille's blindness was the result of a ghastly accident. At the age of three, he stabbed himself in the right eye with a leather-working knife in his father's harness shop. His left eye was lost to sympathetic ophthalmia, a rare autoimmune condition whereby the immune system, suddenly exposed to a rush of antigens from the injured eye, effectively classifies these as foreign and starts attacking the healthy eye.
39. Mellor (2006).

Chapter 7

1. http://www.tellme.com, http://www.google.com/goog411.
2. I will confine the discussion here to spoken language. Obviously, for deaf people who use signed languages such as American Sign Language, the particular processes that I will be discussing are different. However the nature of the problem—the mapping from a physical signal into a mental representation—is identical whether we are talking about signed or spoken languages.
3. The speech displays in this chapter were produced using the freely available Praat software available from http//www.fon.hum.uva.nl/praat/.
4. This is from a version of Goog411 that was fielded in 2007. There have since been updates to the interaction.
5. We already mentioned the CMU lexicon in Chapter 3, where I used it to compute an approximate number of syllables for English.
6. The performance vis-à-vis English is particularly of interest in the case of Mandarin Chinese. Chinese is a *tone language*, meaning that a particular phone sequence may mean different things depending upon the intonation that is applied to the word. Since conventional ASR technology routinely discards tonal information, there is no way in an ASR system to distinguish two words that differ only in tone. This means that ASR systems for Chinese are dependent even more than English ASR systems are on context to disambiguate otherwise phonetically-similar words.
7. It is worth mentioning at this point that the annotations necessary in a large unit-selection system, or for that matter even in a much smaller diphone system, are rarely done by hand: having a phonetician go through and mark up speech with phonetic information is a time-consuming and thus expensive proposition. Rather what is typically done is that an ASR system is used in *forced alignment* mode to segment the speech: since the speaker for a TTS unit database is reading from a text, we know what the reader said. So instead of a full-blown ASR system where a language model is used to determine what was said, in this case we know what was said. However we do not know where the boundaries of the individual sounds are, so we give the uttered sequence of phones (which we can compute from the text that was read) to the ASR system's acoustic model, and let it decide where it 'wants' to place the acoustic boundaries between the phones.

Chapter 8

1. An excellent summary of the early history of translation can be found on John Hutchins' website, for example, http://www.hutchinsweb.me.uk/Milestones-1.pdf
2. Ibid.
3. Weaver's Memorandum can be read in full at http://www.mt-archive.info/ Weaver-1949.pdf
4. We will have more to say about post-editing below. Pre-editing has mostly been restricted to installations of MT systems at corporations. Thus, Caterpillar developed a restricted language called 'Caterpillar Technical English', for the purpose of more accurate translation of technical manuals.
5. Hutchins (2005).
6. Pierce is credited with inventing the term 'transistor'.
7. Slocum (1985).
8. Chevalier et al. (1978); Slocum (1985).
9. Not every weather report sticks precisely within the strict stylistic guidelines, though according to Slocum (1985) the majority of the text that is not handled is a result of misspellings, or dropped data due to network issues.
10. In a similar way, the United States National Oceanic and Atmospheric Administration's deployment of a unit-selection synthesizer for the task of reading weather reports over NOAA Weather Radio benefits from the limited domain of this application. See Chapter 7.
11. Pierre Isabelle, personal communication.
12. From http://www.tolweb.org/Pezizomycotina/29296.
13. Lewis Carroll (1865). *Alice's Adventures in Wonderland*. German translation from *Alice im Wunderland*, Dodo-Verlag, Books on Demand, 2003.
14. Papineni *et al.* (2002).

Chapter 9

1. The discussion here follows work I did with my colleagues Jianying Hu and Hao Chen, Sproat *et al.* (1998).
2. Fried-Oken (2008).
3. For example, the Educational Testing Service's e-rater system for rating essays (Attali and Burstein 2006), or pronunciation testing for second-language learners in the Versant system from Pearson.
4. Anderson and Rainie (2008: 99).
5. See, e.g., Zittel *et al.* (2008).
6. A poem or song-writing machine is less of an issue, since at least lyrical songs and poems do not require one to produce a coherent plot, and furthermore the constraints of rhyme and meter in many ways make it *easier* for a machine to produce plausible output.
7. Hafez (2007).

Bibliography

Adler, M., 1973. *The Writing Machine*. George Allen and Unwin, London.

Aleff, H. P., 1982. The board game on the Phaistos disk, electronic book.

Allen, J., 2000. *Middle Egyptian: An Introduction to the Language and Culture of Hieroglyphs*. Cambridge University Press, New York.

Anderson, J. Q., and Rainie, L., December 2008. The future of the Internet III. Tech. rep., Pew Internet and American Life Project, http://www.pewinternet.org/PPF/r/270/report_display.asp

Attali, Y., and Burstein, J., 2006. Automated essay scoring with e-rater v. 2.0. *Journal of Technology, Learning, and Assessment* 4 (3).

Barthel, T., 1958. *Grundlagen zur Entzifferung der Osterinselschrift*. Cram, de Gruyter, Hamburg.

Baxter, W., 2001. An etymological dictionary of common Chinese characters, www-personal.umich.edu/~wbaxter/etymdict.html (accessed 21 October 2009).

Becker, J., 1984. Multilingual word processing. *Scientific American*, July, 96–107.

Bliss, C., 1965. *Semantography*. Semantography (Blissymbolics) Publications, Sydney.

Bor, J., 2005. The political economy of AIDS leadership in developing countries: an exploratory analysis. Justice Africa GAIN Brief 7, December.www.justiceafrica.org/wp-content/uploads/2006/06/Bor_PoliticalEconomyofAIDSLeadership.pdf (accessed 21 October 2009).

Chadwick, J., 1958. *The Decipherment of Linear B*. Cambridge University Press, Cambridge.

Chadwick, J., 1987. *Linear B and Related Scripts*. University of California Press, Berkeley.

Chang, K.-C., 1980. *Shang Civilization*. Yale University Press, New Haven, CT.

Chevalier, M., Dansereau, J., and Poulin, G., 1978. TAUM-METEO: description du système. Technical report, Groupe TAUM, Université de Montréal, Montréal.

Christensen, C., 1997. *The Innovator's Dilemma: When New Technologies Cause Great Firms to Fail*. Harvard Business School Press, Boston, MA.

Clammer, J. R., 1976. *Literacy and Social Change: A Case Study of Fiji*. E. J. Brill, Leiden.

Couture, P., 1984. Sir Henry Creswicke Rawlinson: Pioneer cuneiformist. *Biblical Archaeologist*, September, 143–5.

Current, R., 1954. *The Typewriter and the Men who Made it*. University of Illinois Press, Urbana, IL.

Cutler, I. M., and SoRelle, R., 1910. *Rational Typewriting*. Gregg Publishing Company, New York.

Darwin, E., 1806–7. *The Temple of Nature; or, The Origin of Society*. J. Johnson, London.

de Kerckhove, D., and Lumsden, C. (eds), 1988. *The Alphabet and the Brain.* Berlin. Springer.

DeFrancis, J., 1984. *The Chinese Language: Fact and Fantasy.* University of Hawaii Press, Honolulu, HI.

DeFrancis, J., 1989. *Visible Speech: The Diverse Oneness of Writing Systems.* University of Hawaii Press, Honolulu, HI.

Dudley, H., and Tarnoczy, T., 1950. The speaking machine of Wolfgang von Kempelen. *Journal of the Acoustical Society of America* 22 (1), 151–66.

Dvorak, A., Merrick, N., Dealey, W., and Ford, G. C., 1936. *Typewriting Behavior.* American Book Company, New York.

Ehrmann, B., 2003. *Lost Christianities: The Battles for Scripture and the Faiths We Never Knew.* Oxford University Press, New York.

Eisenberg, J., 2008. The Phaistos disk: A one hundred-year-old hoax? *Minerva*, July/ August, 9–24.

Elfenbein, J., 1998. Brahui. In: Steever, S. (ed.), *The Dravidian Languages.* Routledge, London.

Everett, D., 2005. Cultural constraints on grammar and cognition in Pirahã: Another look at the design features of human language. *Current Anthroplogy* 46 (4), 621–46.

Farmer, S., 1998. *Syncretism in the West: Pico's 900 Theses (1486): The Evolution of Traditional Religious and Philosophical Systems: With a Revised Text, English Translation, and Commentary* (Hardcover). Medieval & Renaissance Texts and Studies, Tempe, AZ.

Farmer, S., Henderson, J., and Witzel, M., 2002. Neurobiology, layered texts and correlative cosmologies; a cross-cultural framework for premodern history. *Bulletin of the Museum of Far Eastern Antiquities* 72, 48–90, www.safarmer.com/neuro-correlative.pdf (accessed 21 October 2009).

Farmer, S., Sproat, R., and Witzel, M., 2004. The collapse of the Indus-script thesis: The myth of a literate Harappan civilization. *Electronic Journal of Vedic Studies* 11 (2).

Faucounau, J., 1975. *Le déchiffrement du disque de Phaistos. Preuves et Consequences.* Harmattan, Paris.

Fischer, S., 1997a. *Glyphbreaker.* Springer, New York.

Fischer, S., 1997b. *Rongorongo: The Easter Island Script: History, Traditions, Texts.* Oxford Studies in Anthropological Linguistics, 14. Oxford University Press, Oxford.

Fried-Oken, M., 2008. Augmentative and alternative communication treatment for persons with primary progressive aphasia. *Perspectives on Augmentative and Alternative Communication* 17, 99–104.

Gelb, I., 1963. *A Study of Writing*, 2nd edn. Chicago University Press, Chicago, IL.

Gnanadesikan, A., 2008. *The Writing Revolution: Cuneiform to the Internet.* Wiley-Blackwell, Malden, MA.

Godart, L., 1995. *The Phaistos Disc, The Enigma of an Aegean Script.* Itanos.

Goody, J., 1977. *The Domestication of the Savage Mind.* Cambridge University Press, New York.

Goody, J., and Watt, I., 1968. The consequences of literacy. In: Goody, J. (ed.), *Literacy in Traditional Societies*. Cambridge University Press, New York, pp. 27–68.

Griesser, M., 2008. Referential calls signal predator behavior in a group-living bird species. *Current Biology*, 8 January, 18, 69–73.

Guy, J., 1990. On the lunar calendar of tablet Mamari. *Journal de la Societé des Océanistes* 91 (2), 135–49.

Hafez, K., 2007. *The Myth of Media Globalization*. Polity Press, Malden, MA.

Haile, G., 1996. Ethiopic writing. In: Daniels, P., and Bright, W. (eds), *The World's Writing Systems*. Oxford University Press, New York, pp. 569–76.

Hannas, W., 2003. *The Writing on the Wall: How Asian Orthography Curbs Creativity*. University of Pennsylvania, Philadelphia.

Harris, R., 1995. *Signs of Writing*. Routledge, London.

Harris, W. V., 1989. *Ancient Literacy*. Harvard University Press, Cambridge, MA.

Hauser, M., Chomsky, N., and Fitch, W. T., 2002. The faculty of language: what is it, who has it, and how did it evolve? *Science*, November, 298, 1569–79.

Heyerdahl, T., 1958. *Aku-Aku: The Secret of Easter Island*. Allen & Unwin, London.

Hunnicutt, S., 1986. Bliss symbol-to-speech conversion: 'Blisstalk'. *Journal of the American Voice I/O Society* 3, 19–38.

Hutchins, J., 2005. The first public demonstration of machine translation: the Georgetown-IBM system, 7 January 1954. www.hutchinsweb.me.uk/GU-IBM-2005.pdf (accessed 21 October 2009).

Hutchins, J., and Lovtskii, E., 2000. Petr (Petrovich) Troyanskii (1894–1950): a Forgotten Pioneer of Machine Translation. *Machine Translation* 15 (3), 187–221.

Isabelle, P., and Bourbeau, L., 1985. TAUM-AVIATION: its technical features and some experimental results. *Computational Linguistics* 11 (1), 18–27.

Jacobsen, K., 1997. Danish watchmaker created the Chinese Morse system. *Morsum Magnificat* 51, 14–19.

Jurafsky, D., and Martin, J., 2008. *Speech and Language Processing: an Introduction to Natural Language Processing, Computational Linguistics, and Speech Recognition*, 2nd edn. Prentice Hall, Upper Saddle River, NJ.

Keep, C., 1997. The cultural work of the typewriter girl. *Victorian Studies* 40 (3), 401–26.

Keightley, D., 1978. *Sources of Shang History: The Oracle-Bone Inscriptions of Bronze Age China*. Berkeley. University of California Press.

King, R., 1996. Korean Hankul. In: Daniels, P., and Bright, W. (eds), *The World's Writing Systems*. Oxford University Press, New York, pp. 218–27.

Kipling, R., 1913. *From Sea to Sea: Letters of Travel, Volume II*. Vol. XVI of *The Works of Rudyard Kipling*. Charles Scribner, New York.

Lehman, W., and Faust, L., 1951. *A Grammar of Formal Written Japanese*. Harvard University Press, Cambridge, MA, Ch. Supplement: Kokuji, by R. P. Alexander.

Lévi-Strauss, C., 1970. *The Raw and the Cooked*, tr. by John and Doreen Weightman. Harper & Row, New York.

Liebowitz, S. J., and Margolis, S., 1990. The fable of the keys. *Journal of Law & Economics*, April, 33, 1–25.

Light, L., and Anderson, P., 1993. Typewriter keyboards via simulated annealing. *AI Expert*, September.

McLuhan, M., and Logan, R. K., 1977. Alphabet, mother of invention. *Et Cetera*, December, 373–83.

Mahadevan, I., 2003. *Early Tamil Epigraphy: From the Earliest Times to the Sixth Century AD*. Harvard Oriental Series, Chennai and Cambridge, MA.

Massey, K., and Massey, K., 2000. Mysteries of History !!Solved!! Massey Electronic Publishing, http://home.att.net/~phaistosdisk/mystery.PDF (accessed 21 October 2009).

Mellor, C. M., 2006. *Louis Braille: A Touch of Genius*. National Braille Press, Boston, MA.

Moorhouse, A., 1953. *The Triumph of the Alphabet: A History of Writing*. Henry Schuman, New York.

Morais, J., Bertelson, P., Cary, L., and Alegria, J., 1986. Literacy training and speech segmentation. *Cognition* 24, 45–64.

Netzer, Y., 2006. Semantic authoring for Blissymbols augmented communication using multilingual text generation. PhD thesis, Ben-Gurion University of the Negev, Beer-Sheva.

Oppenheim, A. L., 1959. On an operational device in Mesopotamian bureaucracy. *Journal of Near Eastern Studies* 18, 121–8.

Papineni, K., Roukos, S., Ward, T., and Zhu, W., 2002. BLEU: a method for automatic evaluation of machine translation. In: *40th Annual meeting of the Association for Computational Linguistics*, pp. 311–18.

Parkinson, R., 1999. *Cracking Codes: The Rosetta Stone and Decipherment*. University of California Press, Berkeley.

Parpola, A., 1970. The Indus script decipherment: the situation at the end of 1969. *Journal of Tamil Studies* 2 (1), 89–109.

Parpola, A., 1994. *Deciphering the Indus Script*. Cambridge University Press, New York.

Parpola, A., Koskenniemi, S., Parpola, S., and Aalto, P., 1969. Decipherment of the Proto-Dravidian inscriptions of the Indus civilization: first announcement. Tech. rep., Scandinavian Institute of Asian Studies, Copenhagen.

Pernier, L., 1908. Il disco di Phaestos con caratteri pittografici. *Ausonia: Rivista della Società di Archeologia e Storia dell'Arte* 3.

Pierce, J., Carroll, J., et al., 1966. Language and machines: computers in translation and linguistics—ALPAC report. Tech. rep., National Academy of Sciences, National Research Council, Washington, DC.

Pinker, S., 2002. *The Blank Slate: The Modern Denial of Human Nature*. Viking Adult, New York.

Pope, M., 1999. *The Story of Decipherment: From Egyptian Hieroglyphs to Maya Script*. Thames and Hudson, New York.

Pratt, K., 2006. *Everlasting Flower: A History of Korea*. Reaktion Books, London.

Rabiner, L., and Schafer, R., 1978. *Digital Processing of Speech Signals*. Prentice Hall, London.

Ramsey, S. R., 1989. *The Languages of China*. Princeton University Press, Princeton, NJ.

Rao, R., Yadav, N., Vahia, M., Joglekar, H., Adhikari, R., and Mahadevan, I., 2009. Entropic evidence for linguistic structure in the Indus script. *Science*, May, 324, 1165.

Rjabchikov, S., 1999. The Proto-Palestinian, Proto-Sinaian and Proto-Byblian inscriptions: a Slavonic key, http://public.kubsu.ru/~usro2898/sl3.htm, and see also http://public.kubsu.ru/~usro2898/disk.htm.

Robinson, A., 2002. *The Man who Deciphered Linear B: The Story of Michael Ventris*. Thames and Hudson, London.

Robinson, A., 2006a. *The Last Man who Knew Everything: Thomas Young, the Anonymous Polymath who Proved Newton Wrong, Explained How we See, Cured the Sick, and Deciphered the Rosetta Stone, among other Feats of Genius*. Pi Press, New York.

Robinson, A., 2006b. *The Story of Writing: Alphabets, Hieroglyphs and Pictograms*. Thames and Hudson, London.

Robinson, A., 2009. *Lost Languages: The Enigma of the World's Undeciphered Scripts*, 2nd edn. Thames and Hudson, New York.

Rogers, H., 2005. *Writing Systems: A Linguistic Approach*. Blackwell, Malden, MA.

Routledge, K. S., 1919. *The Mystery of Easter Island: The Story of an Expedition*. Hazel, Watson and Viney, London.

Sampson, G., 1985. *Writing Systems*. Stanford University Press, Stanford, CA.

Sankarananda, S., 1968. *Decipherment of Inscriptions on the Phaistos Disc of Crete*. Abhedananda Academy of Culture, Calcutta.

Sanz, C., Call, J., and Morgan, D., 2009. Design complexity in termite-fishing tools of chimpanzees (*Pan troglodytes*). *Royal Society Biological Letters* 5, 293–6.

Schmandt-Besserat, D., 1996. *How Writing Came About*. University of Texas Press, Austin, TX.

Shannon, C., 1949. Communication theory of secrecy systems. *Bell System Technical Journal* 28, 656–715.

Shi, D., 1996. The Yi script. In: Daniels, P., and Bright, W. (eds), *The World's Writing Systems*. Oxford University Press, New York, pp. 239–43.

Shu, H., and Anderson, R. C., 1997. Role of radical awareness in the character and word acquisition of Chinese children. *Reading Research Quarterly* 32 (1), 78–89.

Shufelt, J., 2005. The trickster as an instrument of enlightenment: George Psalmanazar and the writings of Jonathan Swift. *History of European Ideas* 31, 147–71.

Sinha, A., 2003. A beautiful mind: Attribution and intentionality in wild bonnet macaques. *Current Science* 85 (7), 1021–30.

Slocum, J., 1985. A survey of machine translation: its history, current status, and future prospects. *Computational Linguistics* 11 (1), 1–17.

Smith, J., 1996. Japanese writing. In: Daniels, P., and Bright, W. (eds), *The World's Writing Systems*. Oxford University Press, New York, pp. 209–17.

Sproat, R., 2004. Review of Hannas: *The Writing on the Wall*. *Language* 81 (1), 251–4.

Sproat, R., 2008. Review of Zhao and Baldauf: *Planning Chinese Characters: Reaction, Evolution or Revolution? Written Language and Literacy* 11 (2), 229–34.

Sproat, R., Hu, J., and Chen, H., 1998. EMU: An e-mail preprocessor for text-to-speech. In: *IEEE Signal Processing Society 1998 Workshop on Multimedia Signal Processing*. Los Angeles.

Stork, D. (ed.), 1997. *HAL's Legacy: '2001's' Computer as Dream and Reality*. MIT Press, Cambridge, MA.

Trauth, K., Hora, S., and Guzowski, R., 1993. Expert judgment of markers to deter human intrusion into the Waste Isolation Plant. Tech. Rep. SAND92–1382.UC–721, Sandia National Laboratories.

Ventris, M., 1940. Introducing the Minoan Language, *American Journal of Archaeology* 44 (4), 494–520.

Ventris, M., 1988. *Work notes on Minoan language research and other unedited papers*, ed. A. Sacconi. Edizioni dell'Ateneo, Rome.

Ventris, M., and Chadwick, J., 1956. *Documents in Mycenaean Greek*. Cambridge University Press, Cambridge.

Weller, C., 1918. *The Early History of the Typewriter*. Chase & Shepherd, La Porte, IN.

Wershler-Henry, D., 2005. *The Iron Whim: A Fragmented History of Typewriting*. Cornell University Press, Ithaca, NY.

Young, T., 1845. *Course of Lectures on Natural Philosophy and the Mechanical Arts*. Taylor and Walton, London.

Zhao, S., and Baldauf, R., 2008. *Planning Chinese Characters: Reaction, Evolution or Revolution? Language Policy*, 9. Springer, Dordrecht.

Zittel, C., Engel, G., Nanni, R., and Karafyllis, N. (eds), 2008. *Philosophies of Technology. Intersections: Yearbook for Early Modern Studies*, 11, volumes 1–2. Brill, Leiden.

Index